Timor-Leste's Bill of Rights

A Preliminary History

Timor-Leste's Bill of Rights

A Preliminary History

ANNEMARIE DEVEREUX

Foreword by Adérito de Jesus Soares

Australian
National
University

PRESS

ANU PRESS

Published by ANU Press
The Australian National University
Acton ACT 2601, Australia
Email: anupress@anu.edu.au
This title is also available online at http://press.anu.edu.au

National Library of Australia Cataloguing-in-Publication entry

Creator: Devereux, Annemarie, author.

Title: Timor Leste's bill of rights : a preliminary history /
                 Annemarie Devereux.

ISBN: 9781925022384 (paperback) 9781925022391 (ebook)

Subjects: Human rights--Timor-Leste.
                 Civil rights--Timor-Leste.
                 Political participation--Timor-Leste.
                 Nation-building--Timor-Leste.
                 Timor-Leste--Constitutional history.
                 Timor-Leste--Politics and government--2002– .

Dewey Number: 959.87

Cover design and layout by ANU Press

Cover photo: Members of the Constituent Assembly applauding during the signing ceremony
on 22 March 2002 in which the final text of the Constitution was adopted (AP via AAP/Firdia
Lisnawati).

Contents

Foreword

Reading this book brings me back to one of the most exciting periods in Timor's history – the six months of our constitutional debate. The original timeframe granted by the United Nations was actually shorter. I recall joking in the early sitting days of the Constituent Assembly: 'Better we draft a 60-article Constitution, given that we only have 60 effective working days.' Eventually, the timeframe was extended, after some lobbying and public pressure. Following my involvement in the resistance effort that preceded independence, I was again privileged to be a part of the making of my country's history, in drafting the first Constitution of the Democratic Republic of Timor-Leste. The six-month process of constitutional drafting was a great democratic exercise for many Timorese, despite the differences between the political parties, time constraints and other shortcomings. The author of this book, Dr Annemarie Devereux, who was a direct observer and adviser to the Constituent Assembly during the whole process, captures very well the rich debate in the Constituent Assembly. This book is a testimony to that debate and will serve to enhance the understanding of the debates for future scholars, lawyers and the people of Timor-Leste.

In the debates over human rights protections, members of the Constituent Assembly fell into one of two broad groups. The first group (consisting of a majority of members) were quite straightforward in considering the importance of adopting a Bill of Rights within the Constitution. This group was very genuine in the sense that they were motivated by the desire to prevent a repetition of the human rights atrocities faced by Timorese, especially under the illegal Indonesian occupation. They were determined that a human rights vocabulary should be an integral part of the new Constitution. The second group (a minority of members) were concerned with the means of realising those rights, repeatedly asking the question, 'Can the State fulfill all these basic rights for the people?' Concerns voiced during these debates regarding human rights continue to be echoed today: 'Povu seidauk hetan be'e mós' (The people have no clean water); 'Povu la iha aseso ba saude' (The people have no healthcare); and 'Labarik dalan-ibun la hetan protesaun husi estadu' (Street children are not protected by the state). Notwithstanding these challenges, today we all say that we have to uphold the Constitution, which includes upholding human rights. In spite of minor differences between the members of the Assembly on the unresolved issue of justiciability (that is, whether claims for human rights could be enforced through the courts), most were supportive of the Bill of Rights included in the Constitution.

Today we are watching the practice of democracy in Timor-Leste, based on its Constitution. There are gaps here and there, but it is interesting to observe in the years since the Constituent Assembly, how the fulfillment of rights is being reconciled with the various competing priorities facing Timor-Leste. The determination of the members of the Constituent Assembly in adopting the Bill of Rights has meaning only if the State takes the measures necessary to realise those rights. Can the Timorese realise their Bill of Rights and prove wrong the Orwellian statement that 'some are more equal than others'? Only time will tell.

Adérito de Jesus Soares

Former Chair of the Systematisation and Harmonisation Committee of the Constituent Assembly, and former Anti-Corruption Commissioner of Timor-Leste

Acknowledgments

There is a range of people that I would like to thank for their support in finalising this volume. I would like to express my thanks to the Human Rights Unit of UNTAET (at that time headed by Patrick Burgess) for the opportunity to work on the constitutional process as part of my engagement with the United Nations. I was fortunate to work with many wonderful colleagues in that unit, as well as many human rights proponents in civil society and within the Constituent Assembly.

Adérito de Jesus Soares has been a wonderful supporter and facilitator of this project and I owe him a particular debt of gratitude. I was fortunate to first work with Adérito in his NGO days, before he was elected to the Constituent Assembly. Within the Assembly, Adérito became Chair of the Systematisation and Harmonisation Committee. In addition to his kind foreword for this study, Adérito generously gave several days of his time to working through with me several untranslated days of the Assembly's sittings (21–22 December 2001), and facilitated my initial access to the Parliamentary Secretariat and Archives. In addition, he has always been willing to provide his expert opinion and encouragement.

My sincere thanks are expressed to Adelino Guterres, the Director-General of the Parliamentary Secretariat (during my visit in 2007) and João Rui Amaral, Director General of the Parliamentary Secretariat (during my visit in 2012), for arranging my access to the Assembly records held by the Parliament, after approval was received by the respective Presidents of the Parliament (initially Lú Olo, and later Vicente Guterres). Agostinho da Silva and Matias Benevidas at the Parliamentary Audio-Visual Section were of great help in locating the relevant recordings, including overcoming difficulties with corrupted discs. Keryn Clarke, Pedro da Silva, Lia Kent, Anjet Lanting, Armindo Maia, Ana Mequita, João Nataf and Budi Hernawan provided much appreciated assistance in interpreting discrete sections of Assembly discussions, with Bibi Ahmed and Zeca Branco providing translations of several written submissions. For sharing their collections of documents and/or responding to queries concerning documentation, I would also like to thank Nancy Lutz (Carter Center), Anthony Regan (ANU), The Asia Foundation, Fr Frank Brennan SJ, Keryn Clarke (previously of OXFAM), as well as the offices of UNOTIL, UNICEF, UNIFEM, and Yayasan HAK. My thanks also to Alessandra Ronchi (an adviser to the Timorese Parliament) and Martine Perret (of UNMIT) for responding to queries concerning photographs of the Assembly in action.

Whilst much of the work on this study has been completed as an adjunct to my international legal practice, I have profoundly benefited from periods of concentrated research and writing at the Australian Catholic University in 2007 (where this study was commenced) and The Australian National University in mid-2012, and would like to record my sincere thanks to both institutions for their support in this regard. My thanks to ANU Press for their support in publishing this study (including a grant for the copyediting), to the anonymous reviewers for their helpful comments, to the editorial staff, in particular Emily Tinker and David Gardiner, for guiding me through the publication process and to John Owen for his copyediting.

Finally, I remain truly grateful for the support of my family and friends, who have accompanied me as this study was undertaken. At times, the challenges in producing this volume seemed daunting, and it was the encouragement of my family and friends and the example set by all those who have fought and continue to struggle for human rights in Timor-Leste that emboldened me to persist.

Abbreviations

ASDT: *Associação Social-Democrata Timorense* (Association for Timorese Social Democrats)

CA/Assembly: Constituent Assembly

CNRT: *Conselho Nacional da Resistência de Timor-Leste* (National Council for Timorese Resistance)

FALANTIL: *Forças Armadas de Libertação Nacional de Timor-Leste* (Armed Forces for the National Liberation of Timor-Leste)

FRETILIN: *Frente Revolucionària do Timor-Leste Independente* (Revolutionary Front for an Independent Timor-Leste)

ICCPR: International Covenant on Civil and Political Rights

ICESCR: International Covenant on Economic, Social and Cultural Rights

KOTA: *Klibur Oan Timor Asuwain* (Association of Timorese Heroes)

PD: *Partido Democrático* (Democratic Party)

PDC: *Partido Democrata Cristão* (Christian Democratic Party)

PL: *Partai Liberal* (Liberal Party)

PNT: *Partido Nasionalista Timorense* (Timorese Nationalist Party)

PPT: *Partido do Povo de Timor* (People's Party of Timor)

PSD: *Partido Social Democrata* (Social Democrat Party)

PST: *Partido Socialista de Timor* (Socialist Party of Timor)

SRSG: (United Nations) Special Representative of the Secretary-General

UDC/PDC: *União Democrata-Cristão de Timor* (Christian Democratic Union of Timor)

UDHR: Universal Declaration of Human Rights

UDT: *União Democrática Timorense* (Timorese Democratic Union)

UN: United Nations

UNTAET: United Nations Transitional Administration in East Timor

Part I

Introduction

On 20 May 2002, the Constitution of the Democratic Republic of Timor-Leste[1] came into force. Some two months prior to this, the 88 members of Timor's Constituent Assembly adopted the final text and took part in a formal signing ceremony. As each member was called up to the podium, it was a time both of solemnity and celebration. Not all members had voted in favour of the final text[2] and the previous six months of the Assembly's operation had witnessed a number of vigorous debates. However, during the ceremonial sitting, all members signed the Constitution, displaying pride in the significance of the occasion. After a long and bitter struggle for independence, a Constitution had been adopted which detailed the way power was to be governed in the new State of Timor-Leste.

Exploring the history of the Constitution

Unfortunately, to date there has been little in the way of publicly available documentation or analysis concerning the substantive constitutional debates. One can find a number of accounts and critiques of the Constituent Assembly election and the process of constitution making.[3] There are also analyses of the final text of the Constitution[4] and comparisons with other Constitutions.[5] However, there is no history of the debates on particular clauses and so a

---

1 *Constituição da República Democrática de Timor-Leste* [Constitution of the Democratic Republic of Timor-Leste], 2002, as published in the *Jornal da República*, 2003, Série I, No 1, 1st Suplemento (4 June 2003), 1. Hereinafter, it is referred to as the 'Constitution'.

2 The final text of the Constitution was adopted by a vote of 72:14:1 (with 1 absence). Those represented in the 14 votes against/abstentions were drawn from the ranks of PD, PSD and UDT representatives, many of whom objected that the Assembly had not sufficiently considered the views of the public and minority parties.

3 See A Baltazar, 'An Overview of the Constitution Drafting Process in East Timor' (2004) *East Timor Law Journal* 9; M Brandt, *Constitutional Assistance in Post-Conflict Countries: The UN Experience: Cambodia, East Timor and Afghanistan* (UNDP, 2005); L Aucoin and M Brandt, 'East Timor's Constitutional Passage to Independence', in USIP (LE Miller (ed.)), *Framing the State in Times of Transition: Case Studies in Constitution Making* (USIP, 2010); R Garrison, *The Role of Constitution-Building Processes in Democratisation: Case Study: East Timor* (IDEA, 2005); DB Soares, M Maley, J Fox, and A Regan, *Elections and Constitution Making in East Timor* (ANU 2003); and J Wallis, *Constitution Making during State Building* (Cambridge University Press, 2014).

4 Timor-Leste Legal Education Project, *An Introduction to Constitutional Law in Timor-Leste*, supported by USAID, The Asia Foundation and Stanford Law School (undated); H Charlesworth, 'The Constitution of East Timor' (2003) 1 *International Journal of Constitutional Law* 325.

5 For a comprehensive analysis of the Timorese Constitution particularly vis-à-vis lusophone precedents, see Direitos Humanos – Centro de Investigação Interdisciplinar (Coordinator: Pedro Carlos Bacelar de Vasconcelos), *Constituição Anotado: República Democrática de Timor-Leste* (Empresa Diario do Minho, 2011). See too W Binchy, 'The Constitution of Timor-Leste in Comparative Experience' in W Binchy (ed.), *Timor-Leste: Challenges for Justice and Human Rights in the Shadow of the Past* (Clarus Press, 2009) 261.

paucity of material answering such questions as what was the intention of this provision; what questions were asked about this provision; were alternative formulations considered?

This study aims to remedy in part this deficit by focusing on the treatment of one particularly important subject matter: that of the protection of human rights. It examines in detail the history of debates concerning the guarantees within Part II of the Constitution entitled *Fundamental Rights, Duties, Freedoms and Guarantees*. For the sake of convenience, this study uses the generic term 'Bill of Rights' to refer to this part of Timor-Leste's Constitution. This book brings together information relating to each section within the Bill of Rights, presenting:

- a section-by-section analysis of the human rights provisions within the Constitution;
- progressive texts produced during the process of the Constituent Assembly;
- highlights of the arguments put forward within the Constituent Assembly concerning the draft provisions, including alternative proposals advanced;
- submissions made by Timorese officials, civil society and international bodies; and
- the results of consultation with the broader community before and during the constitutional process.

It is designed to be useful in particular to judges and legal practitioners called upon to interpret the Constitution,[6] government officials and civil society actors involved in human rights work, as well as students of history and constitutional law in Timor-Leste and internationally. Knowing the genesis of provisions and contemporary understandings may also assist in informing discussions on potential amendments in the future, given that the Constitution allows for periodic amendment of the Constitution every six years.[7] It is hoped that its publication will also serve as a means of making more accessible some of the records of the constitutional process and may stimulate further research on these historic deliberations. As this study relies upon and presents material in a translated form, its results will necessarily be preliminary in nature and may be subject to revision by future researchers who are able to present material in its original form (whether Tetum, Portuguese, Bahasa Indonesian or English).

---

6   To date, Timorese courts have not referred to the history of clauses in judgments concerning the human rights provisions of the Constitution; see, for instance, the decision of the Court of Appeal, case no. 02/2003, *Review of the constitutionality of National Parliamentary Decree 15/1/1 of 6 May 2003, concerning 'Immigration and Asylum'*, 30 June 2003; and Court of Appeal, case no. 01/2005, *Review of the constitutionality of the Parliamentary Bill of 'Freedom of Assembly and Demonstration'*, 9 May 2005. For a listing of cases in Timorese courts applying provisions of the Bill of Rights, see Direitos Humanos – Centro de Investigação Interdisciplinar, *Constituição Anotado*, above n 5.

7   Section 154 of the Constitution provides that the National Parliament may revise the Constitution after six years have elapsed since the last date on which a law revising the Constitution was published.

Further primary source material may also become available to shed light on the process. Until such time as a comprehensive documentation process is undertaken, however, it is hoped that this 'preliminary history' will make some contribution to illuminating the major contours of debates.

Human rights lie at the very heart of the Timorese Constitution. Its Preamble contains a solemn reaffirmation of determination to 'respect and guarantee human rights and the fundamental rights of the citizen'. Section 1 declares Timor-Leste to be based upon 'the rule of law, the will of the people and the respect for the dignity of the human person'. Over 40 substantive provisions providing for the protection of human rights were included in the finalised text. Its Bill of Rights embraces a wide range of rights: civil, political, economic, social and cultural rights as well as 'third generation' rights such as environmental rights. During the drafting process, a desire to prevent the repetition of violations that had occurred within Timor in the past was strongly evident. Inspiration was also drawn from the protection of rights in comparative Constitutions (particularly those of lusophone nations) and, to a lesser extent, the formulation of rights in international instruments. Although eschewing an explicit right to a remedy through the courts, the Assembly provided for the establishment of an Ombudsman (*Provedor de Direitos Humanos e Justiça*) to receive complaints and empowered the Supreme Court of Justice to conduct reviews of the constitutionality of measures when petitioned by certain bodies/ officials.[8]

With the Constituent Assembly sitting in the post-conflict environment of 2001–02, its members were frequently reminded that the fight for independence was undertaken not simply to gain political independence, but also to deliver freedom and human rights for all Timorese. At the same time, representatives were critically aware of resources constraints, including Timor's status as the poorest nation in the Asia region.[9] With the physical scars of 1999 still evident, the Assembly debated what realistically could be provided by the State, with concerns particularly apparent during discussions of economic and social rights. Notwithstanding these reservations, all members agreed that human rights needed to be at the heart of the new Timor-Leste.

As is outlined further in the next chapter of this study, deliberations on the substantive provisions of the Constitution took place within a short timeframe (October 2001–March 2002). Once the time taken for finalising internal working methods is subtracted from this period, this equates to some five months spent focused on the substance of the Constitution. Formal mechanisms for community

---

8   As noted in the discussion of s 48, there is no general clause concerning enforcement of the Bill of Rights granting, for instance, a right of recourse to the courts in the case of infringement of rights. The right to petition the Supreme Court for an abstract review of constitutionality is limited to particular bodies/officials.
9   UNDP, *Ukan rasik a'an: East Timor – the way ahead* (UNDP, 2002).

input were limited, a matter attracting significant criticism by observers and NGOs at the time. Indeed, the short length of the Assembly's deliberations, the dominance of one political party (FRETILIN) and the limited nature of public participation has been the focus of much of the subsequent commentary on the Timorese Constitution. However, to conclude that the Timorese Constitution was simply a transplant from another legal system (for example, to view the Assembly as having passively adopted the Portuguese Constitution) or a *fait accompli* by one political party is to render invisible the reflections on key issues of power and governance that occurred within the community and Assembly. Through bringing to the fore more details of these debates, it is hoped that future scholars and practitioners will be in a better position to evaluate the dominant influences in the constitutional process and appreciate the ideas generated (even if not always accepted) during this period, within and outside the Constituent Assembly.

The author has a personal connection with the project in several senses. Whilst employed with the Human Rights Unit of the United Nations Transitional Administration in East Timor (UNTAET), she was involved in assisting the Constituent Assembly and other stakeholders with advice (upon request) on means of constitutionally protecting human rights. One of the great privileges of this work was to observe the deliberations of the Assembly and the constitutional process more broadly. Given the UN's desire to ensure the process was, and was seen to be, owned by the Timorese, the UN's role in providing assistance was low key. However, the author was involved in supporting mechanisms for discussion of human rights issues, contributing analyses of draft Constitutional texts, addressing several thematic committees of the Assembly, advising the UN High Commissioner for Human Rights and the Special Representative of the Secretary-General for East Timor (SRSG) on points of engagement and monitoring the process more generally. A deep personal interest in Timor-Leste and its constitutional process developed as a result of this and subsequent work in Timor-Leste. Yet, rather than presenting a personal reflection on the process, this study aims to document the history of debates in a neutral form so as to enrich the ongoing understanding of the Constitution. Recognising the potential for bias arising out of personal involvement, however, care has been taken to engage in broad research with a range of institutions and organisations holding pertinent records to provide as complete a record as possible.

Structure of this study

This study begins with an overview of the constitutional process: explaining the context of the UN administration, the consultations carried out by the UN and civil society in the lead-up to the formal Constituent Assembly process, and the Constituent Assembly process itself. The first chapter also provides a summary of how the human rights clauses developed during the different phases of the process, and ends with some reflections on the major influences. The second part of this volume forms the bulk of this study and presents a section-by-section analysis of the Bill of Rights – highlighting movements in the text and the nature of debates within and outside the Assembly. The discussion of each section is structured around the major phases of the Constituent Assembly proceedings: examining the evolution of the text from the thematic committee stage, through the Systematisation and Harmonisation Committee to the Plenary of the Assembly. In addition to identifying textual changes, the analysis highlights the most salient points from the plenary debates, including the nature of proposed amendments to the text, and details submissions made to the Assembly.

Sources, methodology and caveats

Capturing the history of the text and the discussions of the Bill of Rights – both within and outside the Constituent Assembly – has involved analysis of a wide range of primary materials. Available records included the draft texts produced by the Constituent Assembly and its committees, recordings of the plenary sessions, and submissions presented formally to the Assembly or disseminated at the time of the Assembly's functioning. Contemporaneous press releases of the Constituent Assembly have also been mined, particularly in relation to cross-checking data and providing evidence of the Assembly's formal stance on issues such as timetabling and public consultation.[10] Much of the material used in this study has been drawn from the archives of the Constituent Assembly, now held by the National Parliament, with additional documentation coming from records of the Human Rights Unit of UNTAET, and other interested individuals and organisations, including the personal files of the Chair of the Systematisation and Harmonisation Committee (Adérito de Jesus Soares), The Asia Foundation, Oxfam, UNICEF, and Yayasan HAK. To all who have opened their files so willingly, the author expresses sincere thanks. Likewise, an immeasurable debt of gratitude is owed to those colleagues and friends who have so generously assisted in interpreting or translating material (a full listing of which appears in my acknowledgments). Before presenting the substantive results of this research, a variety of caveats relating to the nature of the source material should be acknowledged. The section below thus outlines the documentation which has been accessed, noting, as relevant, particular

---

10 From week six of the Assembly onwards, the Secretariat, with assistance from the international NGO Internews, commenced producing a daily press release that focused on key decisions of the Assembly: for example, adoption of sections, timetabling decisions and the reading out of particular letters received by the Assembly.

limitations of the material. It draws attention to the particular complexity of the 'language factor' in the constitutional process, and highlights particular methodological decisions that have been taken in navigating these challenges.

Available documentation relating to the Constituent Assembly process

Draft texts of the Bill of Rights

Fortunately, the successive draft texts of the Bill of Rights provisions survive and can be examined in detail. Four versions of the text are extracted in this volume.[11] Starting from the earliest draft, they are:

> (1) **Thematic Committee I's text** of 7 November 2001.

Thematic Committee I was the committee made responsible for producing the first draft of provisions on the topics of 'Duties, Rights and Freedoms; Defence and National Security'. Their text and accompanying report at the end of their deliberations was produced in Portuguese only. Annex III of the committee's report contained their finalised text, with underlining used to illustrate changes from the FRETILIN draft text.[12]

> (2) the 'streamlined' text produced by the **Systematisation and Harmonisation Committee** and approved by the Plenary on 30 November 2001.

This text was produced following the completion of all thematic committee reports, and represented the first full draft text. It is this text which was used as the basis for plenary debates. The Portuguese version of this text was approved 'in principle' by the Plenary on 30 November, with a Bahasa Indonesian version being produced subsequently. An English version was also made available in the following week.[13]

> (3) the revised **version used for the public consultation process**, approved by the Plenary on 9 February 2002.

---

11 There were several additional interim texts generated during the process – in particular a text produced in early January by the Secretariat showing changes made by the Plenary until that date, and another created immediately after the public consultation process, showing changes which were the subject of consensus between the political party benches. Each has been used in informing the analysis presented in this study, but they are not quoted separately given their nature more as working documents rather than formal drafts.
12 Thematic Committee I, 'Final Report', 7 November 2001, [Portuguese], copy on file with the author.
13 A copy of this text in Portuguese can be accessed at www.etan.org/et2002a/february/10-16/11etapro. htm (accessed September 2014). For reasons explained further in the text under 'The language factor', the English version of this text presented in this study departs from the contemporary Assembly translation (also available on this website) in order to ensure consistency with the form of translation in the official English translation of the final Constitution.

This text was produced by the Systematisation and Harmonisation Committee following the plenary debate. It incorporated the changes made during the plenary session, as well as some further amendments and was approved by representatives of the thematic committees and party benches. On 9 February 2002, the Plenary approved this version for distribution for the public consultation process. The text was disseminated in its original Portuguese form, as well as in Bahasa Indonesian, Tetum and English.[14]

(4) the **final text** as adopted on 22 March 2002.

This text was approved and adopted by the Assembly through a roll-call vote. The original text was Portuguese, though translations were produced in Bahasa Indonesian, English and Tetum.[15]

As explained further in the discussion of the 'language factor' below, this study has relied upon the successive Portuguese texts as the 'original text' and presents the texts in English with a streamlined translation which uses the official English translation of the final Constitution (as used by the Government of Timor-Leste) as the base version.

Constituent Assembly deliberations

Thematic Committee I of the Constituent Assembly: Thematic Committee I's proceedings were not easily accessible for observers at the time. Nor were there any recordings of proceedings kept for posterity. Documentation of the thematic committee's deliberations is thus largely limited to its formal Final Report presented to the Assembly. This report, however, is extremely useful in detailing the source of draft provisions and key decisions of the committee. Office holders of the committee also produced an abbreviated summary of its public hearing (in Bahasa Indonesian).

Plenary discussions of the Constituent Assembly: The Assembly foresaw detailed records being kept of its deliberations. Under the Internal Rules and Procedures of the Assembly, for example, the technical secretariat was tasked with preparing minutes of each plenary session and a Gazette of the Assembly, together with preparing the summary of the deliberations of the Plenary and the

---

14 A copy of this text in Portuguese can be found at www.etan.org/et2002a/february/10-16/11etapro. htm (accessed September 2014). For reasons explained further in the text under 'The language factor', the English version of this text presented in this study departs from the contemporary Assembly translation (also available on this website) in order to ensure consistency with the form of translation in the official English translation of the final Constitution.

15 The final text of the Constitution can be found at www.timor-leste.gov.tl/wp-content/uploads/2010/03/ Constituicao_RDTL_PT.pdf (Portuguese); and the official English translation at www.timor-leste.gov.tl/wp-content/uploads/2010/03/Constitution_RDTL_ENG.pdf (English) (accessed September 2014). For ease of access, a copy of the Bill of Rights in its original Portuguese form is presented in Annex I.

committees for public information.[16] In reality, the amount of record keeping (at least that which is currently accessible in the Parliamentary archives) appears to have been more limited. Of particular interest amongst surviving records are the:

Recordings of the plenary debates: No 'Hansard' exists of the plenary discussions of the Assembly. Fortunately, recordings were made of the plenary sessions in their multilingual format and these are retained on compact discs in the Parliamentary Audio-Visual Section. The recordings are not perfect. At times, handover times between interpreters, equipment failures and electricity outages created breaks in both the simultaneous interpreting and the recordings. In addition, with the passage of time, some of the recordings themselves have now deteriorated. The persistence of parliamentary staff in recovering material from corrupted compact discs was most appreciated. Notwithstanding their efforts, in some cases the damage to the discs could not be completely repaired, such that there are additional gaps in the recordings provided to the author. Contemporary notes of the author and/or other monitors have been used to supplement the record. Notwithstanding their limitations, the surviving recordings form a remarkable and valuable resource for retaining the history of the debates. It is to be hoped that in the future, transcription of these debates will be possible in the original languages and translation at least in the official languages of Timor – an epic task given the volume of debates and the language issues involved.

Records of amendments: Whilst the National Parliament's holdings include the text and voting records for some of the early successful amendments, the Secretariat was not able to locate records for all successful amendments, or indeed any of the unsuccessful amendments, put to the Plenary of the Assembly. Reliance has had to be placed on the information provided during the plenary sessions for these amendments. The interpreters (and some Assembly members) experienced particular difficulties when amendments were read out, for example, in Bahasa Indonesian, with the Bench on occasion being asked to provide Tetum translations for the benefit of Assembly members. In this study, translation of some of the amendments has been facilitated by noting the similarities with provisions in other Constitutions, particularly the Portuguese Constitution. Hopefully at some time in the future the written records of all amendments will be rediscovered and so be accessible to future researchers.

Records of global votes: The technical secretariat produced a record of the Assembly's 'global votes' on all provisions and there are partial records of the

---

16   Internal Rules and Procedures of the Constituent Assembly, s 65(3).

official vote on successful proposals for amendments.[17] As of the time of the author's research in 2007, access was gained to an annotated version of the text before the Plenary in December 2001, with stamped votes and attached successful amendments for ss 16–48. No similar document could be found for ss 49–61.

Systematisation and Harmonisation Committee: The outcome of this committee's deliberations is manifest in the draft texts produced: in particular the draft texts following analysis of the thematic committee's deliberations; the completion of the plenary debates; and following the public consultation process. The specific reasoning of the Systematisation and Harmonisation Committee is not as accessible, however, given that many of the committee's deliberations took place in closed meetings. Although the author attended some of the early open sessions of the committee, no full record of the committee's proceedings or deliberations was located in the Assembly's files. Besides producing the draft constitutional texts, the Systematisation and Harmonisation Committee produced a key report summarising the results of the formal consultations (drawing together individual District reports and written submissions received) which has been used to structure the discussion of external submissions in Part 2.[18]

Submissions made to the Constituent Assembly: The Parliamentary Library and Archives have retained copies of submissions made to the Assembly, which were formally registered as received by the Secretariat. Not all submissions appear to have been captured through this formal process, so the author has supplemented this research with recourse to submissions held by other interested bodies, including the Human Rights Unit of UNTAET, The Asia Foundation, Yayasan HAK, UNIFEM, UNICEF, and the personal files of the Chair of the Systematisation and Harmonisation Committee.

Deteriorating nature of the archival record

It is of some concern that the records of the Constitutent Assembly maintained by the National Parliament appear to be languishing and in some cases deteriorating. At the time of carrying out this research, the location of records relating to the Assembly was diffuse – with some records held in the Executive office of the Secretariat, others in the general Secretariat section and others in the Archives of the Parliament. No central index of holdings existed to assist location of relevant records. During the author's second research visit, there were some instances in which previously accessible documentation could no

---

17 Very occasionally, a discrepancy between the Secretariat's record of global votes and the recording of the actual vote was discovered. In these cases, the vote from the recording has been preferred and the discrepancy noted in a footnote.

18 In Part 2 of this study, it is noted whether submissions were included in this summary report, or were otherwise received by the Assembly.

longer be found (for example, the copy of the text being considered by the Plenary annotated with the amendments adopted for ss 16–48 located in 2007). Whilst resources limitations may present a real challenge, it is to be hoped that in future years, renewed efforts will be taken to preserve and organise this historic material as an important part of Timor's legal history.

The 'language factor' of the Constituent Assembly

The most evident complexity in compiling and analysing information related to the Constituent Assembly might be termed the 'language factor'. The Internal Rules and Procedures of the Assembly designated Portuguese and Tetum as the languages to be used in the Constituent Assembly. Provision was also made for members to use Bahasa Indonesian or English.[19] In reality, Tetum was the most commonly used language for expressing opinions, followed by Portuguese. A few members spoke in Bahasa Indonesian, particularly when proposing amendments (most frequently members of the Democratic Party (PD)). It was not uncommon, however, for members to use several languages in the course of their interventions. Proposals that were put forward from the floor of the Assembly were largely in Portuguese, though a few were submitted in Bahasa Indonesian. Written texts of the draft Constitution were produced first in Portuguese and then translated into Bahasa and English, and sometimes Tetum. It was the Portuguese version of the draft text, however, that was regarded as the original version throughout the drafting process.

Many of the younger members of the Constituent Assembly were not fully conversant in Portuguese,[20] whilst some members of the Assembly (including the President of the Assembly) did not speak Bahasa Indonesian. As part of the UN support for the process, simultaneous interpreting of plenary sessions was offered, though there were days when the absence of staff meant that no interpreting was available. Interpreting facilities were only offered in the main room of the Constituent Assembly and were not available for committee deliberations. Submissions were also made to the Assembly from officials and civil society groups in varying languages: Tetum, Portuguese, Bahasa Indonesian and English. Unless an individual/group provided translations of their submissions, these submissions remain available only in the original language.

As a predominant English speaker, the author has relied heavily on translated and interpreted material. In the course of navigating the available sources and making decisions on what to include in this study, some specific methodological decisions have been taken which are outlined further below.

---

19   Internal Rules and Procedures of the Constituent Assembly, s 5.
20   At an early stage of proceedings, 31 members of the Assembly indicated that they would like the Bahasa Indonesian version of the draft text.

Some challenges in using translated and interpreted material

Translations of the draft texts: In relation to the written documentation left by the Assembly, in particular, the draft texts produced by committees or adopted by the Plenary, differences are apparent in the Assembly translations of successive texts. This means that, for instance, one can look at contemporary English versions of successive draft texts and believe there has been a change in the language, when recourse to the same texts in Portuguese reveals no such change. In such cases, the variance in the English versions relates to a difference in translation (or an error in translation), rather than an amendment to the text. Particularly common in this respect were matters such as *'todo o cidadão'* being wrongly translated as 'everyone' rather than 'every citizen' in the distributed English text. At other times, variations occurred in the ordering of terms. Some differences were relatively benign and relate most probably to individual translators' preferences, or a refinement of the translation over time. On a few occasions, phrases or whole subsections were incorrectly retained or omitted in the process of translation. This was an irritant for Assembly members – leading to sporadic debate over whether clauses had been adequately translated, in particular, whether the Bahasa Indonesian version was identical to the Portuguese text being debated. These translation issues also raise particular issues for recreating the drafting history.

There are also two versions of the final text in English, albeit reflecting relatively minor differences. One translation appears in a pamphlet produced by the Assembly. The other version, incorporating some minor refinements, is presented on the Government of Timor-Leste's website as the official English version and appears in the United Nations compilation of laws for Timor-Leste.[21] Having recourse to what was gazetted in the *Jornal da República* unfortunately does not resolve the issue since the Constitution was published only in Portuguese and Tetum in that source.[22] However, the website of the *Jornal da República* links to the United Nations compilation of laws version for laws made during the UNTAET period (including the English version of the Constitution).[23] In light of its continued usage by the Government of Timor-Leste, it is this second-mentioned text that has been used as the official translation of the Constitution.

Reliance on the Portuguese 'original text' and streamlining the translation of draft texts to the official translation: In order to reflect the clauses being

---

21 This version can be found on the government's website at www.timor-leste.gov.tl/wp-content/uploads/2010/03/Constitution_RDTL_ENG.pdf (English) (accessed September 2014).

22 The Portuguese and Tetum versions of the Constitution appear in the *Jornal da República*, 2003, Série 1, No 1, 1st Suplemento (4 June 2003) 1.

23 For the link to the Constitution in the UN's compilation of laws for East Timor from the website of the *Jornal da República*, see www.jornal.gov.tl/lawsTL/RDTL-Law/index-e.htm (accessed September 2014). Whilst the UN website includes a general disclaimer that its translations have no official status, its adoption by Timorese authorities (through the *Jornal*) has been taken into account in this study.

debated, primary reliance has been placed on the successive Portuguese texts as the 'original texts'. Translation of these texts into English for presentation in this volume has been 'streamlined' according to the form of translation employed in the official translation of the final text. Thus where the Portuguese text of a clause did not change from one text to the final text, the official English language version of the final text is reproduced. At times this has involved departing from the contemporaneous Assembly translations of draft texts submitted to and approved by the Plenary.

Replicating verbatim the Assembly translations of draft texts without exception was considered. However, in the course of analysis, it became apparent that this approach risked leading either to an overestimation of changes made by the Assembly in some cases (where the Portuguese text remained consistent, but the English translation changed), or an underestimation of changes (where the English translation failed to mirror changes in the Portuguese text), or might otherwise prove misleading (where significant errors were made in the translation). As the primary purpose of this study is to assist in the ongoing understanding of the Constitution, a 'streamlined' approach to translation using the official English translation as the base standard, seemed to better reflect the major contours of debates. This decision has also been taken against the background that only a minority of participants and observers were looking at the English version of the text. Assembly members, for instance, were using primarily the Portuguese or Bahasa texts as the basis of their deliberations. Many of the changes made for the purpose of streamlining are minor. Yet where significant changes have been made to an Assembly produced translation, these changes are noted.

Using the official translation of the final Constitution means that some phrases reproduced in this study may appear awkward or grammatically questionable to the native English speaker. Readers familiar with both Portuguese and English who compare the final Portuguese text and the official translation may consider that an alternative form of wording might have been preferable on occasion, and may pick up some inconsistencies in the official translation. However, with the exception of a few instances in which either clarifying words have been added in square brackets to assist understanding (for example, inserting 'ethnic' after 'ethnical'), a phrase overlooked in translation has been reinserted or an extraneous space has been removed, the translation preferred in the official English version of the Constitution has been retained.

Interpretation of plenary debates: The highlights of the plenary debates presented in this volume rely heavily on contemporary or subsequent interpretations. Fortunately, on many days of the Assembly, simultaneous interpreting into English was available through the sound system to observers and it has been captured on the recordings. The UN-employed interpreters performed well in a demanding environment, but there was some unevenness in the quality of interpretation provided. Interpreters had not necessarily been specifically trained for simultaneous work. In general, interpreters had been hired to translate from one language into another (for example, from Tetum to English). When Assembly members themselves used a variety of languages in their interventions (for example, Tetum and Portuguese, or Tetum and Bahasa), interpreters were not always able to follow proceedings. As noted earlier, handover times and equipment failures created breaks in both the simultaneous interpreting and the recordings available. On several days of the Assembly's sittings (particularly in the days leading up to Christmas 2001), no English interpreters were present.

In relation to these days (and in relation to gaps or significant ambiguities encountered in the interpretation on other days), the author has benefited profoundly from the generous assistance of many colleagues and friends in listening to the recordings and providing summarised interpretation. Whilst all care has been taken in using this material, the potential for error or misunderstanding in using these interpretations (rather than verbatim transcripts) must be acknowledged. Should any such errors be noted, comments would be most welcomed by the author. Finally, the focus has been on faithfully presenting the major points of interventions, even if at times this results in some awkwardness when presented in the English language.

Notwithstanding these caveats, this 'preliminary history' is offered to assist those seeking the details of Timorese constitutional history and to stimulate further research in this field. Ultimately, it is hoped that this volume will do justice in highlighting the aspirations voiced both within and outside the Assembly during the constitutional process, and that reflecting on these aspirations will in turn assist to nurture the ongoing commitment to translating these human rights guarantees into reality.

Overview of the Constitution-Making Process in Timor-Leste

From September 2001 until March 2002, an elected Constituent Assembly deliberated on a Constitution for what was to become the Democratic Republic of Timor-Leste. At the time of its functioning, Timor was being governed by the United Nations Transitional Administration in East Timor (UNTAET) pursuant to a Security Council mandate.[1] The United Nations' assumption of power followed an international military intervention to restore peace and security in Timor. It was necessitated by the widespread atrocities that occurred before and after the Popular Consultation of August 1999, in which an overwhelming majority of Timorese voted for independence from Indonesia. By the time the constitutional process was taking place, Timor was a post-conflict country in two senses. Firstly, it was recovering from the immediate events of 1999. Secondly, in a longer-term sense, it was bearing the scars of an ongoing resistance against Indonesian control since 1975 and a civil war in 1974–75 after the withdrawal of the Portuguese colonial powers.[2] Finalisation of a Constitution was viewed as a vital component in order for power to be transferred from the United Nations to Timorese authorities. It was also a process anticipated by Timorese political groupings during the Resistance as a means of delivering the fruits of the struggle for independence. The final text came into force on 20 May 2002, the date which is termed the 'restoration of independence' in Timor-Leste.[3] Incorporating the base rules governing the exercise of power in Timor, the Constitution entrenched within it a wide range of human rights protections.

Deciding on the shape of the constitutional process

The lead-up to the Assembly reflected both UN and Timorese political leadership imperatives.

For the UN, the drafting and adoption of a Constitution was regarded as a key milestone on the path to Timor-Leste's independence and the transfer of power

---

1   SC Resolution 1272 (1999), 4057th meeting, UN Doc S/RES/1272 (25 October 1999), established the United Nations Transitional Administration in East Timor (UNTAET).

2   The history of Timor as a former colony of Portugal from the sixteenth century, the civil war in Timor (1974–1975), and Indonesia's invasion and consolidation of control is well documented in Chapter 3 of the report of the *Comissão de Acolhimento, Verdade e Reconcilição de Timor-Leste* (CAVR) available online at www. cavr-timorleste.org/en/chegaReport.htm (accessed September 2014).

3   The language of the 'restoration of independence' recognises the Unilateral Declaration of Independence by FRETILIN on 28 November 1975, shortly before the Indonesian invasion.

from the UN to the new State's authorities. The Assistant Secretary-General for Peacekeeping, Hedi Annabi, listed this as one of the key benchmarks for the political transition in April 2000, noting that consultations on the type of process to be undertaken were ongoing.[4] As early as May 2000, the Director of UNTAET's Political Affairs Department, Peter Galbraith, was already speaking of a specific model for the process, namely having an elected Constituent Assembly to draft and adopt a Constitution.[5] The Special Representative of the Secretary-General for East Timor (SRSG) and Transitional Administrator, Sergio Vieira de Mello, was less directive in his approach. In August 2000, the SRSG referred to two models for the constitutional process.[6] The first involved an (appointed) Constitutional Commission preparing a draft Constitution after carrying out a constitutional dialogue with the community. The provisional Constitution would be subject to a referendum at the same time as elections for a Constituent Assembly, a body which would be tasked with finalising the Constitution.[7] The second alternative mooted was for an elected Constituent Assembly to itself draft the Constitution. The election of the Constituent Assembly would take place after a broad-based constitutional debate. Consideration of other appropriate models was also encouraged.[8]

This forum for Vieira de Mello's August speech was the National Congress of the National Council for Timorese Resistance (CNRT), an umbrella group of most major political parties, formed in 1998 to bring together parties in the fight for independence.[9] Following Indonesia's withdrawal and the establishment of UNTAET, it became the most powerful political grouping in Timor. Its President was Xanana Gusmão, the charismatic leader of the Resistance, who went on to be later elected Timor-Leste's President, and then Prime Minister. The tenor of the SRSG's prepared remarks at this Congress showed a preference for the first, more expansive model, though within a month, the tide of UN thinking had turned back to the 'one-stop Constituent Assembly' model favoured by

---

4 Verbatim Record of the 4133rd meeting, UN SCOR, *The situation in East Timor*, UN Doc S/PV.4133 (27 April 2000) 4. Assisting the East Timorese to develop a Constitution was foreshadowed as one of the functions for a UN Administration in the report to the Security Council leading up to the creation of UNTAET: See *Report of the Secretary-General on the Situation in East Timor*, UN Doc S/1999/1024 (4 October 1999), para 28.

5 Speech of Peter Galbraith, Director of UNTAET's Political, Constitutional and Electoral Affairs Department ('Political Affairs Department') at the Tibar meeting of the CNRT, quoted in L Aucoin and M Brandt, 'East Timor's Constitutional Passage to Independence', in USIP (LE Miller (ed.)), *Framing the State in Times of Transition: Case Studies in Constitution Making* (USIP, 2010) 245, 251.

6 Speech of Sergio Vieira de Mello, SRSG, to the CNRT Congress, 21 August 2000, as annexed to the UNTAET Daily Press Release, 21 August 2000, available online at www.un.org/en/peacekeeping/missions/past/etimor/DB/DB210800.HTM (accessed September 2014).

7 Ibid para 16.

8 Ibid para 17.

9 The CNRT (whose Portuguese full title was *Conselho Nacional de Resistência Timorense*) was the successor organisation to the *Conselho Nacional de Resistência Maubere* (National Council of Maubere Resistance (CNRM)), formed in 1987.

the UNTAET Political Affairs Department.[10] Galbraith argued that an elected Constituent Assembly would have greater legitimacy in making decisions about a Constitution since 'all constitutional decisions will be derivative of a founding democratic act, the election of the Constituent Assembly'.[11] Some commentators have referred to underlying pressure from the international community to 'complete a costly mission as swiftly as possible' as an equally strong motivating force.[12]

East Timorese opinion was somewhat divided, though the dominant political elite increasingly coalesced in support of a rapid transition to independence. In the aftermath of the Popular Consultation of 1999, some Timorese leaders had considered a five-year transition to independence ideal, whereas others favoured a more abbreviated two- to three-year period.[13] Due to increasing tension between UNTAET and Timorese counterparts, a broadening consensus developed in favour of the quicker transition.[14] In August 2000, the National Congress of the CNRT recommended a two-stage process: with an expert commission engaging in full public consultation; and drafting a Constitution which would be considered and adopted by an elected Constituent Assembly.[15] By December 2000, Gusmão, on behalf of the CNRT, tabled a political timetable to hasten the movement towards independence in the National Council. The National Council was a body created by UNTAET to undertake the function of legislative review. Composed of 36 Timorese members appointed by the UN Transitional Administrator, it was to be the 'forum for all legislative matters related to the exercise of the legislative authority of the Transitional Administrator'.[16] Amongst its members were representatives of the CNRT, other political parties, the Catholic, Muslim, and Protestant faiths, and civil society together with a representative from each of the 13 Districts and three UNTAET staff. The CNRT timetable foreshadowed an extremely rapid process – with the election of a Constituent Assembly on 30 August 2001 (the anniversary of the Popular Consultation), followed by the Assembly having 90 days to deliberate on a Constitution. The anticipated adoption date for the Constitution was 15 December 2001, after which the Constituent Assembly would be converted into

---

10   A Goldstone, 'Building a State and "State-building": East Timor and the UN, 1999–2012', in M Berdal and D Zaum, *Political Economy of State Building: Power after Peace* (Routledge, 2013) 209, 217–218; J Wallis, *Constitution Making during State Building* (Cambridge University Press, 2014) 83. See too the remarks of the SRSG to the Security Council during discussion of *The situation in East Timor*, Verbatim Record of the 4203rd meeting, UN SCOR, UN Doc S/PV.4203 (29 September 2000) 5.

11   Peter Galbraith, Cabinet Member for Political Affairs and the Timor Sea, Testimony to the National Council, 20 January 2001, copy on file with the author.

12   S Ingram, 'Building the wrong peace: Reviewing the United Nations Transitional Administration in East Timor (UNTAET) through a political settlement lens' (2012) 64(1) *Political Science* 3, 14.

13   A Goldstone, 'UNTAET with Hindsight: The Peculiarities of Politics in an Incomplete State' (2004) 10(1) *Global Governance* 83, 88.

14   Ibid.

15   CNRT, *Outcomes of the CNRT National Congress*, 21–30 August 2000, Dili, Commission V, 27–28.

16   UNTAET Regulation No 2000/24 on the Establishment of a National Council, s 1.1.

a National Parliament. Implicit in this proposal was that the Constitution would be adopted by a vote of the Assembly, rather than a referendum. Prior to the elections for the Assembly, there was to be a breathtaking array of activities: the promulgation of an electoral law, the registration of political parties, the signing of a Pact for National Unity, civic and voter education, and community consultation on the Constitution.[17] Whilst there was some dissension within the National Council concerning Gusmão's failure to consult prior to tabling this timetable, the timetable was adopted in principle on 12 December 2000, reportedly following Xanana Gusmão's threat to resign.[18]

The National Council convened a public hearing on the proposed timetable from 14–24 January 2001 in Dili. During this hearing, several prominent human rights NGOs and some political parties argued that the timetable was too limited. Civil society organisations were in the lead in Timor in arguing for a participatory process of constitution-making and had sought input from experts from Thailand and South Africa, in particular, concerning comparative models. Yayasan HAK, one of the leading human rights NGOs in Timor, for instance, suggested having a Constitutional Commission established to consult widely and develop a draft Constitution that would then be considered by an elected Constituent Assembly. This was similar to the first model advanced by Vieira de Mello and was the model incorporated in a draft Regulation proposed by the HAK representative (see further below). The Catholic Church mooted the adoption of a transitional interim constitution. The National Council was not moved. On 23 February 2001, it endorsed the draft Regulation prepared by UNTAET based upon the original CNRT schedule.[19]

This did not totally quell debate. In a further push for a more consultative process, an NGO representative on the National Council, Aniceto Guterres, put forward a draft Regulation which would have established an independent Constitutional Commission.[20] Under the initiative, commissioners were to be inclusive in the sense of having professionals, representatives of youth, women, the church and civil society. The commission was to work for 12 months across the nation, with separate phases including public information, debate, consultation, reporting, and drafting. In this last phase, the commission was seen

---

17   For details of the CNRT Proposed Political Timetable for Independence, see Appendix 1, of P Walsh, *East Timor's political parties and groupings: Briefing Notes*, ACFOA Development Issues 9 (ACFOA, 2001) 30.

18   R Garrison, *The Role of Constitution-Building Processes in Democratisation: Case Study: East Timor* (IDEA, 2005) 11–12. Wallis reports that Gusmão relented (from his threat to resign) after the National Council agreed to hold public hearings to generate recommendations: Wallis, above n 10, 81.

19   Goldstone, 'UNTAET with Hindsight', above n 13, 88, has noted there were 'justified suspicions that it [the National Council approval] was in fact shaped by UN imperatives'.

20   Aucoin and Brandt, above n 5, 258–259; M Brandt, *Constitutional Assistance in Post-Conflict Countries: The UN, Experience: Cambodia, East Timor and Afghanistan* (UNDP, 2005) 14.

as assisting the Constituent Assembly with the drafting of the Constitution.[21] This draft Regulation sparked a heated debate. Support was forthcoming from powerful figures like Gusmão (who had become a convert to the cause of greater community consultation), but vigorous opposition emanated from the UNTAET Political Affairs Department and FRETILIN members of the National Council.[22] FRETILIN (which was to become the dominant political party in the Assembly) fundamentally disagreed with this approach – preferring to place primary reliance on the electoral process as the means of public consultation. Eventually the proposal was rejected by the National Council, at which point Gusmão resigned from its ranks.

After the CNRT schedule and the UNTAET Regulation were adopted, the NGO Forum took their concerns direct to the Security Council. In an open letter sent in March 2001, the NGO Forum expressed fears that a three-month Constituent Assembly would mean virtually no additional consultation with the community. The Assembly would be under 'enormous pressure to deliver the document that will declare the independence of East Timor'[23] and Timorese would be robbed of 'their right to contribute to the future of their country and … alienate[d]… from the very document that should voice their aspirations'. The Forum urged that any Constitution adopted under this process be seen as temporary, an 'Interim Constitution, allowing more time for broad-based input and consultation'.[24]

The Regulation governing the elections for the Constituent Assembly was approved by the National Council and Cabinet of the Transitional Government and promulgated by the SRSG. Despite the National Council's rejection of the Constitutional Commission Regulation,[25] a more limited form of Constitutional Commission was established by virtue of a Directive promulgated by the SRSG.[26]

Regulation 2001/2 governing the election of the Constituent Assembly

Under UNTAET Regulation 2001/2 on the Election of a Constituent Assembly to Prepare a Constitution for an Independent and Democratic East Timor of 16 March 2001, human rights were expressed to be one of the primary purposes for drafting a Constitution. Section 1.1 stated:

---

21 Details of this proposal are outlined in Aucoin and Brandt, above n 5, 258–260, and Brandt, above n 20, 16.

22 Aucoin and Brandt, above n 5, 259–260.

23 NGO Forum, Letter to members of the Security Council, 17 March 2001, available online at www.etan. org/news/2001a/03ngoconst.htm (accessed September 2014).

24 Ibid.

25 Goldstone, 'UNTAET with Hindsight', above n 13, 94. Goldstone recalls that the National Council accepted the argument advanced particularly by FRETILIN that the Constitutional Commissions were 'an attempt by UNTAET to undermine the autonomy of the Constituent Assembly': 94.

26 UNTAET Directive 2001/3 on the Establishment of Constitutional Commissions for East Timor.

> In order to implement the decision of the people of East Timor in the popular consultation of 30 August 1999 and so as to protect the inalienable human rights of the people of East Timor including freedom of conscience, freedom of expression, freedom of association and freedom from all forms of discrimination, there shall be a Constituent Assembly to prepare a Constitution for an independent and democratic East Timor.

The Assembly was to consist of 88 members: 13 District representatives voted for directly through a 'first past the post' system and 75 national representatives voted for on the basis of proportional representation (ss 3, 36 and 37). Sixty members needed to vote in favour of the Constitution for its adoption (s 2.2). A 90-day period was permitted for deliberations (s 2.3). The Regulation also stipulated that the Assembly was to 'give due consideration' to the views expressed during any Constitutional Commissions (s 2.4). At the same time as drafting the Constitution, the Assembly was charged with approving legislation submitted to it by the Transitional Administrator (s 2.5).

One of the more contested topics discussed was a proposal to embed a quota for female candidates in the electoral law. REDE Feto Timor Lorosae, an umbrella group of 16 women's organisations, proposed that at least 30 per cent of the candidates of political parties be women, and further that they be placed in winnable positions through being named as every third candidate.[27] Although the National Council originally agreed in principle to the inclusion of such a quota, opposition came from both segments of the UN (in particular the UN Electoral Assistance Division, and the Political Affairs Division), political parties and some development partners.[28] In the final form of the Regulation adopted by the National Council, no quota was included. The push for women's representation did, however, result in increased funding for the training of potential female candidates, and the introduction of incentive payments – with parties that included at least 30 per cent women candidates being given extra airtime on UNTAET-run radio and television.[29]

The election for the Constituent Assembly was held on 30 August 2001. The date chosen was hugely symbolic, being the second anniversary of the Popular Consultation in which 78.5 per cent of the population of Timor voted for independence vis-à-vis Indonesia. On election day, there was a turnout of more than 90 per cent.[30] Sixteen political parties participated in the election, with

---

27 M Pires, 'East Timor and the Debate on Quotas', Regional Workshop on the Implementation of Quotas: Asian Experiences, Jakarta, September 2002, 2.

28 Ibid 3.

29 Ibid 4.

30 A voter turnout of 91.3 per cent was quoted in the UNTAET Daily Briefing, 5 September 2001, available online at www.un.org/en/peacekeeping/missions/past/etimor/DB/db050901.htm (accessed September 2014).

five candidates running as independents. Twelve of the 16 parties garnered sufficient votes to be represented in the national seats. Four parties accounted for over 82 per cent of the vote: FRETILIN (57.37), Democratic Party/PD (8.72), Social Democratic Party/PSD (8.18) and Social Democratic Association of Timor/ ASDT (7.84).[31] Twenty-four women (27 per cent) were elected to the Assembly.[32] With FRETILIN also amassing 12 of the 13 District seats, its members constituted an overwhelming majority of the Constituent Assembly – some 55 of the 88 members.

Community views expressed prior to the Assembly

Whilst the Constituent Assembly began sitting in September 2001, the constitutional dialogue within Timor started much earlier. One could look, for instance, at the discussions leading up to the adoption of draft texts by political parties: for FRETILIN, culminating in the 1998 adoption of a draft Constitution in Melbourne (Australia); for PSD, a conference in Portugal leading to the adoption of a Constitution prepared by Professor Miranda. The fruits of these discussions were reflected in the draft texts put forward in the early stages of the Assembly process. A total of five parties put forward draft texts for the Constitution, with the FRETILIN text often adopted as the base text.

Less well reflected in the Constituent Assembly process were the dialogues within Timor which had taken place in the immediate lead-up to the Assembly process. Two deserve particular attention: the UNTAET-organised Constitutional Commission process and the parallel Yayasan HAK/Fokupers consultation (an NGO initiative).

(UNTAET) Constitutional Commission process

Prior to the elections, UNTAET organised a two-month Constitutional Commission process to explain the constitutional process and gather information from the community as to its views on a future Constitution. Constitutional Commissions for each District were established by the SRSG on 30 March 2001 under UNTAET Directive 2001/3 on the Establishment of Constitutional Commissions for East Timor. Whilst members of the commissions were appointed by the Transitional Administrator, appointment was on the basis of

---

31　Figures from the Independent Electoral Commission quoted in L de Sousa, 'Some Facts and Comments on the East Timor 2001 Constituent Assembly Election' (2001) *Lusotopie* 299 at 307.

32　UNTAET Daily Briefing, 6 September 2001, available online at www.un.org/en/peacekeeping/missions/ past/etimor/DB/db060901.htm (accessed September 2014).

recommendations received from District Administrators acting in collaboration with the District Advisory Council.[33] Each District Administration submitted a list of 10 candidates to a selection panel. The selection panel consisted of representatives from REDE Feto Timor Lorosae (a network of women's rights organisations), the University of Dili, the Catholic Church, and a youth organisation Presidium Juventude. Candidates for the Constituent Assembly were prohibited from being Constitutional Commissioners.[34] The Constitutional Affairs Branch of the Department of Political Affairs, UNTAET, explained that the concept of the Constitutional Commissions arose because of a belief that it was 'essential that the future Constitution, reflecting the "basic laws of the nation", should incorporate the aspirations of the East Timorese people, what they themselves want and believe is right for East Timor'.[35] The process was not without controversy. The NGO Forum, for instance, refused to nominate persons to act as commissioners or even sit on the selection panel. It wrote to the Director of the Political Department of UNTAET objecting that the timeframe for the commissions was too short to permit meaningful consultations, that the process for nominations, training and guidance for commissioners was inadequate in the timeframe and finally that it was unclear how the commission intended to influence the work of the Assembly.[36]

Constitutional Commissions were required to carry out at least one public hearing in each of the sub-districts of each District, a total of 65 sub-districts.[37] The commissions were asked to consult with local leaders and other prominent persons, the Church, NGOs and community groups.[38] During the period June to July 2001, over 200 public hearings were organised, involving more than 38,000 people.[39]

Whilst this commission process was to be the most extensive consultation process undertaken, and the reports were formally handed over to the Assembly by the SRSG, the results were barely referred to by members of the Assembly. In the author's hearing, the reports of the Constitutional Commission were only referred to once during the debates of the Bill of Rights and thus had

---

33   UNTAET Directive 2001/3, s 6.

34   Ibid s 6.4.

35   'A Report on the National Constitutional Consultation in East Timor, June–July 2001', (Report finalised and distributed by the Constitutional Affairs Branch, Department of Political Affairs, UNTAET), September 2001, copy on file with the author, Foreword. The Executive Summary of this report can be found at www.un.org/peace/etimor/DB/db190901.htm (accessed September 2014).

36   Quoted in Brandt, above n 20, 14. Note that Adérito Soares (who was later to be a FRETILIN member of the Constituent Assembly and Chair of the Systematisation and Harmonisation Committee) was a co-signatory of this letter.

37   UNTAET Directive 2001/3, s 9.1.

38   'A Report on the National Constitutional Consultation', above n 35, Foreword.

39   Ibid.

very little tangible effect on the process.[40] Assembly members seem to have regarded the Constitutional Commission process as illegitimate and certainly not determinative, viewing the commission as an UNTAET creation, involving unelected personnel. The Constitutional Commissions were also criticised by civil society groups as operating for too short a time, with inadequate civics education, thereby denying the community the opportunity to provide meaningful input. The International Federation for East Timor, for instance, decried the inadequacy of the commissions having 'only 45 days to educate a mostly illiterate public on complex constitutional issues and gather input'.[41] Notwithstanding the limitations of the process, it remains interesting to look at community expectations as expressed during these consultations.

The report of the Constitutional Commissions consisted of 13 individual District reports compiled in one document. Looking through these District reports, human rights shine out as a topic regarded as being of particular importance, with protection of most of the internationally recognised human rights being called for by communities. Particular stress was laid on rights connected with equality (equality before the law and equality of opportunity), but a wide range of rights cropped up in discussions. These included access to justice and fair trial rights, rights to life, privacy, education, health, family and an adequate standard of living. Freedoms mentioned included movement, expression, association and worship. Issues around land rights enjoyed some prominence alongside the need to protect the environment. More isolated references were made to the right to use any language as a means of communication, the right to enjoy a fair share of development, and the right to 'achievement and sport'. Some participants mentioned the importance of prohibiting the death penalty.

Everyday concerns of life were apparent in the specificity with which rights were discussed – such as the right to lease land,[42] the extent of rights over ancestral lands and the need for resolution of land conflicts arising from post-1999 developments.[43] Price control of products to ensure livelihoods was also regarded as desirable, as was State control over Timor's natural resources and the environment.[44] A concern with moral and social issues was also manifest. In the District of Aileu, for example, feedback included calls for a prohibition on abortion, polygamy or polyandry[45] (a topic raised repeatedly in other Districts);

---

40   The one occasion on which the Constitutional Commission Report was referred to in the author's hearing was in the discussion of s 32, with Jacob Xavier (PPT) making reference to the community's desire for justice.
41   International Federation for East Timor, 'Elections in the Context of Nation Building Preliminary Report', Press Release distributed at a press conference at Yayasan HAK, Dili, 3 September 2001; quoted in Brandt, above n 20, 13.
42   'A Report on the National Constitutional Consultation', above n 35, 23 (Aileu District).
43   Ibid 37–38 (Ainaro District).
44   Ibid 93 (Dili District).
45   Ibid 19–20.

narcotics (including production of morphine), pornography and gambling.[46] In Bobonaro, the dowry system and marriage rights each provoked particular discussion.[47] Issues of religion and culture enjoyed particular prominence. Differing views were expressed as to whether to be open to all religions or recognise Catholicism as the State religion. Some concern was evidenced in several Districts with protecting Timorese culture – both minority cultures within Timor[48] and protection of Timorese culture from foreign influence.[49] Those who had suffered as a result of the struggle for independence – in particular orphaned children, widows, war veterans – were identified as deserving of particular assistance in Ermera.[50] Reference was also made to citizens' duty to help defend the country when under attack.[51] The situation of women, and domestic violence in particular, was raised most explicitly in Oecussi, with calls for the Constitution to outlaw violence against women.[52] Reflecting previous and ongoing divisions within society, the Oecussi consultation report also included the view that all Timorese should enjoy equal rights, and rights of persons should not be limited, even if they were ex-militia or pro-autonomy or former criminals.[53]

Yayasan HAK/Fokupers consultation

Yayasan HAK (the Law, Human Rights and Justice Foundation) and Fokupers (the Communication Forum for East Timor Women), two of the leading human rights organisations in Timor, organised a parallel consultation with communities across East Timor during the period March–July 2001. Dialogues were held in the 13 Districts, involving some 1,267 people. Invitations were sent to religious and community leaders, political organisations, organisations representing women and youth, traditional leaders and other groups. Of the total number of persons participating, 200 (15.78 per cent) were described as coming from 'organisations including women's groups', 117 (9.23 per cent) 'young people', 88 (6.94 per cent) from political parties, 13 (1.02 per cent) from religious organisations and 839 (66.21 per cent) 'community leaders' and 'common people'.[54] Participants came from different employment backgrounds such as those involved with fishing, teachers, students, traders, journalists, government officials, members of the

---

46   Ibid 20.
47   Ibid 67–70.
48   This matter was raised for instance in the Dili District: Ibid 98–99.
49   This matter was raised for instance in Covalima: Ibid 82.
50   Ibid 110–111.
51   Ibid.
52   Ibid 166–168.
53   Ibid 166.
54   Yayasan HAK, 'People's Opinion on Constitution: A Report of Dialogue on Constitution', September 2001, copy on file with the author, 2. Whilst the consultations were carried out by Yayasan HAK in conjunction with Fokupers, the report was published by Yayasan HAK and thus is cited accordingly.

military and police forces. The report also noted that participants ranged from the university educated to persons without formal education.[55] (The figures unfortunately, did not include a gender breakdown of participants.)

At the outset, some concerns were expressed by participants that there was little hope of their views being taken into account, given the lateness of the education and dialogue process. Paulina from Dili, for instance, wondered: 'What guarantee can you give that the ideas and opinions we offer here will make it into the constitution building process? Maybe this is just a formality and there is already a draft constitution prepared for debate.'[56] Similarly, Bonifacio Mondonça of Suai was quoted as saying: 'Who knows, with the time constraint, the political elite have prepared a draft constitution in their drawer to be adopted, and the whole process will become rubbish [wasted] and useless, just for formality.'[57]

The NGO report stated that this was a common view throughout the 13 Districts, being linked also to perceptions that communities had been left unaided during the 24 years of struggle against Indonesian occupation, whilst in 1999 decisions were taken by others (namely the UN). The report stated '[o]ften people were treated as if they know nothing, so everything has to be decided by others.'[58] Calls were made for a consultative process. Hostility was expressed to the adoption of draft texts made by one or two parties, or 'foreign made drafts'[59] and the involvement of foreigners in the drafting process.[60]

There was awareness of the role of the Constitution, and sometimes it was expressed in traditional terms:

> People are aware that the Constitution is the fundamental law (*lei inan* or *lei boot*) or the source of all the laws that will be decided in East Timor. The participants of the dialogues realize that the Constitution is also a social contract among all East Timorese people on how the East Timorese people as a whole organize and govern themselves in their life as a nation. The determination and the will of the people to participate in the process are a very good starting point to lay the foundation for a democratic East Timor. It is regrettable if these hopes are broken, as it would not only mean that the aspirations of the people are negated, but it would remove the legitimacy of the Constitution itself. Respecting the will of the people and taking their voices into consideration is the

---

55   Ibid.
56   Ibid 3.
57   Ibid 5.
58   Ibid 5.
59   Ibid 7.
60   Ibid.

only way to establish democracy, where people hold the sovereignty, although the legislative authority is in the hands of their representatives in the Constituent Assembly.[61]

Of course, this NGO consultation report was compiled partly as an advocacy document – in particular, to support the case for greater consultation with civil society. Notwithstanding this context, the document does provide a richness of views concerning the constitutional process and key human rights concerns.

The NGO report noted that the issue of human rights was brought up at every meeting, attributing this to the history of abuses experienced:

> During the Portuguese colonization and later Indonesian occupation, people have suffered and have been subjected to various forms of human rights violation in many ways. Torture, restrictions on movement from one place to another, arbitrary arrests, unlawful imprisonment, extra-judicial executions, restrictions on freedom of expression and opinion, restriction on freedom of association, and denial of the right to health care.[62]

Support was evidenced for explicitly protecting human rights through adopting the articles of international human rights instruments or formulating new sections with the principles and spirit of those in the instruments, as well as by making sure that other sections of the Constitution would not be interpreted in such a way as to open the way for human rights violations. In the field of civil and political rights, the list comprised freedom from fear, freedom from violent actions and arbitrary action, State guarantees of everyone's freedom of belief, thought, speech, assembly, and the freedom to choose one's spouse. Perceptions of the fragility of the political situation were manifest in a certain wariness concerning political activities. Calls were made for the Constitution to stipulate criteria for the establishment of political parties and to limit 'certain political organizations that clearly pose a threat to the nation's life'.[63]

Economic, social and cultural rights also featured strongly. Calls were made for recognition of the right of all to participate in and enjoy the fruits of development. Practical questions were raised as to how people were to obtain the money to pay for electricity and water.[64] A comprehensive, non-discriminatory education system funded by the government was called for,[65] as well as specific programs to support the education of older persons who had not been able to

---

61   Ibid 7.
62   Ibid 28.
63   Ibid 21.
64   Ibid 25.
65   Ibid 24.

access education during the Indonesian era.[66] Some participants specifically recalled revolutionary aspects of the struggle in advocating anti-colonialism, anti-feudalism, egalitarianism and women's participation.[67] One participant called for an education system based on that proposed and practised by Vicente Reis (Sahe);[68] that is, applying 'a participatory egalitarian method which values both teachers and students'.[69] Women's education was also identified as a particular need, given the high illiteracy rate among women. Support was also given to inclusion of a State obligation to protect elderly people, widows, orphans, and adults who had not had the opportunity to be educated as a result of poverty or those who had abandoned their studies due to their involvement in the struggle. The State needed to pay special attention to the former guerilla fighters who were now too old to earn their own living.[70] Health services were also commonly raised. Government was to be required to provide healthcare free of charge.[71] Social security was highlighted, particularly for the victims of war (as per the Constitutional Commission reports).[72] Land issues enjoyed particular prominence, with recognition of the need to unravel the different sources of land rights: from Portuguese colonial laws, Timorese customary laws and Indonesian laws – and the need to fulfil 'people's sense of justice'.[73] It was recognised that this would need considerable study. An immediate measure favoured, however, was to prohibit foreigners from owning land.[74]

The desirability of a strong emphasis on non-discrimination and equality in the Constitution was also clear. Women and men were to be treated equally under the Constitution.[75] The long period of colonialism and oppression was seen as having placed women in the lowest position in the society, such that the Constitution needed to ensure women were 'given the chance to develop themselves and to participate in all aspect[s] of the nation'.[76] Moises from Bazartete, for example, linked equality to the liberation struggle for Timor: 'The principle of our revolution is that women and men have an equal role in the struggle for independence. So, it is desirable that women can also enjoy the result of our struggle.'[77]

---

66   Ibid 26.

67   Ibid 25.

68   Vicente Reis (Sahe) was one of the founders of FRETILIN and a resistance fighter against the Indonesian occupation. He was appointed the Minister for Labour and Social Welfare after the Unilateral Declaration of Independence of FRETILIN in 1975.

69   Yayasan HAK, 'People's Opinion on Constitution', above n 54, 25–26.

70   Ibid 29.

71   Ibid 26.

72   Ibid 23–24.

73   Ibid 23.

74   Ibid 24.

75   Ibid 29.

76   Ibid.

77   Ibid.

Issues of social relations (marriage, violence against women) were also raised prominently. The historical context in which polygamy took place was acknowledged (with guerilla fighters getting married again during the struggle). A system of monogamy was preferred (rather than women being treated as 'second wife' or 'third wife') with individuals having a free choice of spouses in the future.[78] The prevalence of violence against women was decried, with calls for the Constitution to mandate the State to take actions to effectively combat violence against women and to implement protection and rehabilitation measures for victims.[79] A reminder was given that many women had been victims of sexual violence during the Indonesian occupation, including some who were forced to become wives of the occupying forces.[80]

Copies of both the reports of the Constitutional Commission and the Yayasan HAK/Fokupers's consultation were handed over during the first week of the Assembly's sittings.

The operation of the Constituent Assembly

Constituent Assembly members were sworn in on 15 September 2001, with the administration of an oath which included a commitment to uphold human rights.[81] The first substantive sitting day of the Assembly was 17 September, at which time the SRSG handed over the results of the Constitutional Commission to the Assembly. Under its original timetable, the Assembly was to have 90 days only to draft the Constitution. Notwithstanding this time pressure, 21 of the first 90 days were occupied with discussions on presiding officers and how the Assembly should proceed – in particular what rules of procedure should apply.[82] On the first day, a 'Bureau discussion' of the heads of the political parties, together with UNTAET's Political Affairs decided that the SRSG and Transitional Administrator, Sergio Vieira de Mello, should sit as the interim Speaker pending the election of the Assembly's office-holders. Francisco Guterres ('Lú Olo'), a FRETILIN member of Parliament with a distinguished record as a Falantil fighter, was elected unopposed as President of the Assembly. Two Vice-Presidents were elected: Francisco Xavier do Amaral (ASDT)[83] and

---

78   Ibid 30.

79   Ibid.

80   Ibid.

81   *Report of the UN High Commissioner for Human Rights on the situation of human rights in East Timor*, UN Doc E/CN.4/2002/39 (1 March 2002) para 45.

82   Brandt, above n 20, 16.

83   Xavier do Amaral had been a founding member of FRETILIN, and was declared as the first President of Timor following FRETILIN's Unilateral Declaration of Independence in 1975.

Arlindo Marçal (PDC). A 'political Secretariat' was also elected, tasked with creating a record of proceedings each day. Those elected were all FRETILIN members: António Capeda, Judit Ximenes, and Maria Teresa Hono Lay Correia.

The first day of proceedings also witnessed some tussles, essentially aimed at establishing the Assembly's power. Thus, for instance, Mari Alkatiri (FRETILIN, Chief Minister of the Second Transitional Government) queried the ceremony planned by the UN Secretariat for a handing over of keys by the *liurai* (traditional leaders) to the Assembly. Alkatiri's objection centred on there being only one representative of power, namely the Assembly, a body that already included District representatives. There could not be parallel power structures, making any handover ceremony from traditional leaders to the Assembly inappropriate. The issue was not resolved, but left to the following day. The issue quietly lapsed with no such ceremony taking place. Debate also surrounded a UNDP-organised orientation seminar planned without the Assembly's request. During the course of this debate, Alkatiri pointed out that he had not taken the oath in the swearing-in ceremony because he had not been consulted on its terms. The seminar was put off but proceeded as planned the next day following discussion with representatives of political parties.

In order to draft a set of internal rules of procedure, a seven-member multi-party committee was established.[84] Whilst there appears to have been some internal wrangling within this committee (with Lucia Lobato (PSD) expressing public dissatisfaction with the dominant role of Ana Pessoa (FRETILIN)), the committee presented a draft set of rules to the Assembly for its consideration. Debate continued on these rules from the second to the fourth weeks. At times, debate was quite heated. Minority parties (in particular PD, PSD and UDT) evinced frustration that their suggested amendments were not being given appropriate consideration. After reaching boiling point, closed door discussions took place which resulted in an improved atmosphere and greater consideration of amendments.

In the final Internal Rules and Procedure adopted, a nine-step process was agreed upon:

(a) Presentation by Members or parliamentary party groups of proposals to systematise the constitutional text [which meant providing draft structures/outlines of the Constitution];

(b) Designation of a committee to advise on the proposals of systematisation;

---

84 The committee consisted of Adérito Soares (FRETILIN), Lucia Lobato (PSD), Eusébio Guterres (PD), António Ximenes (PDC), Manuel Tilman (KOTA), Isabel Fereirra (UDT), and Ana Pessoa (FRETILIN).

(c) Approval of the systematic structure of the Constitution and designation of thematic committees for the drafting of each title or chapter of the Constitution;

(d) General as well as specific debate on each title or chapter of the Constitution based on the proposals presented to this end;

(e) Establishment of a committee to harmonise the approved proposals and final drafting of the constitutional text;

(f) Approval of the final [draft] text of the Constitution;

(g) Following its approval, the final text shall be fully disseminated throughout all sectors of civil society, which shall be invited to make representations within a period of one week;

(h) Analysis, discussion and debate on the comments received from the public;

(i) Global and final approval of the Constitution.[85]

This procedure was generally adhered to, though each step did not take an equal amount of time. In reality, the Assembly considered the substance of the text in three major stages:

(1) Discussions in the thematic committees during the period mid-October to early November 2001.

(2) Plenary debate from mid December 2001 to late January 2002, culminating in a revised text which was adopted on 9 February 2002 [86] and subsequently released for the purpose of the one-week consultation period commencing in late February.

(3) A brief discussion in the Plenary of the Assembly in mid-March 2002 of the results of the one-week consultation leading to some amendments, with the approval of the final text and the signing ceremony on 22 March 2002.

In between each of these steps, the Systematisation and Harmonisation Committee was active in undertaking further deliberations and revisions of the text.

Time period: While the Regulation establishing the Assembly set a 90-day timeframe for the Assembly to produce a Constitution, it was also envisaged

---

85   Section 5(a)-(i) of the Internal Rules and Procedures of the Constituent Assembly, contemporary unofficial translation.

86   This text was approved 65:0:13 (with 10 absent).

that the Assembly might seek and be granted such extensions of time as proved necessary for it to complete its task.[87] During the Assembly's operations, the impetus for keeping to a tight timeframe came very much from within the Assembly, particularly the President of the Assembly, Lú Olo, and the FRETILIN Bench. From the earliest stages of proceedings, questions were raised about the 90-day framework at various fora – including press conferences, workshops and in petitions to the Assembly. The suggestion made by Father José Antonio of the Catholic Church, and supported by Assembly Watch, was to regard any text produced as an interim text, with an independent commission to function in four–seven years to revise the Constitution.[88] Other calls were made for the Assembly to request an extension of its mandate. However, the official responses maintained the desirability of the existing framework. On 15 November 2001, Lú Olo, for instance, spoke at a press conference about this topic. The official press release records his view that '[t]he CA did not want to ask for extensions now, because having a deadline helped members to focus their energies on the task'. He also expressed confidence that the Assembly would meet its deadline 'because there was a lot of consensus among the members and good debate during the thematic committees' deliberations'.[89] It was not until 13 December 2001, a matter of days before the expiration of the initial 90-day period, that a vote was taken to extend the deliberations. The date chosen was 25 January 2002, bearing in mind the next discussion of the Security Council scheduled for late January. By 21 December, an element of caution had entered into the explanation of Lú Olo about the likelihood of meeting this deadline: 'It was not enough,' he said, 'simply to write the constitution and present it to the people, the CA needed to listen to the different institutions groups and institutions to get their input.'[90] That the Assembly would not complete its deliberations in January became increasingly apparent, and spurred an intervention from eight members of the US Congress expressing concern that 'external pressures' were forcing the Assembly to rush the process. They encouraged the Assembly to extend its sittings by two months.[91] On 21 January 2002, the Assembly resolved to extend the constitution writing period to March.[92]

---

87   The Assembly encapsulated this understanding in s 6(1) of its Internal Rules and Procedures which provided that whilst the Assembly would use every effort to meet the three-month deadline, should this not be possible, it would propose to the Transitional Administrator an extension of time.

88   Assembly Watch submission (on Renetil letterhead), Letter to the President of the Constituent Assembly, 29 October 2001 [Tetum]. See too the submission of the NGO Working Group on the Constitution, 'Recommendations to the Constituent Assembly', undated but circa October 2001, also supporting adoption of an Interim Constitution.

89   Summary of the press conference included in the Constituent Assembly Press Release, 15 November 2001.

90   Summary of the press conference included in the Constituent Assembly Press Release, 21 December 2001.

91   Letter from eight Members of the US Congress (Kucinich, Lee, Smith, Weiner, Baldwin, Sanders, Evans and Farr) to the President of the Constituent Assembly, dated 10 January 2002.

92   The decision in January was to extend the Assembly until 9 March; however, this was extended subsequently to 22 March when it became apparent that further time was necessary.

Voting methods: UNTAET Regulation 2001/2 provided that the Constitution was to be adopted by an affirmative vote of 60 of the 88 Assembly members. This was interpreted as governing only the vote for the overall adoption of the Constitution. The Internal Rules and Procedures for the Assembly stated that voting on individual sections needed only a simple majority (of those present).[93] On the first day of proceedings, a decision was taken that votes during sessions should be open, rather than secret. Greater disagreement surrounded whether sections should be adopted by vote or by consensus. Minority parties were concerned in particular about the voting bloc of FRETILIN. Given FRETILIN's numbers in the Assembly, they would have a majority sufficient to pass individual sections, even if not sufficient numbers for the global vote on the Constitution. Clementino Amaral (KOTA), supported by Vicente Guterres (UDC/PDC) proposed a new section in the rules to recognise the Assembly's obligation to build consensus. A consensus-based model was portrayed as the Timorese way. Vote taking should only be regarded as a tool of last resort. The proposal was, however, rejected. Most who spoke against the proposal were from FRETILIN. They argued that voting was itself the proper methodology to determine if there was consensus.[94] Voting also had the advantage of offering a speedy and transparent form of decision making. During discussions on the rules, there was a reopening of whether vote taking should be secret or open (again against a background of potentially opening up spaces for more individual decision making rather than party voting). The open vote system was, however, retained.

Substantive discussions of the Assembly

The operation of the thematic committees: mid-October–early November 2001

Four thematic committees were established and given the following subject area mandates:

- Thematic Committee I: Duties, Rights and Freedoms; Defence and National Security (the primary committee for human rights issues)
- Thematic Committee II: State organisation; Organisation of Political Parties/ Systems
- Thematic Committee III: Economic, Social and Financial Organisation
- Thematic Committee IV: Fundamental Principles, Final and Transitional Arrangements, Amendments

---

93   Internal Rules and Procedures of the Constituent Assembly, s 57.
94   Some FRETILIN members also spoke in favour of a consensus model.

Although the rules specified that thematic groups were to be composed of 20 members, the Assembly decided variations from this number were permissible provided the balance of parties was maintained. Thematic Committee I itself comprised 21 members (see Annex II for the full listing of members). Paulo Assis Belo (PD) was elected as President, with two FRETILIN members as Secretary (Adalgisa Soares Ximenes) and Rapporteur (Vicente Soares Faria). Thematic committees were originally given 10 days only to consider the subjects within their areas of competence, though most took longer.

Significant lobbying took place from NGOs to ensure that thematic committees held public hearings.[95] Article 29 of the Internal Rules and Procedures dealt with this subject, and as a result of a PD amendment, the Assembly endorsed the policy that thematic committees 'shall hold public hearings for interested groups', though the text of s 29(2) (which appeared to leave hearings to the discretion of committees) remained unaltered. A member of the Assembly's Technical Committee reported his understanding that thematic committees would hold public hearings, but that committees would determine who was invited. All thematic committees did in fact hold public hearings, though at least one submission from Assembly Watch called upon the Assembly to augment these hearings with public hearings during the plenary debates.[96]

At the end of their deliberations, each thematic committee provided a report containing the draft text which they had adopted, together with a record of the votes for provisions and some detail concerning the methodology employed by the committee.

Production of a draft text by the Systematisation and Harmonisation Committee

The four reports were then collated and analysed by the Systematisation and Harmonisation Committee with a view to creating a full streamlined text for the Plenary's consideration. In addition to having meetings with the full membership of the committee over three days, the office holders of the committee met legal experts from Portugal, Mozambique and Cape Verde. As a result of these deliberations, both stylistic and substantive changes were made to the text. Some, but not all, were marked for further consideration by the Plenary of the Constituent Assembly. On 29 November 2001, the Systematisation and

---

95   Note that the NGO Working Group on the Constitution not only called for public hearings by each of the specialist committees, but had also advocated that the committees consider different models of responding to key issues. The Group recommended that committees hear from experts, other members of civil society and members of the public; that the records of the Constitutional Commissions be taken into account, and that there be public hearings of the Assembly itself: 'Recommendations to the Constituent Assembly', undated, but circa October 2001.

96   Assembly Watch submission (on Renetil letterhead), Letter to the President of the Constituent Assembly, 29 October 2001 [Tetum].

Harmonisation Committee submitted a full draft text to the Plenary of the Assembly. The Plenary approved the Portuguese version of this draft on 30 November 2001. Public release of these documents was not automatic, but was the subject of some debate (see further under 'Contemporary access to draft texts'). The eventual decision of the Assembly was that the draft text would be made available to the public.

The Systematisation and Harmonisation Committee played a more major role in shaping the text than their title might suggest.[97] This committee comprised 42 members drawn from 12 political parties.[98] With 24 representatives, FRETILIN was numerically dominant. However, as this committee did not operate on a voting system, the impact of the FRETILIN bloc was not as significant as in other fora.[99] The office holders were to prove particularly influential: namely Adérito Soares (FRETILIN) as President/Chair; Vicente Guterres (UDC/PDC) as Secretary; and Manuel Tilman (KOTA) as Rapporteur. At several stages of the process, the committee made amendments to the text before its presentation to the Plenary. As noted above, this was apparent on the face of the draft text produced by the Systematisation and Harmonisation Committee based upon the thematic committee reports in late November 2001. It was equally evident when the text was revised following the plenary debates. At times, changes were put forward as suggestions, or as bolded text, with explanations provided for the suggested changes. At other times, amendments were simply integrated and justifications provided only if/when the change was queried by a member of the Assembly. As will be apparent in the section-by-section discussion, some of the changes related to streamlining the text or 'technical'/'stylistic' changes, while others were of a more substantive nature.

The plenary debates: December 2001 – February 2002

The initial pace of the Plenary's deliberations on the draft sections was slow, with separate formal discussions and votes on the title of each section, and then each subsection in turn. Voting of those in favour, against and abstaining was undertaken separately, which led to an average of two sections being passed in a day. Within two weeks of the Assembly commencing discussion on the draft text, it was apparent that this pace would not allow the Assembly to complete its task within its agreed timeframe. At the same time as proposing to extend its deadline to 25 January 2001, the Assembly re-examined its methodology. Following a discussion on 14 December 2001, the President of the Assembly, Lú Olo, announced the streamlined process on 18 December. Henceforth members would vote only on the complete sections, unless there was a specific proposal

---

97 The Portuguese title of the Committee was *Comissão de Sistematização e Harmonização*.
98 The Internal Rules and Procedure provided for a membership of 42: 24 members from Fretilin, four from PD, and three each from PSD and ASDT, and the heads of the parliamentary party groups: s 25.
99 See Annex II for the full listing of membership of the Systematisation and Harmonisation Committee.

concerning a subsection. Stricter time limits and restrictions to the numbers of speakers were also introduced, and the hours of deliberations of the Assembly were increased. Under this amended regime, the pace of decision making thereafter rapidly increased.

A solid FRETILIN bloc vote appeared in relation to many of the Assembly's votes. Indeed at times it appeared to observers that a significant number of FRETILIN members voted for or against a proposal based on the attitude demonstrated by the leadership such as Lú Olo (who as President of the Assembly sat facing the membership).[100] Since FRETILIN constituted the majority of the Assembly, such a bloc vote was able to hold sway. Some members of minority parties voiced frustration that their amendments were not genuinely considered (that voting patterns depended on who was proposing the amendment, rather than the merits of the amendment).[101] This led one commentator to conclude that 'ultimately the constitution was not the product of genuine legal and intellectual debate but merely the result of consensus among FRETILIN leaders'.[102] Certainly, in the plenary sessions of the Assembly, a litany of amendments proposed by minority parties failed. Amendments proposed by FRETILIN members or supported by a cross-party selection of members had a greater chance of success. A small number of FRETILIN members notably voiced contrary opinions and voted on an individual basis, siding with minority parties during discussions. On other occasions, hesitance about controversial matters, particularly those touching upon matters of culture or religion, led to significant numbers of members abstaining rather than rejecting particular amendments outright.

Revision of the text for the public consultation process: early February 2002

Immediately following the end of the plenary debate of the whole draft Constitution, the Systematisation and Harmonisation Committee undertook further editing of the text to produce a revised text. According to its report, its methodology included discussions with the office holders of the four thematic committees, 'jurist members' of the Assembly and 'foreign jurists'. Amendments again included grammatical, stylistic and substantive changes.[103] The title of the

---

100   Carter Center, *The East Timor Political and Election Observation Project: Final Project Report* (April 2004) 43. See also D Soares, 'The challenges of drafting a Constitution' in DB Soares, M Maley, J Fox and A Regan, *Elections and Constitution Making in East Timor* (ANU 2003) 25, 29.

101   Ibid. The same view was advanced subsequently in a personal communication between a Constituent Assembly member and the author.

102   Wallis, above n 10, 96. Wallis has quoted one source saying that no more than 12–14 members appeared really across the issues in the Assembly, with the remainder voting according to party lines, though this seems a particularly harsh judgment: 95.

103   The Systematisation and Harmonisation Committee described its methodology in a document entitled 'Report and Script', undated, but postdating its meeting on 19 January 2002. It was included as Annex VIII in a summary of the work of the Constituent Assembly in the Assembly records.

revised text produced indicated that it had been approved by the heads of the parliamentary party groups and the officials of the thematic committees, before being approved by the Plenary. On 9 February 2002, this text was approved as the text to be distributed for the purpose of the consultations.

The one-week public consultation process in the week of 25 February 2002

Only a one-week period of community consultation had been provided for in the Assembly's Internal Rules and Procedures. Proposals for more lengthy engagement predated, and continued to be agitated for during, the Assembly's deliberations. Baltazar reports that many of the minority parties originally proposed one month's public consultation between March and early April 2002, but that FRETILIN and ASDT favoured a one-week consultation.[104] Similarly, when the methodology for the public consultation was debated, Baltazar reports that a 'scientific formula' for collecting data was proposed by PD, PSD and UDT, but was rejected again by FRETILIN and ASDT, who considered that briefing audiences and questions/answers would be sufficient.[105]

From the FRETILIN side of politics, an often-encountered attitude was that extensive consultation with the community was unnecessary. Assembly members, they argued, had been elected on the basis of their views and as such the Assembly could formulate the Constitution on the basis of that mandate. Stress was laid on the model of representative democracy. Even after the public consultation period was agreed upon, some hesitancy remained. At the press conference on 29 November 2001, for instance, Lú Olo was reported to have said that he was willing to allow organisations to come up with suggestions and ideas which might be incorporated at a later date, such as in one or two years' time. Agreeing that the period of the one-week consultation was short, Lú Olo nonetheless considered that the situation in East Timor was unique:

> Other countries took years to complete their constitutional process. The fact that the information campaign would need to take place in the rainy season would also complicate the process, but Lú Olo said Constituent Assembly members would do their best to inform people in the Districts. During the information process members would be going out to the Districts to explain the constitution to the people. They would not only be giving out copies of the text, but would also be listening to the people's comments, so that if necessary changes can be made.[106]

---

104 A Baltazar, 'An Overview of the Constitution Drafting Process in East Timor' (2004) *East Timor Law Journal* 9. The minority parties Baltazar lists as preferring the one-month consultation period were KOTA, PD, PSD, PST, UDC, and PDC.
105 Ibid.
106 Constituent Assembly Press Release, 6 December 2001.

In the context of discussing their revised calendar of work (having opted to seek an extension to 25 January), José Reis (FRETILIN) proposed delaying any discussion with the community until after the text was finalised on 25 January, due to pressures of time to complete deliberations on the text. Any recommendations for change arising out of such discussions (which he initially termed 'socialisation') would then be forwarded to the Transitional Administrator or Security Council. Although this proposal was rejected in a vote of 29:22:30, members' interventions displayed ongoing divisions within the Assembly as to the necessity for consultation versus socialisation (explanation) of the text.[107] When bringing the debate to a close, Lú Olo sought to reconcile the two perspectives – arguing that the process of socialisation would also involve seeking feedback, and accepting the importance of bringing the Constitution back to the people.

In a continuing campaign for a more participatory process, the Assembly Watch Team sent a letter to the Constituent Assembly, read out on 4 February 2002, asking the Assembly to extend the information campaign from one week to two months and to allow for two weeks to analyse the results.[108] The Assembly Watch Team also called for people's opinions to be published before the Assembly considered its response. At the press conference on 8 February, Lú Olo was again asked whether a one-week information campaign was sufficient. He affirmed that it was.[109]

The methodology for the consultation was divulged on 28 January 2002. Members were to divide into 13 groups, with each group to spend one week visiting one District each, disseminating the text of the draft and listening to people's views. Whilst the consultation period was scheduled to commence on 23 February, initial days were spent travelling to the Districts. Thus the real consultation occurred between 25 February and 2 March 2002. Copies of the draft Constitution were produced in Portuguese, Tetum, Bahasa and English, but generally were received by communities only a day or so before the consultation.[110] In some cases, copies were received only hours before the consultation meeting.[111] One commentator, Michele Brandt, who was then coordinator of The Asia Foundation's assistance program to the Constituent Assembly, has described in detail the difficulties associated with the consultation and the resulting frustration within some communities. Due to a lack of

---

107   The debate took place in the plenary session of 14 December 2001.

108   Letter from the Assembly Watch Team to the President of the Constituent Assembly, 31 January 2002 [Bahasa Indonesian].

109   Constituent Assembly Press Release, 8 February 2002.

110   Joanne Wallis has noted that while a total of 25,500 copies of the draft Constitution in Indonesian, Portuguese and English were distributed on 20 February, the 35,000 copies of the Tetum version were distributed only on 25 February: Wallis, above n 10, 103.

111   UNTAET Daily Press Briefing, 1 March 2002, available online at www.un.org/en/peacekeeping/missions/past/etimor/DB/db010302.htm (accessed September 2014).

forward planning, a variety of logistical challenges arose relating to obtaining necessary funds and resources, including cars, helicopters, and communication devices.[112] Whilst these were addressed through UN and The Asia Foundation assistance, Brandt's account highlights how the rushed process impacted on the consultations and the Assembly's later analysis of feedback:

> Because of the rush and poor Secretariat planning, many citizens received the drafts the day the Assembly members arrived. In some areas, the public ripped up their copies of the constitution in protest and declared the process a sham because there was no time to read the draft, prepare comments and properly participate.

> Each team of Assembly members had a different methodology for holding consultation meetings. Some spent the entire period explaining the draft to the public. Others listened to hundreds of citizens come forward to give their views on the draft. This resulted in a skewed process with only some groups having commentary to report to the Assembly. Even after the one-week consultation period, the CA continued to debate whether the draft would be open to change based on the public's comments.

> … The East Timor Constituent Assembly did not decide how to consider the views until they returned to Dili. Some CA members, at least in private, still maintained that the process was an exercise in public relations only. Nonetheless, there was public pressure to consider the views that had been collected.[113]

The shortness of the time period for consultations and the limited information available ahead of time meant that in many Districts, the hearings involved large segments of socialisation rather than consultation.[114] For many attendees at meetings, information may also have come from radio and television coverage of the Assembly, rather than the distribution of its formal documentation. In the report of the consultations, it was apparent that those with the most knowledge of the draft text were affiliated with political parties or NGOs.

Commentators have been particularly scathing about this short period of public consultation.[115] Without doubt, the one-week period and the methodology employed was insufficient for the community to study the proposed text and provide feedback in any detailed fashion. In a televised panel discussion, Bishop Belo spoke of the one-week period as tantamount to 'teasing' the Timorese community. Both the Bishop and Xanana Gusmão made calls for the

---

112   Brandt, above n 20, 17.
113   Ibid.
114   See too R Garrison, above n 18, 20.
115   Della-Giacoma, for instance, has characterised the consultations as 'rushed, poorly conceived and executed, peripheral, shallow and tokenistic': quoted in Wallis, above n 10, 105.

Assembly to pursue consultations during the month of March. Xanana Gusmão began to delink the finalisation of the Constitution and looming independence, suggesting that 'a Constitution is the pillar of a nation. It is the mother of law, and it should be properly legitimized by the people.'[116] HAK was similarly critical of the one-week consultation period:

> We cannot make mistakes, again and again, by calling consultation what is in effect a ready-made monologue between those that are already making decisions on behalf of the East Timorese people. And we certainly cannot make this mistake when it relates to the constitution, which has to be a living document reflecting how the East Timorese as a people see themselves, relate to themselves, and finally, after many centuries, govern themselves.[117]

Plenary discussion of the consultations and final debates: 12–22 March 2002

On 12 March 2002, the Systematisation and Harmonisation Committee handed over their report summarising the results of the District consultations, and written submissions received.[118] Their report also included recommendations for changes to some 45 sections, based on the consultations.[119] The Assembly agreed that this report would be considered within parliamentary party groups who would then provide feedback to the Systematisation and Harmonisation Committee, with a view to determining if there was consensus around the proposed amendments. On 15 March, the committee reported back on the results of the discussions. Those matters which already enjoyed consensus were considered adopted. Members were said to be free to raise matters which were not the subject of consensus, or other issues. One member of the Assembly, João Carrascalão (UDT), was particularly vocal in his criticism of the pace of the process and the quality of the summary report of the consultations. According to Carrascalão, there were issues raised during the consultation which were not included in the summary report, and conversely, on occasion, suggestions advanced by only a single individual appeared in the report. He expressed dissatisfaction that a small committee was deciding on these issues, and

---

116 Quoted in Brandt, above n 20, 17. The views of Bishop Belo are also discussed in this source.
117 Ibid 24. This was referring to the insufficiency of public hearings on the initial decision making re the constitutional process – i.e. the January 2001 hearing.
118 The submissions listed are relatively limited and number only nine. These were from the Transitional Administrator, Chief Minister (not on human rights matters), Minister for Foreign Affairs, Vice-Minister for Justice, Minister for Health, Haburas Foundation, East Timor Study Group, Asia Foundation and the Timor-Lorosa'e Journalists' Association . It is not clear on what basis submissions were included, but it may have been date of receipt (with these submissions representing those lodged from late February to early March 2002).
119 One recommendation was also inserted concerning the (yet to be adopted) Preamble. The recommendations emanated from the Bench of the Systematisation and Harmonisation Committee.

suggested instead that each point be debated. The President of the Assembly, however, closed down this discussion on the basis that the Systematisation and Harmonisation Committee had been given the authority by the Assembly to undertake this analysis. Adérito Soares, the Chair of the committee, sought to be conciliatory in affirming an intention not to close the doors to anyone who wished to raise issues. In the end, some 60 per cent of recommendations of the Systematisation and Harmonisation Committee were the subject of consensus and were adopted. Although several minority parties urged a full debate on each of the remaining recommendations (and any further recommendations), debate focused primarily on issues of particular symbolic importance, in particular the flag and the national anthem, as well as the Preamble and the relationship between church and State. Only a few additional proposals were put to the floor of the Assembly.

Final adoption and signing of the Constitution: 22 March 2002

The final vote to adopt the Constitution was 72:14:1 (with 1 absence). This vote was undertaken via a nominal roll count – that is, each member's name was called out, and he/she indicated his/her position. Those represented in the 14 votes against were drawn from the ranks of PD and PSD, with one UDT representative.[120] Aquilino Guterres (PD) and Mariano Sabino Lopes (PD) were amongst those who voted against the text, expressing frustration that the final text did not take sufficient account of the views of people.[121] The dominance of the FRETILIN text was also raised, as was the perception that the text incorporated a FRETILIN view of history. João Carrascalão (UDT) was the member who abstained in the vote, expressing concern about the limited time for popular consultation and the way in which restrictions of time for the drafting process had resulted in limitations in the Constitution itself. By the afternoon, when the signing ceremony took place, all members (including those who had voted against/abstained in relation to the draft text) signed the final text of the constitution.

An overview of the drafting process concerning human rights in the Constitution

Thematic Committee I (Duties, Rights and Freedoms; Defence and National Security)

Prior to Thematic Committee I's commencement, the Assembly agreed upon a draft structure of the Constitution, based on the proposal put forward by the

---

120   PD and PSD members voted against the final text, along with Quitéria da Costa (UDT). João Carrascalão abstained in this vote.

121   Author's contemporary notes.

Systematisation and Harmonisation Committee. It took into account proposals put forward by nine political parties.[122] The draft structure for the Bill of Rights was as follows:

Part II – Fundamental Rights, Duties and Freedoms

Title 1 – General Principles

Title II – Personal Rights, Freedoms and Guarantees

Title III – Economic, Social and Cultural Rights and Duties

Thematic Committee I began its deliberations on 17 October 2001, having been given a notional 10 working days to formulate a draft set of provisions pertaining to its areas of responsibility. Thematic committees were given fairly minimal directions in how to conduct their deliberations from the Internal Rules and Procedures. Thematic Committee I's meetings were generally open, though little information was made publicly available as to how to access meetings.[123] Committee hearings were held in small side conference rooms with limited seating for observers. Discussion took place primarily in Tetum, with no translation available. Proceedings of the committee were not recorded, and no records of the deliberations produced other than the final report which contained the details of the proposals and the voting records.

One of the first actions of Thematic Committee I was to plan its public hearing. This was scheduled for 22 October 2001. Whilst the committee was responsible for both human rights and defence matters, invitees were weighted towards the human rights side of the equation. The attendees were drawn from:

- the Catholic Church (Bishop Belo, Bishop Nascimento and Father José Antonio da Costa received an invitation. The Bishops indicated they were unable to attend but were represented by Father Antonio);
- REDE Feto Timor Lorosae (Jesuina Soares Cabral and Teresinha Cardoso), a network of 16 women's rights organisations;
- Yayasan HAK (Aniceto Guterres and Joaquim Fonseca), a human rights NGO;
- Timor Lorosa'e Journalists' Association (TLJA) (Hugo Fernandes);
- Haburas Foundation (Demetrio Amaral de Carvalho) an environmental NGO;

---

122 According to the records of the Systematisation and Harmonisation Committee and Thematic Committee I, there were outlines of this Part from nine parties: FRETILIN, UDT, PSD, PPT, PD, PL, PNT, PST, and KOTA. The FRETILIN, UDT and PSD outlines were the most comprehensive.
123 The Internal Rules and Procedures of the Constituent Assembly left the decision as to whether meetings were open to each committee: s 43(2). The Constituent Assembly's Fact Sheet No. 1, distributed by the Constituent Assembly, noted that all thematic committee meetings were open to the public and accessible provided persons coming to the Assembly brought means of identification.

- UNTAET Human Rights Unit/Working Group on Future Institutions (Annemarie Devereux and Bendito dos Santos); and

- UNICEF (Yoshiteru Uramoto).[124]

The first speaker at the public hearing was Father José Antonio, appearing on behalf of the Catholic Church. Father Antonio referred to the importance of the Constitution as a document of the people, and that, like a tree, it needed to have strong roots. He spoke with particular reference to the rights of the family, speaking in favour of freedom to choose one's spouse and to form a family. Raising issues of procreation, Father Antonio advocated freedom from forced sterilisation, and the desirability of prohibiting abortion. Guarantees with respect to the provision of education, health and social assistance were supported. Father Antonio saw the (Catholic) Church and State operating separately but in coordination, with the State consulting the Church in relation to its social programs. Given the plurality of faiths in Timor, the State should not take on a role of determining a national religion. Some concern was expressed that Timorese culture had been adulterated by the cultures of its colonisers. In the course of his presentation, Father Antonio requested that the Church be given copies of any existing drafts such as those of FRETILIN, KOTA and PSD, so that comments could be provided. That such a request needed to be made in the public hearing reflected the lack of contemporary access to relevant texts.

A representative of the Human Rights Unit of UNTAET (the author) was asked to address the topic of economic, social and cultural rights. Together with another member of the Working Group on Future Human Rights Institutions (Bendito Soares),[125] the Human Rights Unit also addressed the committee on the topic of enforcement of human rights, including through a national human rights commission. UNICEF and the Committee for Child Rights in East Timor's Constitution presented draft provisions for the protection of children's rights, whilst REDE Feto Timor Lorosae and the Gender and Constitution Working Group introduced and spoke about the Women's Charter of Rights in East Timor.[126] Specific attention was focused on the need to address high levels of maternal and infant mortality and domestic violence, as well as the situation of victims of the conflict. Stress was laid upon ensuring equality of rights between spouses. Yayasan HAK referred to the long-standing denial of human rights in

---

124 An invitation was also extended to Filomena Reis of the NGO Working Group on the Constitution.

125 The Working Group on Future Human Rights Institutions was a coalition of human rights NGOs and the Human Rights Unit of UNTAET.

126 The Women's Charter of Rights in East Timor had been developed through consultations with Timorese women, led by the Women and the Constitution Working Group (also called the Gender and Constitution Working Group). It was presented to the SRSG in September 2001 and was subsequently presented to the Assembly, supported by over 8,000 signatures.

Timor, and advanced a broad-ranging submission concerning all categories of rights, recalling the indivisibility of all types of rights. HAK also highlighted specific gaps in the FRETILIN party's draft text.

Protection of environmental rights was the focus of the intervention of the Haburas Foundation. Stress was laid on the need for government action: for example, to seek cheap oil, so people would no longer destroy forests for firewood. Draft provisions concerning freedom of expression and information were presented by the Timor Lorosa'e Journalists' Association (TLJA). TLJA stressed the importance of guaranteeing freedom of the press, prohibiting censorship of the press, and ensuring the individual's access to information.

In the course of their interactions with speakers, committee members raised issues such as how to deal with the topic of religious conversion, divorce, abortion, religious cults, and freedom to choose one's spouse. The amalgamation of cultures in Timor (in particular from Portuguese colonial times and from the Indonesian occupation) was mentioned, as were the difficulties faced by street children. In relation to enforcement of rights, there was some discussion of the relationship between a national human rights commission and a court. Several committee members emphasised the need for specific protection of women's rights. With a paucity of documentation concerning Thematic Committee I's deliberations, it is difficult to evaluate the influence of the public hearing on committee members. There is one specific case in which a provision was explicitly linked to the suggestion of an NGO – namely the protection of environmental rights proposed by the Haburas Foundation. Other presentations may have been considered in a background fashion during deliberations. From the existing records, most of the committee's deliberations focused more specifically on textual proposals drawn from existing political parties' drafts.

Deliberations on the individual sections within the Bill of Rights commenced on 18 October 2001 and finished with the production of the committee's report on 7 November 2001.[127] The primary texts that the committee had before it were the draft provisions in the FRETILIN, PSD and KOTA texts. On their second day of deliberations, the committee decided to use the FRETILIN Global Project text as the basis for their discussion.

Over the course of Thematic Committee I's deliberations, six new sections were introduced to the FRETILIN draft,[128] with the majority emanating from PSD and KOTA suggestions. These additional clauses focused on rights of children, rights

---

127 Thematic Committee I made an original allocation of time per subject, providing one day for General Principles; three days for Personal Rights, Freedoms and Guarantees; three days for Economic, Social and Cultural Rights and Duties and two days for Defense and National Security.
128 The new sections were known in the 7 November 2001 Thematic Committee text as 17A, 18A, 18B, 21A, 45A, 48A.

of Timorese abroad and of strangers in Timor-Leste, access to courts, rights of consumers and the right to housing. A significant number of amendments were also made to existing FRETILIN clauses, as shown in the section-by-section analysis in Part II of this volume. The alterations had the effect of, for instance:

- bolstering the rights of children;
- providing for the inviolability of life;
- prohibiting the transfer of criminal liability, and ensuring that convicted persons maintained the right to enjoy their fundamental rights;
- extending rights over the processing of personal data;
- securing the special protection of women during pregnancy and after childbirth, including the right to maternity leave;
- providing additional workers' rights;
- recognising a right to social security, and a State duty to support and supervise institutions of social solidarity;
- guaranteeing rights of access to the highest levels of education, scientific investigation and artistic creativity, and rights to culture; and
- providing an explicit right to an environment beneficial to human life.

A majority of these amendments were discussed and voted upon by the committee as a whole. A small number were not voted upon, with the Final Report explaining that such changes were either minor editorial changes, consensual additions or general revisions undertaken centrally. Several of these later alterations emanated from recommendations of the Technical Adviser to the committee. The result was a draft which incorporated some 41 human rights clauses covering a wide range of civil, political, economic, social and cultural rights.[129]

In their report, Thematic Committee I sought to explain influences on their thinking beyond the party texts – referring in particular to the constitutions of other continental countries, including Portugal, the results of the Constitutional Commissions, and the reports of other Assembly committees.[130] The committee opted for a 'minimalist' text rather than a detailed, dense text, fearing that the latter would be difficult for citizens to understand.[131] Likewise, the committee avoided 'advanced principles', particularly in the field of environmental rights and what were described as 'fourth generation rights', which were not regarded

---

129   Many provisions at this point, however, applied only to citizens.
130   Thematic Committee I, 'Final Report', 7 November 2001, [Portuguese], 3.
131   Ibid 3–4.

as feasible.[132] Whilst accepting that any Constitutional text must be open to evolve with values and external changes, it was satisfied that the text 'answered the aspirations of the Timorese people'.[133]

Revisions by the Systematisation and Harmonisation Committee

In theory the Systematisation and Harmonisation Committee was focused on producing a streamlined text for the Plenary's consideration. Indeed, once the Committee had the reports of all the thematic committees, it produced a draft version of the full Constitution in late November. In this draft, the Systematisation and Harmonisation Committee also proposed some amendments and, at its own initiative, included a column comparing the provisions of the draft Constitution with the provisions of the Universal Declaration of Human Rights.

Some of the changes made by the Systematisation and Harmonisation Committee to the thematic committee's text were:

- adding in 'sexual orientation' as a ground of prohibited discrimination;
- integrating Thematic Committee IV's suggested clause on the establishment of a Provedor for Justice;
- prohibiting extradition in cases where the offence under the law of the requesting State was punishable by the death penalty or life imprisonment, or there were grounds to assume that the person might be subjected to torture, and inhuman, degrading and cruel treatment;
- requiring that regulation of freedom of expression and information be 'based on the imperative of respect for the Constitution and the dignity of the human person';
- removing the prohibition on 'fascist' or 'totalitarian' organisations, but extending the prohibition to associations 'that promote terrorism';
- decreasing the voting age threshold to 17 years;
- omitting the reference to military service being for a 'limited period';
- adding a new section on freedom of the press; and
- requiring that requisitions and expropriation of property be for a public purpose and that fair compensation be paid.[134]

---

132 Ibid 4.
133 Ibid.
134 Other changes related to limiting the right to self-defence, and making maternity leave 'in accordance with the law'.

Plenary debates of the Constituent Assembly

The Bill of Rights was the subject of debate from 12 December until 22 December 2001, when the Assembly broke for the Christmas period. The initial pace of the Plenary's deliberations on the draft sections was slow. However, as the Assembly was to commence discussion of s 20 (concerning the rights of persons with disabilities), the President of the Assembly, Lú Olo, announced the finalised streamlined process, leading to an increase in the speed of decision-making. Debate also initially diminished, though some minority parties, in particular UDT, PD and Kota, sought to continue a full debate on provisions. Extensive discussion still centred around provisions dealing with the establishment of the Ombudsman (*Provedor de Direitos Humanos e Justiça*), the right to life, detention and legal process rights, the right to marriage and family, freedom of speech and freedom of the press, freedom of assembly and demonstration, and the range of economic and social rights, including education, health and property.

Some of the more significant changes to the draft text which occurred during the plenary debate included:

- deletion of 'sexual orientation' as a ground of non-discrimination, and the addition of 'marital status';
- recognition that all children, regardless of whether they were born in or out of wedlock, would be entitled to equal rights and social protection;
- addition of new sections dealing with the rights of youth and the rights of the elderly;
- deletion of a provision dealing with the rights of foreigners in Timor-Leste;
- inclusion of an alternative section providing for the establishment of the Ombudsman (*Provedor de Direitos Humanos e Justiça*);
- addition of a section establishing a High Authority for the Mass Media;
- addition of a guarantee for an accused to have a right of hearing and defence;
- addition of the right to work, 'regardless of gender', and inclusion of religion as a prohibited ground of dismissal from employment;
- deletion of the requirement to pay fair compensation for requisitioning or expropriation of property;
- addition of a new section dealing with the obligation to pay tax; and
- elimination of a requirement that public education be non-denominational.[135]

Of the amendments passed during the plenary sessions, over half had FRETILIN members as their chief sponsors. Some amendments were successfully proposed by smaller parties, but in those cases cross-party support was vital. FRETILIN's

---

135   Other changes related to requiring written authorisation from judicial authorities before law enforcement officials could enter a home; and recognising a right to social assistance.

dominance may well have had a chilling effect on those considering advancing amendments. On many occasions dissatisfaction with an aspect of an existing clause was expressed without leading to the proposal of a specific amendment.

Revised text produced for the public consultation process

At the conclusion of the plenary debate, a revised text was prepared by the Systematisation and Harmonisation Committee and approved by the heads of the parliamentary party benches and officials of the thematic committees, before being endorsed by the Assembly. It was this version of the text which was disseminated for the purpose of the consultations.

Changes made to the Bill of Rights during this revision (in addition to changes agreed to by the Plenary) included:

- adding a State duty to promote the protection of disabled citizens;
- requiring that the order of arrest or detention of a person be presented before the judge within the legal timeframe;
- extending several rights to all persons (for example, specific arrest/detention-related rights; the right to compensation for those unjustly convicted, *habeas corpus*; the right to honour and privacy; protection from entry into home; and the right to private property);
- narrowing other rights to apply only to citizens: namely, the right to emigrate freely and return to the country; and the right to social assistance and security;
- deleting the provision establishing a High Authority for the Mass Media;
- guaranteeing the freedom of religious denominations to teach religion;
- reinserting a requirement that compensation be paid for expropriation of property; and
- moving into the Bill of Rights a clause on intellectual property rights.[136]

The Systematisation and Harmonisation Committee explained the genesis of some of these changes in the Portuguese text put to the Plenary. Some were the subject of a specific recommendation advanced by the Centre for Peace and Development, and others were identified as coming from the Timor Lorosa'e Journalists' Association. Most, however, were not attributed to any particular source.

---

136   Other changes related to adding ethnic origin as a field regarding which the non-consensual processing of data was prohibited, and providing that the operation of radio and television stations operate under a licence 'in accordance with the law'.

Suggestions arising from the public consultation

Notwithstanding the limitations of the formal consultation process, many community members responded to what they heard or read during the constitutional process about the protection of human rights. The section-by-section analysis in Part 2 of this study outlines the areas in which a recommendation about a particular clause arose during the District consultations. While some points were identical to those which had been raised in the Assembly (such as defining the age of children, youth and the elderly), others displayed a greater social conservatism. Key messages from the District consultations included calls for greater recognition of the place of the Catholic Church within Timor and the desirability of protecting Timorese culture. Concern was also raised about divorce and polygamy. Frequently, suggestions were made to delete certain guarantees, or to leave them to ordinary law.

Recommendations concerning the human rights clauses were also to be found in the formal written submissions referred to in the report of the Systematisation and Harmonisation Committee. These included the recommendations of Timorese office holders (such as the Minister for Foreign Affairs, the Vice-Minister for Justice, and the Minister for Health), national NGOs (Haburas, Timor Lorosa'e Journalists' Association, and the East Timor Study Group) or international actors (including the SRSG and Transitional Administrator, and The Asia Foundation). A strong theme from these submissions was to amend clauses to ensure greater consistency with international human rights standards. This included applying all appropriate human rights to all persons (rather than citizens), providing more stringent safeguards in relation to limitations on rights and states of emergency, and bolstering means of enforcement of rights.

After compiling the summary of suggestions from Districts and written submissions received at this time, the Systematisation and Harmonisation Committee made some 13 recommendations for changes to the Bill of Rights, four of which were identified as coming from District consultation suggestions and nine of which were identified as coming from the written submissions. The four coming from the District consultations related to (i) banning polygamy and polyandry; (ii) adding in a requirement of 'fair compensation' in relation to expropriation of property; (iii) strengthening the right to health and recognising an individual duty to defend and promote health; and (iv) strengthening the right to environment.[137] At least one other of the suggestions identified as coming from the written submissions was similarly raised in District consultations — namely, requiring a *habeas corpus* application to be ruled on more quickly than

---

137 During his oral explanation of the changes agreed to by consensus, Adérito Soares, Chair of the Systematisation and Harmonisation Committee, referred to two of these proposals also being supported by the formal written submissions: linking the call for 'fair compensation' for acquisition of property to the SRSG and The Asia Foundation; and the changes to the right to health to the Minister for Health.

eight days. Notwithstanding this, it is apparent that the majority of amendments endorsed by the Systematisation and Harmonisation Committee came from the written submissions.

Plenary consideration of proposals from the public consultation

Of the 13 recommended changes to the human rights provisions of the Constitution, nine were the subject of political consensus following the public consultation, in particular:

- adding 'language' as a prohibited ground of non-discrimination;
- recognising as non-derogable rights: the rights to be free from torture, slavery or servitude, cruel, inhuman or degrading treatment or punishment, and non-discrimination;
- making rights to freedom of expression and information, freedom of assembly and to demonstrate, freedom of association and freedom of movement applicable to all persons rather than all citizens;
- requiring compensation for expropriation of property to be 'fair';
- strengthening the language around the right of all persons to health and medical assistance; and
- strengthening the right to environment by removing the qualifying words 'in accordance with its capacities'.

One commentator, Brandt, has argued that topics considered too political or sensitive were not considered by the Plenary, with only 'soft' topics being incorporated into the draft at this point.[138] Yet, from a human rights perspective, not all these changes would be regarded as 'soft'.

Four of the Systematisation and Harmonisation Committee's recommendations were not the subject of consensus and so were not adopted; namely, the proposals to:

- amend the language to avoid limiting the rights of persons with disabilities;
- reduce the period in which a court had to decide a *habeas corpus* application from eight days;
- remove a qualification on the right to demonstrate; and
- include a prohibition of polygamy and polyandry, and include language supporting monogamy.

In the relatively brief debate on these and further changes, the Plenary agreed to qualify the obligation to pay taxation 'in accordance with the law'. Other

---

138   Brandt, above n 20, 17.

suggestions were not accepted, specifically a repeated attempt to remove the same limitation from the right to demonstrate, and a proposal to add recognition of companies' obligation to pay taxes.

With voting finishing on these amendments, the stage was set for the final adoption of the Constitution on 22 March 2002.

UN and other international involvement in the process

As the administering authority in Timor-Leste in 2001–02, the UN was clearly heavily involved with the constitutional process – in particular in the regulatory framework for the Constituent Assembly and the establishment and functioning of the Constitutional Commissions. At the same time, divergent attitudes were present within the UN administration as to proper roles for the UN vis-à-vis the Constituent Assembly. Concerned to ensure that the Assembly operate, and be seen to operate, independently (given constitution-making's nature as a sovereign act), UNTAET took a relatively low-key approach during the deliberations.[139] Whilst providing key administrative secretariat support, most of the UN Transitional Administration did not make substantive interventions on the substance of the Constitution. In late February 2002, Sergio Vieira de Mello sent a letter to the Constituent Assembly in his capacity as SRSG rather than Transitional Administrator. The significance of the distinction was that as the formal head of the governmental structure, (that is, the Transitional Administrator) Vieira de Mello did not wish to intervene in the process, but as Special Representative of the Secretary-General, he was comfortable with promoting compliance with UN standards.[140]

The Human Rights Unit of the Mission, where the author was situated, considered that technical assistance and advocacy related to the protection of international human rights was a legitimate part of its role. Fortunately, a certain tacit agreement existed within the Mission that human rights stood as one of the key values of the UN, so that support to Assembly members on these topics or support for civil society initiatives in these areas was acceptable.[141] In a public statement to the Security Council, the SRSG included respect for human rights as part of the ground rules for the constitutional process: 'the final say

---

139   As to the political sensitivities of governance more broadly in the Transitional Administration, see J Morrow and R White, 'The United Nations in Transitional East Timor: International Standards and the Reality of Governance' (2002) *Australian Yearbook of International Law* 1.

140   More generally as to the involvement of UNTAET in the constitutional process, see A Devereux, 'Searching for Clarity: A case-study of UNTAET's application of international human rights norms' in N White and D Klaasen (eds), UN, *Human Rights and Post Conflict Situations* (Manchester University Press, 2005) 309–311.

141   Note that this process predated the *Guidance Note of the Secretary-General: United Nations Assistance to Constitution-making Processes* (2009), which confirms the UN's role in promoting compliance with international human rights norms and standards in Guiding Principle 2.

… will be with the East Timorese; human rights must be adequately protected; and the system adopted must be democratic.'[142] As a result, the Human Rights Unit made available to Assembly members and others its analyses of draft texts, accepted invitations to address thematic committees and provided other forms of technical assistance. At a key point in the debate, use was also made of the Unit's links with the Office of the High Commissioner for Human Rights, resulting in the High Commissioner making a written intervention. Other UN entities outside the Transitional Administration were actively engaged with the process – including UNICEF, UNIFEM and UNHCR, who variously provided submissions or supported initiatives such as working groups or committees to focus on strengthening the constitutional protection of rights related to their mandates. UNDP also supported the provision of some technical advisers to the Assembly and provided financial support for community awareness programs.

Full-time technical advisers were also provided to the Constituent Assembly by other international sources – in particular the Portuguese Parliament and the Inter-Parliamentary Union. While such advisers undoubtedly provided considerable ongoing assistance on matters of analysis and drafting, there is less in the way of publicly available documentation regarding their role. Fortunately for this study, the international technical adviser for Thematic Committee I specifically identified his recommendations within the committee's reports, but other more informal advice is rendered invisible in the archival record. A significant number of short-term consultants were also provided by the international NGO The Asia Foundation, whose submissions are reflected in this study.[143]

Limits to the public information and outreach program of the Assembly

Late development of a public information strategy

Whether by design or lack of resources, the Assembly initially had no real public information strategy, despite advocacy on the issue from human rights NGOs and UNTAET's Human Rights Unit. As a result of an agreement between Internews and the Constituent Assembly, daily press releases began to be produced in late October (some six weeks into the process), recording such information as the progress of committees, and global votes for the adoption of sections during the plenary sessions.

---

142   Sergio Vieira de Mello (SRSG), during discussion of *The situation in East Timor*, Verbatim Record of the 4165th meeting, UN SCOR, UN Doc S/PV/4165 (27 June 2000) 6.

143   Details of The Asia Foundation's program of assistance to the Constituent Assembly can be found in Aucoin and Brandt, above n 5, 266–268.

In the early debates about the internal rules of the Assembly, PD sought an amendment requiring the elected (political) Secretariat to take notes of the proceedings and make them available to the public. This was, however, defeated, with most of the discussion related to note taking being a function for the technical secretariat (the officials providing administrative support to the Assembly) rather than the elected Secretariat, who were also members of the Assembly and thus not in a position to take such detailed notes. The Assembly also voted against a proposal that the thematic committees report on a daily basis and that their minutes be accessible not only by Assembly members but the public. Manuel Tilman, for the Technical Committee, argued that the minutes were internal documents, and that until documents went through the Assembly, they would not be made public. The Assembly voted in favour of the technical secretariat taking minutes of plenary sessions and the President reported ongoing discussions as to means of overcoming budgetary constraints to do this. Daily press releases came to be the major form of official public information regarding deliberations (though the information in such releases was necessarily abbreviated). Coverage on radio and television provided broader access to ongoing debates.

The issue of public access and information was the subject of the most vociferous demonstration outside the Constituent Assembly. The Assembly was housed in what is now the Parliament's building – directly opposite a university. In the second week of the Assembly's sitting, the NGO Working Group on the Constitution[144] organised a demonstration to draw attention to the need for the Assembly to develop mechanisms to ensure public participation in the constitution-making process. Several hundred people (mainly university students) took part. The demonstration was repeatedly referred to in the Assembly as a 'youth delegation'. As the crowd amassed and became vocal, approximately 20–25 police members mobilised to guard the Assembly's fences, and riot police with shields and batons were stationed at the end of the street. After discussions in the Assembly, the President agreed to a delegation of Assembly members meeting with the demonstrators' leaders. The President explained that to permit a direct address to the Assembly would be disruptive and premature given that the Assembly had not commenced substantive discussion. Once negotiations continued, however, both the group and the police presence dissipated. When the delegation reported back to the

---

144   The NGO Working Group on the Constitution was a coalition of NGOs 'wanting to work towards a legitimate and participatory constitutional process'. Its members included Yayasan HAK, the NGO Forum, Caritas Australia, Fokupers, Haburas, KSI (Kadalak Sulimutuk Institute), Lao Hamutuk, Oxfam Australia, the East Timor Jurists' Association, the Bishop Belo Peace Centre and GFFTL (Grupo Feto Foinsa'e Timor-Leste): NGO Working Group on the Constitution, paper entitled 'Building East Timor's Constitution, together', undated, copy on file with the author.

Assembly, a letter of demand was read out which apologised for the actions of some within the crowd, but reiterated their calls for public consultation and greater accessibility of the Assembly to civil society.[145]

Contemporary access to draft texts

The first official publicly released draft text from the Assembly did not occur until after the Plenary adopted the full draft text in late November 2001. While thematic committee hearings had been open to the public, so the content of draft clauses being discussed were known by attendees, including members of civil society, the standing order of the Assembly (reiterated by Lú Olo in early November 2001) was that documentation of the committees was internal in nature. This significantly constrained, but did not totally prevent, copies of draft texts from circulating outside the Assembly during and immediately after the thematic committee stage of the process. When the Systematisation and Harmonisation Committee presented the draft text of 29 November 2001 to the Assembly, a debate arose as to whether the document was a public document or an internal document. Some members relied on the Internal Rules and Procedures to argue that the approved text should remain confidential until the Assembly was ready to conduct its consultations. Others supported release of the text to foster public discussion and knowledge of the Assembly's deliberations. After the Assembly accepted the draft in principle, the decision was taken to make the text public on 30 November. Thereafter, the draft texts of the Assembly were disseminated.

Limits to the level of participatory constitutionalism

As acknowledged above, there were clear limitations in the process carried out in Timor in 2001–02 from the perspective of participatory constitutionalism. A contemporary report of the UN High Commissioner for Human Rights drafted whilst the process was ongoing summed up many of the concerns. By emphasising a representative democratic model of government, the Assembly minimised the right of individuals to participate in political life through contributing to the constitutional process.[146] The High Commissioner highlighted that public hearings by thematic committees, for instance, were of limited duration, held at short notice and involved a small number of invitees. The result was said to be a lack of ownership of the process:

> Accordingly, there is a popular perception that, to a large extent, the drafting process has focused on the prepared drafts of political parties, rather than incorporating comments or suggestions from ongoing

---

145 See NGO Working Group on the Constitution, 'Clarification', 5 October 2001 [Tetum].
146 *Report of the UN High Commissioner for Human Rights on the situation of human rights in East Timor*, UN Doc E/CN.4/2002/39 (1 March 2002) 13.

consultations or the public hearings. As a result, there appears to be a limited sense of ownership of the process amongst civil society and already a questioning of the responsiveness of the Assembly to its constituents.[147]

The report of the High Commissioner drew particular attention to the lack of accessible information concerning Assembly proceedings, which undermined real engagement:

> Initially, the secretariat of the Assembly lacked resources to ensure adequate dissemination of information. In addition, documents being debated by the Assembly are considered to be internal until they are officially approved by the plenary. This has resulted in the draft Constitution being made available to civil society and UNTAET, inter alia, at a very late stage of proceedings, thereby restricting the ability of individuals and groups to provide commentary and analysis and make proposals to the Assembly. While members of the Assembly have repeatedly affirmed the value of public opinions and the need to incorporate them into the constitutional drafting process, it seems that little has actually been done to support a truly consultative process.[148]

Looking back on this contemporaneous judgement, it remains valid. The official one-week consultation period did not serve to remedy the defects, such that community input to the process remained limited.

Influences in shaping the Bill of Rights

In stressing the role of FRETILIN during the Constituent Assembly, many commentators have either downplayed the role of other influences on the constitutional process, or restricted their gaze to focus on a few high-profile actors. Yet, a close examination of the movements in relation to the Bill of Rights suggests a more nuanced narrative should be considered.

It is not uncommon to read critiques of the Timorese constitutional process that assert that there was no real debate on the draft Constitution; that, instead, there was merely adoption of the FRETILIN party draft because of that party's political dominance. Randall Garrison, for instance, states that '[n]either the team of five international constitutional experts brought in by UNTAET, nor the input from public consultations, nor drafts presented by four other political parties brought any serious modifications of the Fretilin draft'.[149] Anthony Goldstone describes

---

147 Ibid.
148 Ibid.
149 Garrison, above n 18, 20.

the Constitution as a 'Fretilin Constitution',[150] whilst Joanne Wallis concludes that the FRETILIN draft (based on Portuguese and Mozambiquan texts) dominated debate, with the result that 'the committee "cut and pasted" from these constitutions, did not take account of "local context" and "occasionally focused on issues that had no relevance" to Timor-Leste'.[151] These commentators have been fairly dismissive of the constitutional process involving any real dialogue or discussion, seeing changes as the result of interventions by a select number of influential individuals or institutions. Goldstone, for instance, recognises changes made to incorporate international human rights and humanitarian law into the Timorese legal system, but attributes them solely to the prompting of then Foreign Minister and Nobel laureate José Ramos Horta.[152] Wallis highlights the effect of submissions from the UN High Commissioner for Human Rights and the Transitional Administrator in persuading the Assembly to amend some of the human rights provisions so that they applied to all persons, regardless of citizenship.[153] A small number of other amendments are ascribed to lobbying by Bishop Belo and the Catholic Church.[154]

One commentator who has provided a broader analysis is William Binchy. Binchy has identified four factors as being influential in relation to the Timorese Constitution: the influence of the Portuguese Constitution; the marks of the recent struggle for independence; the 'cosmopolitanism of its reception of international human rights instruments'; and a 'delicate accommodation with the Catholic Church'.[155] When one reviews the process of considering the Bill of Rights in closer detail, Binchy's analysis with its recognition of a plurality of influences appears preferable. Yet even Binchy's analysis might be usefully augmented by recognising the richness of aspirations being discussed within the Assembly itself, and the influence of civil society actors beyond the Catholic Church.

It is apparent that the draft texts proposed by political parties at an early stage of the Assembly process were central to the Constituent Assembly's deliberations. These texts, often developed by the diaspora during the Resistance struggle, owed much to the Portuguese Constitution and the Constitutions of other lusophone countries. This is not surprising considering Timor's legal and political history. Timor was a Portuguese colony from the sixteenth century until 1974. and Portugal and its former colonies were strong supporters of the Resistance to the Indonesian invasion and control of Timor-Leste. Many influential members

---

150   Goldstone, 'Building a State', above n 10, 217.
151   Wallis, above n 10, 93.
152   Goldstone, 'Building a State', above n 10, 218.
153   Wallis, above n 10, 106.
154   Ibid 104.
155   W Binchy, 'The Constitution of Timor-Leste in Comparative Perspective', in W Binchy (ed.), *Timor-Leste: Challenges for Justice and Human Rights in the Shadow of the Poor* (Clarus Press, 2009) 261, 262.

of the diaspora found refuge in Portugal and other lusophone countries such as Mozambique. During the debates, one could hear strongly the influence of history in another manner – the experience of human rights violations during Indonesian times and the interlinking of the Resistance with human rights values. Whether it be in discussions about the importance of freedom of the press, reining in police powers or providing for economic and social rights, there was a clear identification between human rights and the struggle over the previous 24 years. All agreed that the adoption of strong guarantees was vital for the future of Timor-Leste. Some of the most heated debates concerned the extent to which the Assembly was remaining faithful to this vision, with accusations on occasion that the Assembly was unnecessarily restricting the ambit of rights.

Politically, the FRETILIN party was certainly dominant within the Assembly and a 'bloc vote' was apparent in relation to consideration of many amendments during plenary sessions. However, in acknowledging this, it is important not to render invisible the significant input of minority parties during the constitutional process. During Thematic Committee I's deliberations, for instance, the FRETILIN draft was used as the basis for discussion, but a significant number of amendments were made to this draft, drawn in particular from alternative PSD and KOTA draft texts. The subtle mechanism of the Systematisation and Harmonisation Committee was another important forum for cross-party discussion. Despite their rather innocuous title, the Systematisation and Harmonisation Committee made or suggested a range of changes to the text, often with a view to bolstering the human rights protections in the Constitution. The office holders of that Committee, comprising one FRETILIN member, one UDC/PDC member and one KOTA member, were to prove particularly influential in guiding deliberations. Even if the plenary sessions of the Assembly presented a challenging environment for minority parties, several critical amendments were passed during the plenary sessions at the prompting of minority parties as well as FRETILIN members.

Opportunities for community engagement with the Constituent Assembly were significantly constrained, and suggestions arising directly from the community through the District consultations had less impact than those coming from organised civil society actors. Amongst civil society actors, the views of the Catholic Church certainly enjoyed particular prominence, and Assembly members were wary of provisions which might unduly interfere with Church operations. This did not equate, however, to uncritical acceptance of its views. A clear undercurrent of several plenary debates (for example, on marriage) was the need to ensure a proper separation of Church and State; to guarantee individuals' rights, rather than leave matters to be settled by Church doctrine alone. Other civil society actors were also influential. Specific mention was made during the debates of views expressed by, for example, Yayasan HAK, REDE Feto Timor Lorosae, the Timor Lorosa'e Journalists' Association, and the environmental NGO Haburas Foundation.

International human rights instruments were referred to sparingly during the debates, though were frequently cited in civil society submissions to the Assembly. The most notable nod to international instruments occurred when the Systematisation and Harmonisation Committee's version of the draft text included a column with comparisons to the Universal Declaration of Human Rights (UDHR). Within the Assembly, there was evident resistance to a wholescale incorporation of rights from international instruments. Stress was laid on the need to ensure that rights adopted were tailored and appropriate to conditions in Timor. Submissions quoting international law were most likely to be considered when expressed at a high level (for example, by the Minister for Foreign Affairs or the UN High Commissioner for Human Rights) or incorporated into revisions advanced by the Systematisation and Harmonisation Committee (for example, extending rights to 'all persons'). Ultimately, whilst the FRETILIN draft remained the dominant textual base for the constitutional process, it is important to acknowledge the contribution of many other actors in shaping the final text, and leaving a legacy of ideas that might be considered in the future.

Conclusion

Examining in detail the debates within and outside the Assembly concerning the shape of human rights provisions permits a deeper appreciation of the major influences on the Bill of Rights. Insight can be obtained into the perceived meaning of the constitutional text and the nature of aspirations being addressed during the process. This study deliberately surveys successive texts and canvasses views expressed by Assembly members (the traditional legislative history), as well as capturing opinions expressed by the Timorese community, civil society and the international community. It will be for future commentators to evaluate whether the promise offered by the Bill of Rights is being actualised.

Part 2 – Section-by-Section Analysis of the Bill of Rights

Explanatory notes for Part 2

Draft texts: The key texts of the draft Constitution presented are:

(1) **Thematic Committee I's text** of 7 November 2001.[1]

(2) The **Systematisation and Harmonisation Committee text** presented to the Assembly on 29 November 2001, and given 'in principle' approval by the Plenary on 30 November 2001.[2] It was this version that was used as the basis for the plenary debates.

(3) The **revised text** approved by the Plenary on 9 February 2002 prior to the **public consultation process**.[3]

(4) The **final text of the Constitution** approved and adopted on 22 March 2002.[4]

As discussed in the Introduction to Part 1, the final text of the Constitution presented in this study is the official translation presented on the Government of Timor-Leste website. In relation to the other texts, the author has looked first to the Portuguese versions of the successive drafts, and has sought to provide a streamlined translation, using the official translation as the base comparator. This has involved some modification of the English language versions produced by the Assembly of the second and third texts listed above.[5]

Presentation of votes: Votes are presented in this study in order of those voting for, against and abstaining. If a vote appears as 42:10:28, it means that 42 persons voted in favour, 10 against and 28 abstained. In most votes, there were members of the Assembly who were not present (or who failed to vote), thus the totals do not necessarily add up to 88 members of the Assembly. For a measure to pass, a majority of those present needed to vote in favour. Thus if 80 members were present, a total of 41 ('40 plus 1') votes in favour was required for the matter to pass.

---

1 Thematic Committee I, 'Final Report', 7 November 2001 [Portuguese]. The finalised text is contained in Annex III of the report.

2 A copy of this text in Portuguese can be accessed at www.etan.org/et2002a/february/10-16/11etapro.htm (accessed September 2014).

3 A copy of this text in Portuguese can be accessed at www.etan.org/et2002a/february/10-16/11etapro.htm (accessed September 2014).

4 The final text of the Constitution of the Democratic Republic of Timor-Leste ('Constitution') can be found at www.timor-leste.gov.tl/wp-content/uploads/2010/03/Constituicao_RDTL_PT.pdf (Portuguese); and the official English translation at www.timor-leste.gov.tl/wp-content/uploads/2010/03/Constitution_RDTL_ENG.pdf (English) (accessed September 2014).

5 For a fuller explanation of the key texts and the methodological approach taken, see the discussion in the Introduction to Part 1.

Plenary debate: In providing details of the debates about each section during the plenary sessions of the Constituent Assembly ('plenary debate'), the focus has been to present the major themes of debates, with illustrations drawn from individual speakers. No attempt has been made to document every comment made during the debate or to record every speaker who addressed the Assembly. Nor are interventions necessarily mentioned in the order of speaking. Instead, comments are grouped in terms of the major points made during the debate. Particular attention has been paid to documenting proposed amendments to sections.

Submissions included: This volume includes both submissions that were analysed by the Systematisation and Harmonisation Committee in their report concerning the public consultation process,[6] as well as other submissions made by civil society, government and international institutions during the constitutional process. A full listing of submissions collected and reviewed by the author is contained in Annex IV. Additional submissions supportive of human rights in general terms are to be found in the Assembly records, including a large number of submissions authored by FRETILIN District Committees. In order to focus on discussions about the choice and wording of human rights to be included in the Constitution, this study quotes only submissions dealing with the detail of the human rights provisions, and focuses on the substantive suggestions made. Many submissions were produced in several languages (including English), allowing quotation of the English language versions. In the cases where submissions were produced in Tetum, Portuguese or Bahasa alone, the translation has been undertaken (or commissioned) by the author.

Terminology: In keeping with the official translation of the Constitution, individual provisions of the Constitution are referred to as 'sections' ('s'). Numbered paragraphs within each section are referred to as 'subsections' ('sub-s'). At the same time, it is recognised that many contemporary actors (including the author) and subsequent commentators commonly use the term 'article' to correspond to the Portuguese term '*artigo*'.[7] During debates, a variety of terms were used to describe component parts of the provisions, including 'paragraphs', 'points' ('*ponto*'), 'lines' ('*linea*') or simply the number of the paragraph. For other sources such as political party projects, Portuguese law or international law, the term 'article' ('art') is used.

---

6 Systematisation and Harmonisation Committee, untitled document submitted to the Assembly on 12 March 2002, summarising the results of the District consultations and written submissions, and containing the proposals from the Bench of the Committee [Portuguese]. It is referred to in this study as the 'Systematisation and Harmonisation Committee's Consultations Report'.

7 Many submissions written in English referred to 'articles' rather than 'sections' of the Constitution. However, in this study, other than where directly quoting submissions, the generic term 'section' is used for consistency purposes and to aid comprehension, given its usage in the official translation.

Presentation of the sections: The sections are presented in chronological order, grouped according to the respective titles under Part II of the Constitution. Draft texts and successfully passed amendments are presented in italics, whilst the final text is presented in bold. The underlining which appears in the Thematic Committee I text is reproduced from the original documentation.[8] It signified the differences between the adopted thematic committee text and the draft presented by the FRETILIN party.

Referencing: In Part 2, a simplified form of referencing is used due to the volume of documentation. Where the source of information is apparent in the text (for example, through a reference to one of the four versions of the draft text listed above, or the Systematisation and Harmonisation Committee's summary of the public consultations), no individual citation has been included. Submissions have, however, been individually cited (and non-sequential shortened references avoided) for the convenience of readers looking only at particular sections.[9]

---

8   Underlining relating to a change of section numbering has not been reproduced.
9   All submissions cited by the author are on file with the author. The location from which they were sourced is noted in Annex IV.

Title I: General Principles (Sections 16–28)

Section 16
(Universality and equality)

1. All citizens are equal before the law, shall exercise the same rights and shall be subject to the same duties.

2. No one shall be discriminated against on grounds of colour, race, marital status, gender, ethnical [ethnic] origin, language, social or economic status, political or ideological convictions, religion, education and physical or mental condition.

(Official translation of the final text)

Drafting history

Thematic Committee I text

Section 16
(Universality of rights)

1. *All citizens are equal before the law, shall exercise the same rights and shall be subject to the same duties.*

2. *No one shall be discriminated against on grounds of colour, race, gender, ethnical [ethnic] origin, social or economic status, political or ideological convictions, religion, education and physical or mental condition.*

Commentary: This section was based on art 16 of the FRETILIN Project[1] and was adopted in a vote of 14:1:4. A slightly longer version of s 16(2) advanced by the office holders of the committee referred also to no one being 'privileged, favored, prejudiced, deprived of any right or exempted from any duty' on the specified grounds. This longer formulation was rejected in a vote of 3:11:6.

---

1 The term 'Project' was used to refer to the draft texts produced by some political parties prior to the constitutional process.

Systematisation and Harmonisation Committee draft text used in the plenary debate

Section 16
(Universality and equality)

1. *All citizens are equal before the law, shall exercise the same rights and shall be subject to the same duties.*

2. *No one shall be discriminated against on grounds of colour, race, gender, sexual orientation, ethnical [ethnic] origin, social or economic status, political or ideological convictions, religion, education and physical or mental condition.*

Commentary: The Systematisation and Harmonisation Committee added in 'sexual orientation' as a ground of prohibited discrimination. The heading was also changed from 'Universality of rights' to 'Universality and equality'.

Plenary debate (12 December 2001)

During the plenary debate, discussion focused on (i) the appropriate terms for the heading and (ii) the sufficiency of the prohibited grounds of discrimination.

Heading

The Systematisation and Harmonisation Committee's change to the heading of the draft section prompted some discussion, in particular as to the significance of the term 'equality'. Manuel Tilman (KOTA), the Rapporteur for the Systematisation and Harmonisation Committee, explained that usage of the term 'equality' was to signify that all citizens, whether big or small, black or white, rich or poor, would be treated equally before the law.[2] Rui António (FRETILIN) and José Reis (FRETILIN) favoured referring to 'Universality of rights' alone, as the clause dealt with the application of rights to all persons. Jacob Fernandes (FRETILIN) also spoke in support of the original thematic committee heading, noting that certain discrimination was permissible, giving the example of a person who could not see clearly being prevented from being a pilot.[3]

Several proposals for amendments to the heading were advanced. Quitéria da Costa (UDT), Manuel Tilman (KOTA), Clementino Amaral (KOTA) and Pedro da Costa (PST) suggested altering the heading to 'Principles of universality and

---

2   Vicente Guterres (UDC/PDC) of the Systematisation and Harmonisation Committee also spoke in favor of retaining the reference to both universality and equality in the heading.

3   José Reis (FRETILIN) also noted the acceptability of treating different things differently, in favouring the reference to universality alone in the heading.

principles of equality'. This was rejected in a vote of 8:33:43.[4] Another proposal was to revert back to 'Universality of rights' (a proposal of Rui António da Cruz (FRETILIN) and other members).[5] While this proposal garnered significant support, it also failed in a vote of 39:16:28. Ultimately, the Systematisation and Harmonisation Committee's text for the heading was adopted in a vote of 53:5:25.

Distinctions between classes of citizens: The reference to equality in the heading and the contents of sub-s (1) proclaiming the equality of citizens prompted a return to debates over the earlier adopted draft s 4. Under draft s 4, those who had 'acquired citizenship' (as opposed to 'original citizenship' by virtue of birth) were ineligible for diplomatic and military posts. Furthermore, the same section foreshadowed later regulation of acquired citizens' access to public office. In the context of debate on s 16, all speakers supported recognition of equality rights. However, several members complained of the inconsistency between proclaiming equal rights in this section and providing for unequal treatment in the earlier adopted s 4.[6] Others argued there was no contradiction in the two sections, with s 4 variously justified as a political matter[7] or a common practice in countries which respected human rights.[8] Draft s 4 was criticised in many submissions[9] and was eventually omitted at a later stage of the constitutional debate. Section 16(1) was adopted without amendment in a vote of 77:0:3.

Consideration of extra grounds of non-discrimination

It was the grounds of prohibited discrimination contained within s 16(2) that dominated discussion during the plenary debate.

Sexual orientation: Most contentious of the grounds considered was that of 'sexual orientation'. Although Thematic Committee I had not included this ground in their draft text, it appeared in the text prepared by the Systematisation

---

4   This vote is written according to the contemporary notes of the author. Unfortunately, it was not captured in the recording provided to the author.

5   According to the recording, the amendment was proposed by Rui António da Cruz (FRETILIN), José Reis (FRETILIN), Vicente Soares Faria (FRETILIN), Armando da Silva (PL) and others whose names were not decipherable by the President of the Assembly, Lú Olo.

6   Those speaking against s 4 in this context included Rui Meneses (PD), Mariano Sabino Lopes (PD), Eusébio Guterres (PD), Aquilino Guterres (PD), Armando da Silva (PL), and Milena Pires (PSD). During the discussion on the heading to the section, Adérito Soares (FRETILIN) also spoke against s 4.

7   Jacob Xavier (PPT).

8   Jacinta Maia (FRETILIN). Others seeing no contradiction included Orsório Florindo (FRETILIN) and Januário Soares (FRETILIN).

9   See for instance, the letter from the UN High Commissioner for Human Rights, Mary Robinson, to the President of the Constituent Assembly, 19 December 2001. A copy of this letter was transmitted by the SRSG to the President of the Assembly on 3 January 2002 and read out to the Assembly on 9 January 2002. In this letter the High Commissioner argued that there was no legitimate basis for discriminating between 'original' and 'acquired citizens'. See too the submission of the Human Rights Unit, UNTAET, 'Summary of select technical comments concerning the East Timorese draft Constitution and its treatment of human rights', December 2001, 1.

and Harmonisation Committee. This discrepancy was noted in the plenary discussion[10] and prompted extensive debate. João Carrascalão (UDT) was one of the most vocal opponents of inclusion of this ground, describing sexual orientation as a condition, a tendency which should be regarded as a private issue. Given that homosexuality was not accepted in all families, Carrascalão voiced concern that singling out sexual orientation in this context might create 'social shock' and provoke attention against homosexuals.[11] It might also lead to the view that other conditions or diseases were not covered in the Constitution. Miguel Soares (FRETILIN) supported João Carrasacalão in opposing the inclusion, arguing that it might create 'contradictions' and confusion at a time when Timor was just starting out as a nation.[12] Other opponents voiced support for the concept of non-discrimination on the basis of sexual orientation, whilst giving a range of rationales for the ground's deletion. Elizario Ferreira (FRETILIN) saw that it would create conflict with the (Catholic) Church. Rui António (FRETILIN) suggested there was a lack of readiness in Timor-Leste to deal with the subject.[13] Vicente Faria (FRETILIN) opined that the issue could be more usefully dealt with through education, or in dealing with health issues (referring to the issue of HIV/AIDS).[14] Armando da Silva (PL) considered that referring to 'sex' was sufficient, fearing that reference to 'sexual orientation' carried a connotation that they were orienting youth.

Defending inclusion of the term, Adérito Soares (FRETILIN, and Chair of the Systematisation and Harmonisation Committee) explained its genesis as the proposal of some members of the Systematisation and Harmonisation Committee. While acknowledging that the text possibly should have been set out in the column detailing suggestions from the Bench rather than appearing in the main body of the text, he remained supportive of its inclusion. Milena Pires (PSD) spoke at particular length on the topic. Whilst recognising the sensitivity of the topic, Pires encouraged the Assembly to deal openly with the issue of sexual orientation. She sensed that people did not wish to talk about the issue, thinking that if the door was closed on the topic, it would disappear. However, if the Assembly wanted the Constitution to be inclusive, the issue of homosexuality needed to be addressed. Responding to earlier comments, Pires noted that homosexuality was not a disease, but was natural, and existed in Timor. As a new nation, the Assembly needed to look at conditions in the country and not discriminate against persons of different sexual orientation. Inclusion of the term in the Constitution would not 'give people ideas', as had been suggested. HIV/AIDS was not transmitted just because of homosexuality. Pires argued that

---

10   Pedro Gomes (ASDT), Adalgisa Ximenes (FRETILIN), Vicente Faria (FRETILIN).
11   João Carrascalão (UDT).
12   Other supporters of João Carrascalão's view included Josefa Soares (FRETILIN).
13   Rui António (FRETILIN).
14   In this context, reference was made to reports of 'foreigners of that sexual orientation' coming to Timor, seemingly linking this to HIV/AIDS in Timor.

the Assembly should have the courage to act against discrimination, including ensuring non-discrimination in the workplace. Francisco Branco (FRETILIN) likewise supported retention of the reference to sexual orientation on the basis that homosexuals had rights just like other citizens.

The vote on retaining 'sexual orientation' in the text failed: 13:52:14.

Following the vote, several members spoke out strongly against the result. Milena Pires (PSD), for example, emphasised the importance of rights for all. Mariano Sabino Lopes (PD) stressed that in supporting non-discrimination against all, he was looking at the reality of Timor and not an overseas country like America or Australia.[15] Homosexual people in Timor, he argued, should not be treated as second- or third-rate citizens.

Additional grounds considered: Birth, Age and Language: 'Birth' was put forward as an additional ground by Clementino Amaral (KOTA), and its inclusion was supported also by Pedro da Costa (PST). Amaral advocated inclusion of this term on the basis that all persons, whether born in the mountains or the city, whether in a palace or a thatched house, should have the same rights. Lucia Lobato (PSD) spoke in favour of non-discrimination against children who were born without a father being around or having any links with the child. Families did not necessarily have the means to look after the children in such circumstances, so there was a need for particular protection. João Carrascalão (UDT) similarly considered 'birth' relevant given the experience of children of rich parents or from a particular family having been viewed as powerful and given preference in employment and other such matters.[16] Others considered 'birth' as unnecessary given the existing references to 'ethnic origin',[17] or the existing protections for children.[18]

'Age' was another ground proposed by Clementino Amaral (KOTA) on the basis that, at times, younger persons were not shown respect by their elders and were not listened to. In support of his proposal, he referred to UNICEF's support for the inclusion of both 'age' and 'birth' as grounds of non-discrimination. Rui Meneses (PD) considered that if 'age' were included, the law would need to define 'age' further. Meneses queried the situation in which a law gave the right to work to the elderly, whereas in reality the elderly were not productive [at work]. The inclusion of 'age' provoked some discussion about the need for a proper understanding of ILO conventions (raised by Eusébio Guterres (PD), and Mariano Sabino Lopes (PD)) on issues such as preventing children from

---

15   This appears to have been a reference to the explanation given by speakers such as Madalena da Silva (FRETILIN) that in voting against the clause, she had been reflecting the situation of those born in Timor, rather than those born overseas.
16   Support also came from Pedro da Costa (PST).
17   Armando da Silva (PL).
18   José Manuel (FRETILIN).

working, whilst ensuring those capable of work were able to do so without facing discrimination. Mariano Sabino Lopes (PD) noted situations where age was part of the criteria for work, giving the example of a maximum age for persons serving in the military.[19] José Manuel da Silva Fernandes (FRETILIN) spoke against inclusion of age, noting there was already a provision concerning children's rights.

'Language' was also put forward as another ground of prohibited discrimination by Pedro Gomes (ASDT), supported by Pedro da Costa (PST). Constância de Jesus (FRETILIN) considered that language was already covered by 'ethnic origin', a view also voiced by Armando da Silva (PL). No specific amendment was put in relation to 'language'.

The proposal to add 'marital status, age and birth' (chief proponent, Clementino Amaral (KOTA))[20] failed to pass in a vote of 21:25:33.

Marital status: The only ground that was successfully added to the list during the plenary session was that of 'marital status' (*'estado civil'*). Its inclusion was proposed by Adérito Soares (FRETILIN), with support emanating from a range of FRETILIN, PD and PL members.[21] Others who spoke in favour included Constância de Jesus (FRETILIN), Adaljiza Magno (FRETILIN), Rui Meneses da Costa (PD), Armando da Silva (PL), Mariano Sabino Lopes (PD), and José Manuel da Silva Fernandes (FRETILIN). During the debate, several specific situations of discrimination faced by women at work were raised, including discrimination on the basis of pregnancy or marriage (that is, being viewed as having family responsibilities).[22] *The addition of marital status passed in a vote of 57:0:22.*[23]

Discussion of adding a reference to freedoms: Mariano Sabino Lopes (PD) noted at several times during the debates that the clause referred to rights and duties, but did not mention freedoms (*'liberdades'*). Other members who spoke in favour of mentioning freedoms more explicitly in this context included Rui Meneses (PD) and Milena Pires (PSD). A written proposal put forward by PD spelt out that equality included equal rights and equal freedoms. The proposal referred also to promoting the realisation of equality through legislative and other measures

---

19   Mariano Sabino Lopes (PD).

20   The original proposal for the inclusion of 'age' and 'birth' came from Clementino Amaral (KOTA), Manuel Tilman (KOTA), João Carrascalão (UDT), and Quitéria da Costa (UDT) according to the recording. Vicente Guterres (UDC/PDC) suggested that this proposal be merged with that of Adérito Soares (regarding marital status) and this was agreed to by Clementino Amaral. Upon the defeat of this amendment, a separate vote took place on the proposal of Adérito Soares.

21   Those who signed the formal submission of the proposal were Adérito Soares (FRETILIN), Eusébio Guterres (PD), Adaljiza Magno (FRETILIN), Armando da Silva (PL) and Cipriana Pereira (FRETILIN).

22   The issue of discrimination faced because of pregnancy was raised specifically by Adaljiza Magno (FRETILIN) and José Manuel (FRETILIN) in speaking in support of the inclusion of 'marital status'.

23   An annotated copy of the draft in the Assembly files recorded this vote as including 20 abstentions; however, the vote called out by Lú Olo was 22 abstentions.

to protect persons who had been disadvantaged by discrimination (a 'special measures' clause). Explicit reference to freedoms was regarded as unnecessary by several members, given the overall contents of the Constitution. Vicente Guterres (UDC/PDC), for instance, referred to the title given to this part of the Constitution ('Fundamental Rights, Duties, Freedoms and Guarantees') and to later sections dealing with specific freedoms. Lú Olo (FRETILIN) similarly thought an addition was unnecessary given that that this section appeared under Title I headed 'General Principles' whereas Title II, for instance, dealt with 'Personal Rights, Freedoms and Guarantees' within the overall part of the Constitution dealing with 'Fundamental Rights, Duties, Freedoms and Guarantees'. António Cardosa Machado (FRETILIN) highlighted the coverage of s 29 in dealing with personal freedom, security and integrity.[24] Adaljiza Magno (FRETILIN) considered that non-discrimination was itself a freedom. During the plenary session, there was no debate on the 'special measures' part of the PD proposal by either the proponents or any opponents.

Mariano Sabino Lopes (PD) suggested that the aim of the proponents might be achieved by simply amending sub-s (1) to add a reference to 'freedoms', an approach also supported by Milena Pires (PSD), who saw the issue more as one of editing than substance. Voting proceeded, however, on the basis of the written proposal. It failed in a vote of 7:44:28.

Voting on the section during the plenary session

Subsection (1) passed: 77:0:3.

Subsection (2) was adopted (as amended): 78:0:1.

The whole section passed: 78:0:1.

Version finalised prior to the public consultation process

Section 16
(Universality and equality)

1. *All citizens are equal before the law, shall exercise the same rights and shall be subject to the same duties.*

2. *No one shall be discriminated against on grounds of colour, race, marital status, gender, ethnical [ethnic] origin, social or economic status, political or ideological convictions, religion, education and physical or mental condition.*

---

24   Draft s 29 became s 30 in the final text.

Representations and submissions

District consultations: The draft section sparked little debate during the District consultations. Only in two Districts were proposals recorded in the compiled report of the Systematisation and Harmonisation Committee. In the Liquiça consultation, a suggestion was made to include protection against discrimination on the basis of sexual orientation. In the Los Palos consultation report, a proposal was advanced to eliminate the whole of sub-s (2), without any further explanation being provided.

Submissions listed in the Systematisation and Harmonisation Committee's Consultations Report: The UN SRSG and Transitional Administrator recommended adding several grounds of non-discrimination, specifically mentioning language and 'other status'. Inclusion of an explicit reference to 'special measures' to redress historical disadvantage in order to avoid doubt as to their permissibility was also recommended.[25] The SRSG also stressed the desirability of the guarantee of non-discrimination applying to all persons.

The Vice-Minister for Justice, Domingos Maria Sarmento, considered ss 16 and 17 needed to be made 'uniform', but did not elaborate further.[26]

Other submissions made during the process: Several external submissions supported the insertion of a 'special measures' provision in the Constitution. In late October 2001, both Yayasan HAK and REDE Feto Timor Lorosae proposed a clause that obliged the State: 'To promote the achievement of equality, legislative and other measures designed to protect or advance persons, or categories of persons, who have been disadvantaged by unfair discrimination, may be taken.'[27] The desirability of a special measures clause was similarly raised by the UNTAET Human Rights Unit[28] and the UN High Commissioner for Human Rights.[29] In these submissions, the type of clause put forward was based upon international precedents: permitting special measures for a limited time to help a historically or otherwise disadvantaged group reach a stage of equal enjoyment of rights.

Additional grounds of prohibited discrimination were advanced in a number of submissions. The Working Group of Child Rights in East Timor's Constitution

---

25   Comments attached to the letter from the UN SRSG and Transitional Administrator, Sergio Vieira de Mello, to heads of the political parties, 22 February 2002.

26   Letter from the Vice-Minister for Justice, Domingos Maria Sarmento, to the President of the Constituent Assembly, 2 March 2002 [Portuguese].

27   Yayasan HAK, 'Civil and Political, Economic, Social and Cultural Rights', undated, but received by the Assembly on 22 October 2001, art 2(3); Letter from REDE Feto Timor Lorosae to the President of the Constituent Assembly, 31 October 2001.

28   Human Rights Unit, UNTAET, 'Thematic Committee One's Proposals for the Protection of Human Rights in the Constitution: An analysis by the HRU', 14 November 2001, 2.

29   Letter from the UN High Commissioner for Human Rights to the President of the Constituent Assembly, 19 December 2001.

argued for inclusion of age and birth in the listing,[30] whilst the Human Rights Unit of UNTAET supported adding the grounds of marital status, pregnancy, parental status, age, parentage and language.[31] Yayasan HAK's October 2001 draft Bill of Rights also made reference to language and sexual orientation, though by March 2002, its submission no longer included reference to sexual orientation.[32]

Specific amendment of this section was suggested to ensure that equality and universality of rights applied to all persons, rather than all citizens. Indeed, the equal application of all rights was a subject raised repeatedly under individual sections. The Human Rights Unit of UNTAET, for instance, drew attention to international law, and supported a revision of the draft Bill of Rights to extend human rights to all persons, with exceptions only for relevant rights such as the right of political participation/right to vote and any necessary exceptions in the field of economic rights.[33] The equal application of rights was one of the major points highlighted in the intervention of the UN High Commissioner for Human Rights,[34] as well as the UN's SRSG and Transitional Administrator.[35] Other interlocutors such as The Asia Foundation and the Minister for Foreign Affairs also raised the issue of rights for all persons in relation to individual sections.[36]

Post-consultation plenary debate

Following the consultation period, the Systematisation and Harmonisation Committee recommended adding 'language' to the section.

'Language' was added to sub-s (2)'s listing of the grounds of prohibited discrimination by virtue of a joint proposal of PST, PDC, PD, FRETILIN, Dist; Ind, PPT, PNT, KOTA, and UDC/PDC.[37]

---

30   Submission of the Working Group for Child Rights in East Timor's Constitution, 14 November 2001. This working group brought together NGOs and UN agencies with an interest in children's rights.

31   Human Rights Unit, UNTAET, 'Summary of select technical comments concerning the East Timorese draft Constitution and its treatment of human rights', December 2001, 2.

32   See Yayasan HAK, 'Civil and Political, Economic, Social and Cultural rights', undated, but received by the Assembly on 22 October 2001, art 2; and 'Draft Proposals for the Constitution of East Timor', received by the Assembly on 15 March 2002, 5 [Bahasa Indonesian].

33   Human Rights Unit, UNTAET, 'Thematic Committee One's Proposals for the Protection of Human Rights in the Constitution: An analysis by the HRU, UNTAET', 14 November 2001, 5.

34   Letter from the UN High Commissioner for Human Rights to the President of the Constituent Assembly, 19 December 2001.

35   Comments attached to the letter from the UN SRSG and Transitional Administrator to heads of the political parties, 22 February 2002.

36   The Asia Foundation, 'Comments and Suggested Amendments to East Timor's Draft Constitution of 9/2/02', undated, but attached to a cover letter to the President of the Constituent Assembly dated 8 March 2002, 5.

37   As indicated on the draft text produced by the Systematisation and Harmonisation Committee on 14 March 2002. This amendment was adopted by the Plenary on 15 March 2002 as part of the agreed package of amendments.

Section 17
(Equality between women and men)

Women and men shall have the same rights and duties in all areas of family, political, economic, social, and cultural life.

(Official translation of the final text)

Drafting history

Thematic Committee I text

Section 17
(Equality between men and women)

Women and men shall have the same rights and duties in all areas of political, economic, social, cultural and family life.

Commentary: The starting point for this section was art 17 of the FRETILIN Project concerning 'Equality of women and protection of children'. The FRETILIN Project had also included a subsection concerning protection of children. In the text advanced by FRETILIN, PDC and ASDT, that subsection was omitted on the basis that it would be moved to a new provision. The reasoning appears likely to reflect an acceptance of arguments put to the committee that protection of children's rights was not only the responsibility of women, but of families, the community and the State.[38]

During Thematic Committee I's deliberations, PSD also proposed a subsection based on art 19(3) of the PSD Project: 'Where there is inequality due to physical, mental, economic, social and other conditions, it is incumbent upon the State and civil society to adopt and take action to allow both men and women equal exercise of their rights.' After a tied first vote of 7:7:4, this proposal was rejected in a second vote of 6:11:2.

The form of the final section (including the amended heading) was proposed by FRETILIN, PDC and ASDT and was adopted in a vote of 17:2:2.

---

38   This was the argument put forward, for instance, by the network of women's organisations, REDE Feto Timor Lorosae in their letter to the President of the Constituent Assembly, 31 October 2001.

Systematisation and Harmonisation Committee draft text used in the plenary debate

Section 17

(Equality between men and women)

Women and men shall have the same rights and duties in all areas of family, political, economic, social and cultural life.[39]

Plenary debate (13 December 2001)

Little discussion surrounded this section in the plenary session of the Assembly. Jacob Xavier (PPT) referred to the earlier discussion of s 7, specifically the paragraph dealing with the State objective of promoting the elevation of women's status of women in society (para (j)). He recalled the suggestion to transfer s 7(j)'s contents into this section.[40] No further interventions were recorded and a vote on the section as drafted proceeded. Other than the ordering of terms in the section, the contents of this section remained consistent from Thematic Committee I's draft text until the final adopted Constitution. It was also the first section to be adopted unanimously by the Plenary.

Voting on the section during the plenary session

The title passed: 80:0:0.

The substance of the section passed: 81:0:0.

The whole section passed: 81:0:0.

Version finalised prior to the public consultation process

Section 17

(Equality between women and men)[41]

Women and men shall have the same rights and duties in all areas of family, political, economic, social and cultural life.

(Identical to final)

---

39 An examination of the Portuguese draft text indicates that the Systematisation and Harmonisation Committee altered the order of words in the section to *'da vida familiar, cultural, social, ecónomica e politica'*. This order remained unchanged in subsequent drafts and was that appearing in the final constitutional text. The translation used for the final text has been used here, rather than that presented in the Assembly translation. It is also noted that the Portuguese text uses singular language referring to 'woman' and 'man'. However, in keeping with the official translation of the final Constitution, these references have been kept in the plural.

40 Jacob Xavier (PPT) repeated this view in a point of order after the vote, and at this time was supported by Adérito Soares (FRETILIN) in his recollection of the Plenary's discussion of s 7. Jacob Fernandes (FRETILIN) indicated disagreement with the text (of s 7(j)). The President of the Assembly, Lú Olo concluded that the section had already been approved and moved to the next section.

41 The ordering of the heading appears to have been changed by the Systematisation and Harmonisation Committee as a stylistic matter.

Representations and submissions

District consultations: In contrast to its smooth passage through the Assembly, this section prompted the expression of various reservations during the District consultations. In particular, concerns were raised as to the clause's potential impact on family life. In Baucau, for instance, a suggestion was made to eliminate the reference to equality in family life. In Ermera, a recommendation was made to affirm the husband as head of the household. Manatuto produced a proposal hinting at similar perceived differences between men and women, stating that 'women and men enjoy the same rights and comply with the same obligations according to their natural characteristics'. Simply eliminating the section as a whole was the solution advocated during the consultation in Oecussi.

The reservations expressed in these community consultations were in stark contrast to the support for the section from NGOs, including women's rights groups.

Submissions listed in the Systematisation and Harmonisation Committee's Consultations Report: None listed.

Other submissions made during the process: The coalition group of women's rights NGOs, REDE Feto Timor Lorosae, were active in calling for more extensive protection of equality rights. In their early submission, REDE proposed an additional clause which would oblige the State to 'provide an institutional mechanism for the protection and the promotion of equality'.[42] This proposal was never taken up during the Assembly debates. REDE also submitted to the Constituent Assembly the 'Women's Charter of Rights in East Timor'. The Charter had been developed through consultations led by the Gender and the Constitution Working Group. It was presented to the SRSG in late September 2001[43] and was subsequently presented to the Assembly, with 8,750 supporting signatures.[44]

The Charter's more detailed 'equality clause' called for equality before the law for women, the prohibition of all forms of discrimination against women, and for the State to be empowered to take 'positive measures to promote equality between men and women'.[45]

---

42 Letter from REDE Feto Timor Lorosae to the President of the Constituent Assembly, 31 October 2001.
43 UNTAET Fact Sheet 11 on Gender Equality Promotion, April 2002; available at http://iknowpolitics.org/sites/default/files/gender20equality20promotion.pdf.
44 The President read out the letter to members of the Constituent Assembly.
45 Women's Charter of Rights in East Timor, art 1.

Section 18
(Child protection)

1. Children shall be entitled to special protection by the family, the community and the State, particularly against all forms of abandonment, discrimination, violence, oppression, sexual abuse and exploitation.

2. Children shall enjoy all rights that are universally recognised, as well as all those that are enshrined in international conventions commonly[46] ratified or approved by the State.

3. Every child born inside or outside wedlock shall enjoy the same rights and social protection.

(Official translation of the final text)

Drafting history

Thematic Committee I text

Section 17A
(Child protection)[47]

1. *Children shall be entitled to special protection by the family, the community and the State, particularly against all forms of abandonment, discrimination, violence, oppression, sexual abuse and exploitation.*[48]

2. *Children shall enjoy all rights that are universally recognised, as well as all those that are enshrined in international conventions commonly ratified or approved by the State.*

Commentary: This section was based in part on art 17(2) of the FRETILIN Project which provided that children had the right to the 'special protection of the family, the community and the State'. The full version of the section was put forward by FRETILIN, PDC and ASDT. The section was adopted in a vote of 17:2:2.

---

46   The Assembly English translations used the term 'normally' ratified. However, the official translation uses the term 'commonly' ratified. The Portuguese term used throughout the drafting process was '*regularmente*' which might also be translated as 'regularly'.

47   The Portuguese version is '*Protecção da criança*' – literally 'protection of children'. The official translation of the final text is 'child protection'.

48   The Portuguese language version throughout used the term most accurately translated as 'a child has the right/is entitled'. However, in the later official English translations (including the translation of the final text), the phrase was translated in the plural form, so the plural form has been preferred here.

The underlined amendment to sub-s (1) appears in the final text prepared by Thematic Committee I (Annex III of their report), but not in the initial account of their decision making (Annex I). It derived from a suggestion of the Technical Adviser to the committee (José Manuel Pinto) whose recommendations were compiled in the committee's report (Annex II). No reference was made in the report as to when/how this suggestion was endorsed by the committee, other than the general footnote appearing at the end of Annex III which explains that additional changes were made as a result of consensus, or a general revision undertaken centrally.

Systematisation and Harmonisation Committee draft text used in the plenary debate

Section 18
(Child protection)

1. *Children shall be entitled to special protection by the family, the community and the State, particularly against all forms of abandonment, discrimination, violence, oppression, sexual abuse and exploitation.*[49]

2. *Children shall enjoy all rights that are universally recognised, as well as all those that are enshrined in international conventions commonly ratified or approved by the State.*

Plenary debate (13 December 2001)

Initial discussion centred on the proper placement of a section on children's rights. Clementino Amaral (KOTA) considered the most appropriate location to be after the provision on family, marriage, and maternity.[50] Speakers including Mariano Sabino (PD) opposed such a move, seeing protection of the family and children's rights as distinct subject matters and preferring the section to remain as originally positioned. No specific proposal to move the section was put to the Plenary, and debate proceeded on the substance of the draft.

Subsection (1): There was some debate about whether the text put forward to the Plenary was that which had been approved by Thematic Committee I. Maria Avalziza Lourdes (FRETILIN) and Vicente Faria (FRETILIN), Rapporteur of Thematic Committee I, thought that the approved phrasing for sub-s (1) extended only to the word 'State' (that is without reference to the specific areas of concern). Faria also sought clarification of who was to provide the protection (the family, the community or the State) and suggested that the section should

---

49   The English Assembly version of the text approved at this point used the term 'especially' rather than 'particularly'. However, the Portuguese term remained *'particularmente'*.
50   Some sympathy for this view was expressed also by Rui Meneses (PD).

specify what protections were covered. Manuel Tilman (KOTA), the Rapporteur of the Systematisation and Harmonisation Committee, defended the draft text stating that it came from Thematic Committee I's Final Report. As a member of Thematic Committee I, Lú Olo (FRETILIN) confirmed that the entire clause had been put to the committee, suggesting that perhaps some of the texts produced had not been complete. As noted above, examining the documentation reveals that the detailed phrasing, 'particularly against all forms of abandonment … exploitation' was not included in the text originally voted upon by the thematic committee and thus did not feature in Annex I of the report. Instead, it came from a suggestion of the Technical Adviser to the committee and was subsequently integrated into the committee's final text.

Clementino Amaral (KOTA) thought the Assembly should add in a reference to 'negligence' in sub-s (1), though Pedro Gomes (ASDT) considered negligence was already covered by the term 'abandonment'.[51] No amendments were put to the Assembly, leading to Clementino Amaral (KOTA) voicing a protest that his amendment had not been considered.

Proposal for an age definition of children: Whether an age definition of children should be specified as the trigger for protection under this section was the subject of extensive debate. Clementino Amaral (KOTA) first raised this issue by tabling a proposal that children be defined as those under 16 years of age. When marriage was mentioned as a defining point in life (that is, the view that when children married, they became adults), the discussion turned to expressions of concern about child marriages and ages at which children should be permitted to marry. Lú Olo (President of the Assembly) noted contradictions in practice: some 14- or 15-year-olds were married, whereas some 80-year-olds were still not married! Mariano Sabino Lopes (PD) spoke in favour of protecting children so that 12- or 14-year-olds would not be permitted to marry.

Manuel Tilman (KOTA) emphasised the need for a definition of 'children'. Manuel Tilman (KOTA) suggested that persons aged 0–16 years be regarded as children,[52] and those aged 17–35 be regarded as youth. In advancing this breakdown of ages, he referred to the need to protect children from marriage, to prohibit children from working and to prevent their participation in war. For those up to 16 years, school should be compulsory. Whilst herself considering that the definition of terms would be best placed in ordinary law rather than the Constitution, Maria Solana (FRETILIN) suggested that as a technical matter, it would be better to say 'under 17' since using 'under 16' would mean only those

---

51   Alfredo da Silva (FRETILIN) also spoke against inclusion of 'negligence' on the basis that later laws could provide the detail of this, and deal with criminal forms of exploitation.

52   Supported also by Quitéria da Costa (UDT).

aged 15 and below would be covered. Support was received from a number of speakers for the importance of defining the concept of children.[53] Others thought it best to leave the definition of the concept to the ordinary law.[54]

In arguing against a definition of age in this context, Mario Carrascalão (PSD) suggested that if this definitional path was followed, it would be necessary also to define when a person was old. Yet this had changed over time. During Portuguese times, for example, a person of 48 years was considered old, whereas now in Portugal, one could be 70 and still young. He also highlighted differences between societies: for example, differences between children in Europe, and those of the same age in Timor. In his view, it was preferable to leave the matter to a later law after a proper study was undertaken, rather than insert an age in the Constitution. Jacob Fernandes (FRETILIN) noted that sub-s (2) referred to international conventions, appearing to suggest that the international definitions could be employed (in particular, the Convention on the Rights of the Child's default age of those under 18 years).

The proposal to include a definition of 'child' as those under 16 years of age (advanced by Clementino Amaral (KOTA et al) failed in a vote of 24:42:17.[55]

In the course of the debate, Adérito Soares (FRETILIN) suggested that since it was not known when Timor would ratify the Convention [on the Rights of the Child], it would be preferable to replace sub-s (2) with a specific reference to the rights which should be protected, making reference to the UNICEF proposal on this subject. The same point was the subject of a specific amendment proposed by Clementino Amaral (KOTA) (discussed further below).

Equality of rights for children born inside or outside of wedlock: The proposal to recognise equality of rights for children born inside or outside of wedlock was advanced by Milena Pires (PSD) and supported by 12 members from PSD, PD, PNT, PL, ASDT, PST, KOTA, PPT and FRETILIN.[56] Pires referred in particular to the experience in Indonesian times of violence against women, as well as the more recent experience of peacekeeping forces fathering children in Timor. It was important not to penalise children born as a result of such circumstances, and to guarantee that all children enjoyed the same rights. After Pires spoke, the proposal was seconded by Adérito Soares (FRETILIN) and Clementino Amaral (KOTA).

---

53   For example, support was voiced by Adérito Soares (FRETILIN), Rui Meneses (PD), Pedro da Costa (PST), and Quitéria da Costa (UDT).

54   Januário Soares (FRETILIN). A similar view was put forward by Maria Solana Fernandes (FRETILIN) and Francisco Jerónimo (FRETILIN).

55   The proponents were not read out at the time of voting, but from the history of the debate appear likely to have included Manuel Tilman (KOTA) and Quiteria da Costa (UDT).

56   The 13 signatories for the proposal were: Milena Pires (PSD), Mario Carrascalão (PSD), Mariano Sabino Lopes (PD), Aliança da Araújo (PNT), Armando da Silva (PL), Pedro Gomes (ASDT), Pedro da Costa (PST), Manuel Tilman (KOTA), Clementino Amaral (KOTA), Jacob Xavier (PPT), Jacob Fernandes (FRETILIN), Adérito Soares (FRETILIN), and Lucia Lobato (PSD).

Debate about this amendment focused on what effect the subsection would have, particularly in relation to social morals. Januário Soares (FRETILIN), for instance, felt the proposal was good in principle, but might be interpreted incorrectly: that it might be read as encouraging people to have children 'in all ways' (out of wedlock). António Ximenes (PDC) feared that the section might give people the opportunity to 'do whatever they want', including living in polygamous arrangements, a situation which PDC did not support. Lucia Lobato (PSD) spoke in favour of the amendment, noting the need to ensure that children born of second or third wives and those born of extramarital affairs were also protected. One member questioned the need for the clause given that the section, by using the general term 'children', already covered all categories of children.[57] Jacob Xavier (PPT) reminded members that there were customary rights for children born in such circumstances, querying which child did not currently enjoy such rights?

In speaking in support of the proposal, Mariano Sabino Lopes (PD) referred to the need to take into account the reality that in Timor during the conflict, some women 'gave themselves' to the military to protect their brothers. Adaljiza Magno (FRETILIN) rebutted criticisms of the clause, stating that it did not 'allow' people to be polygamous, but instead recognised the needs of children in Timor. If children had been born as a result of war, or of persons not marrying, and/or perhaps the mother had limited funds or no work, it was necessary for the State to provide assistance. Magno made reference to art 25 of the Universal Declaration of Human Rights and its recognition that motherhood and children are entitled to special care and attention. She quoted the article in full, including its phraseology that all children, whether born in or out of wedlock, shall enjoy the same social protection. Members should not be afraid that society would become too 'wild' and 'loose' or that people would have children 'left, right and centre'. The issue needed to be explicitly mentioned in the Constitution to ensure there was no discrimination between children. Pedro Gomes (ASDT) also spoke in favour of the provision, noting that during the resistance and after the referendum, 'problems occurred' (seemingly also an oblique reference to sexual assault by Indonesian personnel). Indonesian children were in Timor and thought needed to be given as to how to address that issue.

The proposed amendment to add a clause that '[e]very child born inside or outside wedlock shall enjoy the same rights and social protection' passed in a vote: 43:22:18.[58] It became sub-s (3).

Clementino Amaral (KOTA) objected that his earlier proposal had not been discussed, and so abstained from the vote. The President of the Assembly, Lú Olo, suggested considering his proposal in the afternoon session. Amaral's proposal stated that the

---

57   Flávio da Silva (FRETILIN).

58   Note that the Constituent Assembly's stamped records record the vote as 43:27:10. However, the vote included in this text is that which was read out by Lú Olo during the session (43:22:18).

child enjoyed all the rights that were universally recognised, in particular rights to life, education and health. Further, in all actions concerning him/her, the best interests of the child was to be the primary consideration. The proposal had been originally prepared as a supplement to sub-s (2). However, given that sub-s (2) had already been adopted, Amaral suggested it be considered as a new subsection. Lú Olo saw this addition as unnecessary given that the text already spoke of internationally recognised rights. Amaral acknowledged that the existing text referred to international conventions, but understood its coverage was dependent on ratification of a treaty by the State. He preferred a text which recognised the rights of children in the Constitution, as recommended by UNICEF and the children who had come to the Assembly.[59] However, on the basis of Lú Olo's intervention and the fact that sub-s (2) had already been passed, he was willing to withdraw his proposal.

Voting on the section during the plenary session

The heading passed: 83:0:0.

Subsection (1) passed: 81:0:2.

Subsection (2) passed: 77:0:5.

Subsection (3) (proposed during debate) passed: 43:27:10.

The section as a whole passed: 78:0:0.

Version finalised prior to the public consultation process

Section 18
(Child protection)

1. *Children shall be entitled to special protection by the family, the community and the State, particularly against all forms of abandonment, discrimination, violence, oppression, sexual abuse and exploitation.*

2. *Children shall enjoy all rights that are universally recognised, as well as all those that are enshrined in international conventions commonly ratified or approved by the State.*

3. *Every child born inside or outside wedlock shall enjoy the same rights and social protection.*[60]

(Identical to final)

---

59 On 27 November 2001, some 150 children, aged from 4–13 years, attended the Constituent Assembly, in a visit organised by the Working Group for Child Rights in East Timor (facilitated by UNICEF). In addition to receiving an explanation of the Assembly's functioning, the children sang to Assembly members a song about child rights, including the equality of rights between boys and girls. Several children also directly addressed the Assembly, raising such issues as healthcare, education, and protection from exploitation: Constituent Assembly Press Release, 27 November 2001.

60 In the English Assembly translation, the phrase appeared as 'in or outside' wedlock. The Portuguese text remained '*dentro ou fora*', so the translation for the final text has been preferred.

Representations and submissions

District consultations: In eight Districts (Ainaro, Baucau Dili, Liquiça, Los Palos, Oecusse, Same and Viqueque), reference was made to the need to define the relevant age for children so as to clarify the scope of the section. (The same comment was made in relation to each of ss 18, 19 and 20). In one District, that of Manatuto, it was suggested that the section specify more social and cultural protections for children and young people.

In two Districts, a proposal was made to eliminate sub-s (3) concerning the equal enjoyment of rights by children whether born in or outside wedlock (Los Palos and Viqueque).

Submissions listed in the Systematisation and Harmonisation Committee's Consultations Report: The Minister for Foreign Affairs suggested defining children as all individuals under 18 years of age as well as recognising a right of specific protection against 'neglect'.

Other submissions made during the process: Human rights organisations put forward more elaborate articulations of children's rights for consideration.

Many of these drafts were submitted at the earliest stages of the Assembly's functioning. Yayasan HAK, for instance, in their draft Bill of Rights put forward in late October 2001, supported adding more explicit references to children's rights in the form of a clause:

> Every child has the right to the special protection of the family, the community and the state, which include[s the right]:
>
> a. ... [T]o family and parental care;
> b. To be protected from maltreatment, neglect, abuse or degradation;
> c. To be protected from exploitative labour practices and not to be required to perform work inappropriate to the child's age;
> d. Not to be detained except as a measure of last resort and if detained, to be kept separate from other detained persons over the age of 18 years.[61]

In relation to the draft text produced by the Assembly in February 2002, Yayasan HAK's suggestion was more minimalist – suggesting an additional reference to 'child labour' after 'exploitation'.[62]

---

61 Article 4 of the draft Bill of Rights within Yayasan HAK, 'Civil and Political, Economic, Social and Cultural Rights', undated, but received by the Assembly on 22 October 2001.

62 Yayasan HAK, 'Draft Proposals for the Constitution of East Timor', received by the Assembly on 15 March 2002, 5 [Bahasa Indonesian].

In the context of the public hearing by Thematic Committee I in October 2001, UNICEF and the Working Group for Child Rights in East Timor's Constitution, advanced a detailed clause on child rights:

1. For the purposes of the present Constitution, a *child* means every human being below the age of 18 years.

2. Children have all the rights that are provided under this Constitution.

3. Every child shall enjoy equal rights and freedom, regardless of sex, colour, race, language, religious beliefs, political tendency, birth origin, parentage, social status, wealth or other status.

4. Every child has the rights that are stipulated in the Convention on the Rights of the Child, in particular the right[s]:

    (a) To a name, nationality and family relations from birth;

    (b) To know, and be cared for by both of his or her parents or a legal guardian or, to appropriate alternative care when necessary for the child's best interest;

    (c) To basic nutrition and healthcare, shelter and social services;

    (d) To free primary education and access to secondary education and training;

    (e) To be protected from all forms of violence, torture, rape, sexual abuse, HIV/AIDS, neglect and maltreatment;

    (f) To be protected from all forms of exploitation including sale, sexual exploitation, trafficking, slavery and abduction;

    (g) To be protected from economic exploitation and from performing any work that is hazardous, interferes with the child's education, or is harmful to their healthy physical, mental, social and moral development;

    (h) Not to be detained, except as a measure of last resort, in which case the child may only be held for the shortest appropriate time, separately from persons over 18 years, and treated in a manner, and kept in conditions that take full account of the child's age;

    (i) To legal or appropriate representation and assistance in any civil or criminal proceeding affecting the child;

    (j) Not to be used in armed conflict and to receive special protection in times of conflict; and

(k) To express its views and participate in all decisions affecting their future, in accordance with the age and maturity of the child.

5. Parents, guardians and/or the family bear primary responsibility for the welfare of their children and for their physical, social and moral growth and development. A child temporarily or permanently deprived of his or her family environment, or in whose own best interests cannot be allowed to remain in that environment, including orphaned, separated and refugee children, shall be entitled to special protection, assistance, education, and care provided by the State.

6. The State shall:

(a) Respect and ensure the rights mentioned above;

(b) Undertake all appropriate legislative, administrative and other measures to implement these rights;

(c) Allocate sufficient resources for the realisation of child rights;

(d) Provide special assistance to families and communities for the protection, care and education of vulnerable children, including children with mental or physical disabilities.

7. A child's best interests are paramount in every matter concerning the child.[63]

In mid-November, once Thematic Committee I had finished its deliberations and produced an initial draft, the Working Group for Child Rights in East Timor's Constitution put forward a slightly shorter, but still detailed provision on child rights:[64]

1. For the purposes of the present Constitution, a child means every human being below the age of 18 years. A child's best interests are paramount in every matter concerning the child.

2. All children shall have the rights that are universally recognised, in particular the right to life, to a name and nationality, from birth; and the right to be cared for by his/her parents, with support from the State and the community.

3. Every child also has the right to special protection by the family, community and the State, including from all forms of abuse,

---

63   Working Group for Child Rights in East Timor's Constitution (then named Committee for Child Rights in East Timor's Constitution), 'Draft Articles on Child Rights for East Timor's Constitution', 18 October 2001.
64   Working Group for Child Rights in East Timor's Constitution, Submission of 14 November 2001.

exploitation, violence, neglect, discrimination and deprivation of primary caregivers. They have the right not to be detained, except as a measure of last resort, for the shortest appropriate time; and to legal or appropriate representation and assistance in any civil or criminal proceedings affecting the child.

4. Without discrimination, all children have the right to basic education up to the age of 14 years minimum, and to basic healthcare.

5. The State shall provide special assistance to families and communities for the protection, care and full development of vulnerable children, including separated, orphaned and refugee children, as well as children with mental or physical disabilities.

In late October 2001, REDE Feto Timor Lorosae suggested that there should be a provision stipulating that children had four key rights: namely (i) the right to be cared for by parents and family; (ii) the right to food, shelter and social service; (iii) the right to be protected against torture, suffering and sexual abuse; and (iv) the right not to be subject to carrying out work beyond their age capacity.[65] The National Committee for the Rights of Children in Timor-Leste made a submission supporting recognition of children's rights – focusing on the rights to life, health, study, protection, expression and participation in the life of the nation. Specific mention was made of the defence of refugee children.[66]

The Human Rights Unit of UNTAET also provided comments to the Systematisation and Harmonisation Committee in mid-November 2001, supporting a specific clause on children's rights summarising the provisions of the Convention on the Rights of the Child, referring back to the proposal of the Working Group for Child Rights in East Timor's Constitution.

The East Timor Study Group supported the insertion of age-related definitions in this section, together with the sections on the rights of youth and the rights of seniors.[67]

---

65 Letter from REDE Feto Timor Lorosae to the President of the Constituent Assembly, 31 October 2001. These rights were drawn from art 10 of the Women's Charter of Rights in East Timor.
66 *Comité Nacional de Direito das Criancas de Timor-Leste* (CNDCTL) [National Committee for the Rights of Children of Timor-Leste], undated submission, received by the Assembly on 24 October 2001 [Tetum].
67 East Timor Study Group, 'Debate on the Draft Constitution: Positive and Negative Implications for the Future of East Timor', 20 February 2002, 11 [Tetum].

Section 19
(Youth)

1. The State shall promote and encourage youth initiatives towards the consolidation of national unity, reconstruction, defence and development of the country.

2. The State shall promote education, health and vocational training for the youth as may be practicable.

(Official translation of the final text)

Drafting history

Thematic Committee I text

There was no equivalent provision in the Thematic Committee I text.

Systematisation and Harmonisation Committee draft text used in the plenary debate

The section first appeared as a suggestion by the Bench of the Systematisation and Harmonisation Committee, presented as s 17B in a separate column in the table of the draft text compiled prior to the plenary debate. The suggested text read:

17B
(Youth)

Youth shall enjoy special protection for the exercise of their economic, social and cultural rights, namely:

a. *Access to education, culture and work;*

b. *Vocational training [professional formation].*

This text was never itself subject to a vote, but served to catalyse discussion during the plenary session.

Plenary debate (13 December 2001)

Given its origins as a suggestion of the Bench of the Systematisation and Harmonisation Committee,[68] the Plenary first debated whether there was support for such a clause. The answer was overwhelmingly yes, with some discussion as to whether the clause belonged with the protection of children or in a separate section. A majority of speakers supported a separate section on youth. Mario Carrascalão (PSD) suggested the sequencing seen in the later text with this provision placed between those on children and senior citizens.

Much of the debate concerned the definitional issue of who were 'youth' for the purposes of the section.[69] In this and the interrelated discussions of the definition of 'children', several views were advanced. Manuel Tilman (KOTA) identified youth as those in the 17–35 years age group and stressed the importance of having a definition of youth that could be applied also for youth organisations, noting the existence of youth organisations internationally. Any definition adopted needed to be generic and capable of application at all times. António Ximenes (PDC) viewed youth as those who had not yet formed their families. Mariano Sabino Lopes (PD) thought the approach to understanding youth in Timor needed to be special given the experience of those who had been involved in the struggle for independence. He concluded that it was best for the ordinary law to define the term.[70] Reference was also made to the fact that in resistance-related 'youth meetings', such as those in Portugal, persons with grey hair had been present. In a similar vein, José Manuel (FRETILIN) noted that those who contributed to the Resistance still referred to themselves as youth even if they were 40.

In the course of the debate, frequent reference was made to the sacrifices of youth during the Resistance. Mariano Sabino Lopes (PD), for instance, stressed the importance of recognising the contribution of youth to the Resistance. During the conflict, youth often had no access to education and work. The government needed to address this deficit by taking appropriate measures, including support for vocational courses.[71] Prior to the debate on the additional proposals, there was some disagreement evident as to whether youth required 'special protection', with the suggestion that youth's strength made this wording inappropriate.[72] Pedro da Costa (PST), for instance, considered that given youth's

---

68 The clause was explained by Manuel Tilman (KOTA) and Rapporteur of the Systematisation and Harmonisation Committee.

69 This was first raised by Quitéria da Costa (UDT).

70 Other speakers expressing the view that the definition was best left to ordinary law included Jacob Fernandes (FRETILIN) Armando da Silva (PL) and António Cepada(FRETILIN).

71 Mariano Sabino Lopes (PD), Vicente Guterres (UDC/PDC).

72 Mario Carrascalão (PSD), Januário Soares (FRETILIN).

vitality, they did not need protection, but instead needed assistance. Those supporting the 'special protection' phrasing explained that it was intended to support, for example, training and vocational courses.[73]

Support for having a section with title 'youth' was evidenced in a vote of 81:0:3.

Content of the section

In addition to the original suggestion from the Systematisation and Harmonisation Committee, three proposals for the content of the section were made during the debates: one from FRETILIN, one from PD,[74] and one from KOTA.[75] During the debate, KOTA and PD withdrew their proposals given the FRETILIN proposal that was introduced, and following a number of speakers voicing support for the FRETILIN text.[76] Jacob Fernandes (FRETILIN) speaking to the FRETILIN text explained that a choice had been made to leave the definition/age to ordinary law. The draft section focused on recognising youth's contribution to the Resistance and incorporating the State's duty to promote youth's education, health and training, rather than giving 'special protection' to youth.[77]

The FRETILIN text which was adopted read:

Section 18B
(Youth)

1. *The youth played an important role in the fight for the national liberation and constitute the guarantor for a better future.*

2. *The State shall promote and encourage youth initiatives towards the consolidation of national unity, reconstruction, defence and development of the country.*

3. *The State shall promote education, health and vocational training for the youth as may be practicable.*[78]

This formulation prompted some questioning as to whether the section should be framed in terms of youth and the Resistance, or encapsulate a more generic

---

73   Vicente Guterres (UDC/PDC).

74   The PD proposal specified a State obligation to create mechanisms to guarantee work for young people who did not have access to education due to their involvement with the Resistance.

75   The KOTA proposal incorporated the 17–35 years of age definition of youth.

76   Others speaking in favour of the FRETILIN text included Elizario Ferreira (FRETILIN), and Riak Leman (PSD).

77   Francisco Lay (FRETILIN) in speaking in support of this proposal also mentioned the historical changes in definitions of youth within the Resistance.

78   The written proposal noted that it was presented by the FRETILIN bench and bears the signatures of Jacob Fernandes (FRETILIN), Francisco Branco (FRETILIN), Gregório Saldanha (FRETILIN), Elizario Ferreira (FRETILIN), Noberto Santo (FRETILIN), José Reis (FRETILIN), and Joaquim Barros Soares (FRETILIN) as well as Mariano Sabino Lopes (PD).

formulation concerning youth. Vicente Guterres (UDC/PDC), for instance, considered that a provision on youth and the Resistance might be moved to a transitional section of the Constitution. He also suggested that the term 'construction' might be used rather than 'reconstruction' in sub-s (2) so as to ensure applicability for all time in the future. In his view, 'reconstruction' tended to be a reminder of a specific time. He also noted that difficulties of government could not be an excuse for failure to provide necessary opportunities (in sub-s (3)). No formal amendments to the text, however, were put to the Plenary.

Voting on the section during the plenary session

This draft section was adopted: 73:0:10.[79]

Version finalised prior to the public consultation process

Section 19
(Youth)

1. *The State shall promote and encourage youth initiatives towards the consolidation of national unity, reconstruction, defence and development of the country.*

2. *The State shall promote education, health and vocational training for the youth as may be practicable.*

(Identical to final)

Commentary: This version was shorter than the text adopted in the earlier plenary session in so far as the original sub-s (1) was deleted. An annotation suggested that the wording concerning the contribution of youth to national liberation and youth's role as the guarantee for a better future would be better placed in the Preamble.

Representations and submissions

District consultations: Eight District consultation reports included the suggestion that the relevant age be defined for this section (Ainaro, Baucau, Dili, Liquiça, Los Palos, Oecusse, Same and Viqueque).

The Los Palos report proposed adding that youth were the 'future of the nation', whilst Manatuto proposed specifying more social and cultural protections for children and young people.

Submissions listed in the Systematisation and Harmonisation Committee's Consultations Report: None listed.

---

79 At Lú Olo's suggestion, the section was voted for as a whole, rather than each subsection separately.

Section 20
(Senior citizens)[80]

1. Every senior citizen has the right to special protection by the State.

2. The old age policy entails measures of economic, social and cultural nature designed to provide the elderly with opportunities for personal achievement through active and dignified participation[81] in the community.

(Official translation of the final text)

Drafting history

Thematic Committee I text

There was no equivalent section in the text produced by Thematic Committee I.

Systematisation and Harmonisation Committee draft text used in the plenary debate

There was no equivalent section in the text produced by the Systematisation and Harmonisation Committee draft text prior to the plenary debate.

Plenary debate (14 December 2001)

A new section was proposed during the plenary debate on 14 December 2001 to specifically cover the rights of the elderly. The lead proponent was Mario Carrasacalao (PSD), but co-signatories were drawn from PSD, FRETILIN, UDC/PDC, KOTA, PNT, PSD and ASDT.[82] The new section read:

---

80   The contemporary Assembly translation of the heading from the public consultation version to the final was 'Old age'. However, the official translation uses the term 'Senior citizens' and is thus preferred here. The Portuguese term used in these drafts was '*Terceira idade*', literally 'Third age'.

81   Contemporary Assembly translations from the public consultation version to the final text used the term 'dignifying' participation, but the official translation uses the more grammatically correct term 'dignified' participation and so is preferred here.

82   Signatories included Mario Carrascalão (PSD), Armindina Gusmão (PSD), Milena Pires (PSD), Vidal de Jesus Riak Leman (PSD), Lucia Lobato (PSD), Jacob Fernandes (FRETILIN), Adérito Soares (FRETILIN), Elias Freitas (FRETILIN), Cipriana da Costa, Vicente Guterres (UDC/PDC), Clementino Amaral (KOTA), Aliança da Araújo (PNT), Leandro Isac (PSD), Maria da Costa Valadares (ASDT), Pedro Gomes (ASDT), Feliciano Alves Fatima (ASDT), Constância de Jesus (FRETILIN), Madalena da Silva (FRETILIN), José Soares (FRETILIN), Jacinta de Andrade (FRETILIN), and another member whose signature is unclear. In the plenary debate Mario Carrascalão stated that 46 persons subscribed to the draft section according to consultations prior to the session.

Section 18B
(Old age policy)[83]

1. *Every senior citizen has the right to special protection by the State.*

2. *The old age policy entails measures of economic, social and cultural nature designed to provide the elderly with opportunities for personal achievement through active and dignified participation in the community.*

Relatively little debate surrounded inclusion of a section on this topic. Mario Carrascalão (PSD) explained at the outset that the section had the support of 46 members of the Assembly. It was designed to give special attention to the aged. Carrascalão highlighted the needs of older persons as their physical and intellectual powers diminished and portrayed this section as embracing solidarity with the aged. Particular concern was expressed for the plight of those like farmers, fishermen and carpenters, who might not have enough [money] to support themselves when they were old. Rather than being a proposal emanating from one party bench, Carrascalão stressed that the draft represented the views of several benches. Usage of the term 'policy' in the heading sparked some reaction: with some speakers perceiving an inconsistency with the way other sections were presented (for example, the sections on children and youth).[84] Mario Carrascalão responded that the necessity for government to have a policy on these matters justified inclusion of the term 'policy' in the title.

The initial vote on the creation of such a section passed: 63:5:10.

Manuel Tilman (KOTA) proposed an amendment to recognise a State obligation to promote policies to guarantee the economic security of the elderly. The amendment stipulated that government policies would have to deal with conditions of housing, family and community life so as to avoid and overcome the isolation or social marginalisation of the elderly. The possibility of combining the two texts (the original and the amendment) through appropriate editing was raised by Clementino Amaral (KOTA). The President of the Assembly drew attention to the fact that Clementino Amaral had subscribed to both the original text and the proposed amendment. Manuel Tilman indicated that it would be sufficient if language about the active participation of the elderly to overcome marginalisation and social isolation was adopted, to avoid having two texts before the Plenary.[85] Mario Carrascalão preferred the matter to be put to a separate vote. Manuel Tilman's proposal was defeated in a vote of 34:20:26.[86]

---

83 The same term *'Terceira idade'* was used in this heading. However, here it has been kept as 'old age' given the use of the phrase *'política de terceira idade'* and its translation as 'old age policy' in sub-s (2).

84 Manuel Tilman (KOTA), Adaljiza Magno (FRETILIN).

85 Supported by Vicente Guterres (UDC/PDC).

86 Immediately after the vote on this proposal, the result was read out as 34:20:6 (prompting Adaljiza Magno's comments about this proposal needing a recount in addition to the later recount of sub-s (2) of the section). In the course of this discussion, the vote on Manuel Tilman's proposal was read out as 34:20:26. Unfortunately, the accessible Assembly files include only the global vote on the section.

Another amendment was put forward by Jacob Fernandes (FRETILIN).[87] He proposed a modified sub-s (2) providing that the State, within its possibilities, would promote an old-age policy which encompassed measures to guarantee economic, social and cultural [rights]. It also failed in a vote of 39:14:28.

Voting on the section during the plenary session

Reflecting a certain ambivalence concerning use of the term 'policy' in the heading, the title passed with a positive vote of 42.[88]

Subsection (1) passed: 62:3:15.

Subsection (2) was subject to two rounds of voting due to errors of counting in the first round,[89] with the second round vote recorded as *44:10:26.*

The section as a whole passed: 55:6:19.

Version finalised prior to the public consultation process

Section 20
(Senior citizens)

1. *Every senior citizen has the right to special protection by the State.*[90]

2. *The old age policy entails measures of economic, social and cultural nature designed to provide the elderly with opportunities for personal achievement through active and dignified participation in the community.*

(Identical to final)

Commentary: In this version, the term 'policy' was omitted from the title without explanation. It seemingly reflected the 'harmonised' approach to headings advanced by some speakers during the plenary session.

---

87 The co-sponsors were Flávio da Silva (FRETILIN), Francisco Lelan (FRETILIN), and Elizario Ferreira (FRETILIN).

88 This vote read out was 42:12:6 – which was sufficient for the title to be adopted but, as a later speaker noted, may have been inaccurate given that the total of those voting numbered only 60 on this recorded vote. In the recording, a voice is heard suggesting an abstention vote of 26.

89 Adaljiza Magno (FRETILIN) pointed out that errors were not confined to this vote, but also to others in relation to this section, noting in particular the vote on Manuel Tilman's proposal.

90 At this point, the heading changed to '*terceira idade*'. The Assembly's English translation retained the term 'old age citizen'. However, in keeping with the official translation of the final text, the term 'senior citizen' has been preferred. The Assembly's English translation also incorporated a typographical error in referring to 'signifying' participation in sub-s (2).

Representations and submissions

District consultations: As with the sections on children's and youth's rights, the summary of comments from eight Districts (Ainaro, Baucau, Dili, Liquiça, Los Palos, Oecusse, Same and Viqueque) suggested defining the relevant age for application of the guarantee in order to clarify its intention.

Submissions listed in the Systematisation and Harmonisation Committee's Consultations Report: The Vice-Minister for Justice, Domingos Maria Sarmento, considered that both this section, and s 21 (concerning disabled citizens) were inter-related with s 56 (concerning social security and assistance). He proposed amalgamation of the sections.[91]

---

91 Letter from the Vice-Minister for Justice, Domingos Maria Sarmento, to the President of the Constituent Assembly, 2 March 2002 [Portuguese].

Section 21
(Disabled citizens)[92]

1. A disabled citizen shall enjoy the same rights and shall be subject to the same duties as all other citizens, except for the rights and duties which he or she is unable to exercise or fulfil due to his or her disability.

2. The State shall promote the protection of disabled citizens as may be practicable and in accordance with the law.

(Official translation of the final text)

Drafting history

Thematic Committee I text

Section 18
(Disabled citizens)

A disabled citizen shall enjoy rights and be subject to duties, except for the rights and duties which he or she is unable to exercise or fulfil.

Commentary: This section was based on art 18 of the FRETILIN Project with a change to the heading adopted by consensus. The original FRETILIN heading had been 'Condition of disability' ('*condicação do deficiente*'). The section was adopted in a vote of 17:0:3.

Systematisation and Harmonisation Committee draft text used in the plenary debate

Section 19
(Disabled citizens)

A disabled citizen shall enjoy the same rights and shall be subject to the same duties as all other citizens, except for the rights and duties which he or she is unable to exercise or fulfil.[93]

---

92   The contemporary Assembly translation used the heading 'Disabled citizen'. However, this appears in the plural form in the official translation and has thus been preferred here. The Portuguese term used was '*Cidadão portador de deficiência*'.

93   The contemporary English Assembly translation differed in certain respects from the version presented here, in particular using the language 'except for the exercise of rights or fulfilment of duties for which he

Commentary: In this text, the Systematisation and Harmonisation Committee introduced comparative phrasing into the provision: specifying that the rights and duties to be enjoyed were the 'same' as those enjoyed by 'all other citizens'. A similar change had been recommended by the Technical Adviser, José Manuel Pinto, whose suggestion was included in Annex II of the committee's report.

Plenary debate (18 December)

This section passed without debate. On the morning of 18 December 2001, the new methodology of the Assembly was announced by Lú Olo, whereby members no longer voted on individual subsections, but instead voted only on the complete section, and restrictions were placed on the number and timing of speakers. This appeared to be linked to a desire to hasten the deliberation process. From this point on, both the voting and the discussion of sections was significantly abbreviated.

Voting on the section during the plenary session

The section passed: 76:0:1.

Version finalised prior to the public consultation process

Section 21
(Disabled citizens)

1. *A disabled citizen shall enjoy the same rights and shall be subject to the same duties as all other citizens, except for the rights and duties which he or she is unable to exercise or fulfil due to his or her disability.*

2. *The State shall promote the protection of disabled citizens as may be practicable and in accordance with the law.*

(Identical to final)

Commentary: This version included some small differences to the first subsection and a new sub-s (2).

The amended first subsection specified that the inability to exercise of fulfil rights was 'due to his or her disability', and used the phraseology '*o cidadão portador de deficiência*' rather than '*o cidadão deficiente*': in English, the equivalent of speaking of a citizen who has a disability, rather than a disabled

---

or she is disabled', and employing the active tense ('is subject to the same duties'). However, the Portuguese version remained constant, and thus the translation of the relevant phrases used in the official translation has been preferred.

citizen.[94] The same amendment was made to the heading of the section. The new second subsection concerned the State's duty to promote the protection of disabled citizens. These changes were inserted by the Systematisation and Harmonisation Committee with the agreement of the representatives of the thematic committees and the party benches.

Representations and submissions

District consultations: No comments on this section appear in the summary of District consultations prepared by the Systematisation and Harmonisation Committee.

Submissions listed in the Systematisation and Harmonisation Committee's Consultations Report: The Minister for Foreign Affairs, was concerned at how the text might unintentionally prevent persons from being able to enjoy all their human rights. He noted that international law provided for persons with disabilities to enjoy all rights: for example, under the ICCPR, ICESCR, and drew attention to the drafting of a new treaty on the rights of persons with disabilities.[95]

Post-consultation plenary debate

The Systematisation and Harmonisation Committee recommended eliminating the expression 'exercise or' said to be based on letters received, referring to the letter of the Minister for Foreign Affairs. This may also have reflected submissions like that of the Human Rights Unit of UNTAET recommending removal of the reference to disability rendering a person unfit to exercise rights.[96]

No change was made to the text in the subsequent plenary debate prior to adoption of the final text.

---

94 Despite the change in the Portuguese text, the Assembly translation of both this text and the final text and the official translation of the Constitution retained the term 'a disabled citizen' and thus it has been preferred here. The change to the Portuguese wording had also been a suggestion of the Technical Adviser to Thematic Committee I.

95 Letter from the Minister of State and for Foreign Affairs and Cooperation, Dr José Ramos Horta, to the President of the Constituent Assembly, 25 February 2002.

96 Human Rights Unit, UNTAET, 'Thematic Committee One's Proposals for the Protection of Human Rights in the Constitution: An analysis by the HRU', 14 November 2001, 4; and 'Summary of select technical comments concerning the East Timorese draft Constitution and its treatment of human rights', December 2001, 2.

Section 22
(East Timorese citizens overseas)

East Timorese citizens who are or live overseas shall enjoy protection by the State for the exercise of their rights and shall be subject to duties not incompatible with their absence from the country.

(Official translation of the final text)

Drafting history

Thematic Committee I text

Section 18A
(East Timorese citizens overseas)[97]

East Timorese citizens who are or live overseas shall enjoy protection by the State for the exercise of their rights and shall be subject to duties not incompatible with their absence from the country.

(Identical to final)

Commentary: This provision was based on art 20 of the PSD Project. It was approved unanimously in a vote of 21:0:0.

Systematisation and Harmonisation Committee draft text used in the plenary debate

Section 20
(East Timorese citizens overseas)

East Timorese citizens who are or live overseas shall enjoy protection by the State for the exercise of their rights and shall be subject to duties not incompatible with their absence from the country.

---

97 The Portuguese version was '*Timorenses no estrangeiro*': the same heading appeared in all versions of the draft text, from Thematic Committee I's text through to the final Constitution. While a literal translation might be 'Timorese abroad', all official translations translated the term as 'East Timorese citizens overseas', presumably to provide more context.

Plenary debate (18 December 2001)

This section sparked little debate during the plenary session. António Ximenes (PDC), sought clarification as to whether this provision was intended to provide protection to Timorese who were refugees living in West Timor or Indonesia (referring to those who were 'pro-autonomy' supporters) and/or Timorese who had left Timor in 1975 on and were living in Australia, Portugal or elsewhere. Ximenes thought the section would benefit from being made more specific. Manuel Tilman (KOTA), Rapporteur of the Systematisation and Harmonisation Committee, provided an explanation from that committee's perspective. Whilst agencies like UNHCR and UNTAET and the Minister for Foreign Affairs were focused on the situation of refugees from the 1999 situation, the constitutional provision was intended to be forward-looking. It meant that any Timorese citizens, when overseas, would be able to gain assistance or protection when required from the Embassy/consulate. If, for instance, they committed an offence there, the Timorese consulate should provide them with assistance and access to legal rights [counsel]. Timorese overseas would also be subject to duties – with particular mention made of the duty to vote. Adaljiza Magno (FRETILIN) expressed the view that the provision was perhaps better placed in ordinary law.

Voting on the section during the plenary session

The section passed: 40:30:9.

Version finalised prior to the public consultation process

Section 22
(East Timorese citizens overseas)

East Timorese citizens who are or live overseas shall enjoy protection by the State for the exercise of their rights and shall be subject to duties not incompatible with their absence from the country.

Representations and submissions

District consultations: No specific comments from Districts were recorded in the Systematisation and Harmonisation Committee's summary report of the consultations in relation to the text of this provision.

However, in one District (Manatuto), participants suggested that the Constitution should clearly define the rights of citizens and the rights of foreigners.

In this respect, Thematic Committee I had originally proposed a provision dealing with Foreign Citizens in East Timor, based upon art 21 of the PSD Project. It read:

Section 18B
(Foreigners in East Timor)

The law and international conventions shall establish the rules for comparison of the rights and duties of foreigners who are or live in the territory of East Timor.

It appeared as s 21 in the text which went before the plenary. During the debate on 18 December 2001, a majority of speakers supported deletion of the provision. Ana Pessoa (FRETILIN) proposed its removal. She voiced concern that the provision appeared to be opening the door to the application of all international conventions in an irresponsible, dangerous fashion. In her view, it would be better to consider international conventions on a case-by-case basis, with decisions taken as to whether to ratify or not particular conventions, rather than providing for an open-ended rule applying international conventions in the Constitution. Adaljiza Magno (FRETILIN) was one of several speakers who suggested the matter could be dealt with under ordinary law, thus also supporting its deletion. Francisco Lay (FRETILIN) saw the clause as unnecessary given that there were already provisions concerning foreign investment and the protection of foreigners. Lay also foresaw difficulties in opening wide the door to foreigners given the poverty that existed in the country.[98]

Clementino Amaral (KOTA) sought to allay fears associated with the reference to international conventions, highlighting that before any convention was ratified, it would need to be discussed in the Parliament. Nothing would happen automatically. Rui Meneses da Costa (PD) and Mariano Sabino Lopes (PD) suggested that a modified provision be considered focusing on the security of foreigners. No vote was permitted by the President of the Assembly on this suggestion once the vote was taken for elimination of the section, leading to some debate on the procedural issue.

Vote for the elimination of draft s 21: 53:17:13.

Leandro Isac (PSD), in a speech after this vote, expressed concern that by removing this section the Assembly was thereby discriminating against foreigners living in Timor. Others expressed concern that there would be no clause stipulating the State duty to protect foreigners.[99]

Submissions listed in the Systematisation and Harmonisation Committee's Consultations Report: No submissions were listed as addressing this section

---

98 Francisco Lay was responding in part to the fear expressed by Antonio Ximenes (PDC) that omission of this section would make investors afraid to invest. Others who spoke against the section included Jacob Xavier (PPT), José Lobato (FRETILIN), Norberto Espirito Santo (FRETILIN) and Francisco Lelan (FRETILIN).
99 For example, Rui Meneses (PD), Lucia Lobato (PSD) and Aires Cabral (PNT) also voiced support for the Constitution making some provision for foreigners.

in the summary report. However, The Asia Foundation did query the intended scope of s 22, asking whether it was intended to cover only consular protection, or would also cover the right of citizens overseas to vote in elections. Clarification of this section was regarded as desirable.[100]

---

100   The Asia Foundation, 'Discussion Paper on Draft of East Timorese Constitution', March 2002, 3.

Section 23
(Interpretation of fundamental rights)

Fundamental rights enshrined in the Constitution shall not exclude any other rights provided for by the law and shall be interpreted in accordance with the Universal Declaration of Human Rights.

(Official translation of the final text)

Drafting history

Thematic Committee I text

Section 19
(Interpretation of fundamental rights)

Fundamental rights enshrined in the Constitution shall not exclude any other rights provided for by the law and shall be interpreted in accordance with the Universal Declaration of the Rights of Man.

Commentary: This provision was based on art 19 of the FRETILIN Project. It was approved in a vote of 18:0:2.

Systematisation and Harmonisation Committee draft text used in the plenary debate

Section 22
(Interpretation of fundamental rights)

Fundamental rights enshrined in the Constitution shall not exclude any other rights provided for by the law and shall be interpreted in accordance with the Universal Declaration of Human Rights.

(Identical to final)

Commentary: In this version, the only change made was to correct the reference to the Universal Declaration of Human Rights.

Plenary debate (18 December 2001)

Initial discussion focused on whether the provision presented to the plenary was identical to that adopted by the thematic committee. After this was resolved, the debate turned to the interrelationship between the Constitution and international law: both international human rights law in general and the Universal Declaration of Human Rights (UDHR) in particular.

João Carrascalão (UDT) argued that since the Constitution was the source of law, it should make specific reference to international law and so incorporate its terms, rather than referring to domestic law as the source of additional rights. The language of 'not excluding' other rights in other laws opened the door for laws that did not come under the Constitution. This made it appear as if the Assembly was hiding something. In his view, it was preferable for the Assembly to be explicit about what other rights were intended to be covered. Carrascalão thus supported specifically mentioning international norms of human rights. He noted that the 'original' text (seemingly a reference to the Portuguese Constitution) referred to not excluding rights 'laid down by the law and in the application of rules of international law'. Ana Pessoa (FRETILIN) defended the section as written, arguing that while the Constitution set out fundamental rights, ordinary law might also establish other rights. Here, the UDHR was to be used as an interpretive reference document only. Mari Alkatiri (FRETILIN) spoke against adding a reference to international law norms to sub-s (1) as individual conventions needed to be examined on a case-by-case basis to determine if they should be ratified and given effect to within Timor.

Several speakers spoke of historic commitments to human rights contained in international instruments such as the UDHR. Mariano Sabino Lopes (PD) noted that in the (Timorese) Magna Carta, for instance, reference was made to the UDHR and a promise made that human rights would be protected following independence.[101] Lucia Lobato (PSD) similarly noted that before independence, when people wished to make a petition (concerning human rights), they looked to international law and international conventions for support. Eusébio Guterres (PD) criticised the Assembly's earlier decision to eliminate a clause incorporating international law. He suggested stipulating that the new Constitution did not set aside the UDHR.

Mariana Sabino Lopes (PD), Eusébio Guterres (PD), Rui Meneses (PD), Jerónimo da Silva (FRETILIN) and Lucia Lobato (PSD) proposed an amendment to ensure that interpretation of the Constitution as well as (ordinary) laws would be consistent with the UDHR.[102] It failed in a vote of 13:54:11.

---

101   This is a reference to the *Magna Carta concerning Freedoms, Rights, Duties and Guarantees for the People of East Timor*, adopted at the East Timorese National Convention in the Diaspora, Peniche, on 25 April 1998 which declared acceptance of the UDHR as well as a range of international conventions on human rights and proclaimed that the independent East Timor would be based upon, *inter alia*, 'unyielding support and strict respect for the fundamental freedoms and duties of each and every citizen'.
102   The proposal was made in Bahasa Indonesian.

A second proposal by Manuel Tilman (KOTA) and João Carrascalão (UDT)[103] suggested inserting a reference to the Constitution not excluding other rights provided for in international law. It also failed by a substantial margin of 5:56:16.

Voting on the section during the plenary session

The existing wording of the section passed: 68:4:8.

Version finalised prior to the public consultation process

Section 23
(Interpretation of fundamental rights)

Fundamental rights enshrined in the Constitution shall not exclude any other rights provided for by the law and shall be interpreted in accordance with the Universal Declaration of Human Rights.

Representations and submissions

District consultations: No comments on this section appear in the summary of District consultations prepared by the Systematisation and Harmonisation Committee.

Submissions listed in the Systematisation and Harmonisation Committee's Consultations Report: The Asia Foundation suggested that as human rights norms were constantly evolving, it would be preferable for a court to have the benefit of using any international human rights instruments applicable in the domestic legal system. Accordingly, they recommended adding a reference to 'and any other international human rights instruments or norms that are applicable in the internal legal system of East Timor' to the end of the section.[104] In a second set of comments, The Asia Foundation expressed a preference for an explicit reference to the ICCPR, the ICESCR and developing jurisprudence internationally (in international and national tribunals).[105] The Asia Foundation's draft clause also made the fundamental rights in the Constitution non-exclusive, in the sense of a statement that these rights should not exclude any other rights provided for by law.[106]

---

103 The recording does not capture the details of all the proponents.

104 The Asia Foundation, 'Comments and Suggested Amendments to East Timor's Draft Constitution of 9/2/02', undated, but attached to a cover letter to the President of the Constituent Assembly dated 8 March 2002, 2.

105 The Asia Foundation, 'Discussion Paper on Draft of East Timorese Constitution', March 2002, 3.

106 The Asia Foundation, 'Comments and Suggested Amendments to East Timor's Draft Constitution of 9/2/02', undated, but attached to a cover letter to the President of the Constituent Assembly dated 8 March 2002, 2.

Other submissions made during the process: The thrust of most of the other external suggestions was to broaden the references out to include other international human rights instruments – in particular to include core human rights treaties.

Suggestions for making reference to other treaties or groupings of international instruments had been made by a range of actors, including Yayasan HAK,[107] the Human Rights Unit of UNTAET[108] and REDE Feto Timor Lorosae.[109] Yayasan HAK suggested adding a 'non-exclusion' clause: that the Bill of Rights did not 'deny the existence of any other rights or freedoms that are recognised or conferred by customary law or legislation, to the extent that they are consistent with the Bill'.[110] It also recommended placing an obligation on courts to promote the 'spirit, purport and objects' of the Bill of Rights.[111]

The High Commissioner for Human Rights in late December proposed that the provision be extended to include international human rights treaties and conventions (including the ICCPR, ICESCR, CERD, CEDAW, CRC and the CAT).[112] The Human Rights Unit of UNTAET made a similar suggestion to expand the reference to the range of international human rights instruments, specifically mentioning the utility of the jurisprudence around such instruments (for example, General Comments of UN human rights treaty bodies).[113]

The International Commission of Jurists were concerned that inclusion of the phrase 'rights provided for by the law' made the rights uncertain, and easily removable by the government, though no specific drafting suggestion was advanced.[114]

---

107   Yayasan HAK's draft Bill of Rights included reference to interpreting consistently with the International Bill of Human Rights and permitted recourse to 'foreign law': Yayasan HAK, 'Civil and Political, Economic, Social and Cultural Rights', undated, received by the Assembly on 22 October 2001, art 39.

108   Human Rights Unit, UNTAET, 'Thematic Committee One's Proposals For the Protection of Human Rights in the Constitution: An analysis by the HRU', 14 November 2001, 6, suggesting making reference to the International Bill of Rights.

109   Letter from REDE Feto Timor Lorosae to the President of the Constituent Assembly, 31 October 2001. REDE suggested making reference to the International Bill of Rights, CEDAW and CRC.

110   This suggestion was contained within the draft Bill of Rights in Yayasan HAK, 'Civil and Political, Economic, Social and Cultural Rights', undated but received by the Assembly on 22 October 2001, art 39(3).

111   Ibid.

112   Letter from the UN High Commissioner for Human Rights to the President of the Constituent Assembly, 19 December 2001.

113   Human Rights Unit, UNTAET, 'Summary of select technical comments concerning the East Timorese draft Constitution and its treatment of human rights', December 2001, 3.

114   International Commission of Jurists (Australian Section), 'Commentary on the Draft Constitution Proposed for East Timor by the Constituent Assembly', undated, 5.

Section 24
(Restrictive laws)

1. Restriction of rights, freedoms and guarantees can only be imposed by law in order to safeguard other constitutionally protected rights or interests and in cases clearly provided for by the Constitution.

2. Laws restricting rights, freedoms and guarantees have necessarily a general and abstract nature and may not reduce the extent and scope of the essential contents of constitutional provisions and shall not have a retroactive effect.

(Official translation of the final text)

Drafting history

Thematic Committee I text

Section 20
(Restrictive laws)

1. *Restriction of rights, freedoms and guarantees can only be imposed by law in order to safeguard other constitutionally protected rights or interests and in cases clearly provided for by the Constitution.*

2. *Laws restricting rights, freedoms and guarantees have necessarily a general and abstract nature and may not reduce the extent and scope of the essential contents of constitutional provisions and shall not have a retroactive effect.*

(Identical to final)

Commentary: This provision was based on art 20 of the FRETILIN Project. It was approved unanimously in a vote of 20:0:0.

Systematisation and Harmonisation Committee draft text used in the plenary debate

Section 23

(Restrictive laws)

1. *Restriction of rights, freedoms and guarantees can only be imposed by law in order to safeguard other constitutionally protected rights or interests and in cases clearly provided for by the Constitution.*[115]

2. *Laws restricting rights, freedoms and guarantees have necessarily a general and abstract nature and may not reduce the extent and scope of the essential contents of constitutional provisions and shall not have a retroactive effect.*

Plenary debate (18 December 2001)

Debate on this topic was hampered slightly by complaints about the poor quality of the Bahasa Indonesian translation.

In terms of the substance of the section, a number of questions arose concerning the scope of permissible limitations. Rui Meneses da Costa (PD), for instance, requested clarification from the Systematisation and Harmonisation Committee. When the clause mentioned restrictions being permitted 'by law', which law was being referred to? The Assembly was only now in the process of discussing a Constitution. Lú Olo (FRETILIN) saw the Constitution as the source for later laws. He provided an explanation of the application of the provision. In a time of calamity or when facing imminent invasion, situations which endangered the society, the State might need to take certain decisions – for example, prohibiting movement in a District, or asking people to stay inside.[116] Following this explanation, Vicente Guterres (UDC/PDC), Secretary of the Systematisation and Harmonisation Committee, noted that for completeness, it was necessary to look also at the next section on states of siege and emergency. Any restrictions of rights needed to be in accordance with the law in order to protect rights provided for in the Constitution. Lú Olo felt confident that the draft Constitution had previously defined rights, so that in a specific situation, ordinary law could demark limitations permitted by this provision. When Mario Carrascalão (PSD)

---

115 The English translation approved by the Assembly differed slightly from that presented here, in that it appeared to provide an incorrect translation, referring to 'protected rights *and* interests *or* in cases ...'.

116 As noted in a subtle manner by Vicente Guterres (UDC/PDC) in his subsequent intervention, the explanation provided by the President related more to states of emergency than the ordinary limitation of laws.

queried the meaning of laws of a 'general and abstract nature', suggesting it was too opaque for understanding by non-lawyers, Manuel Tilman (KOTA) explained that the law needed to be concrete in nature and not specific.[117]

Voting on the section during the plenary session

The section passed: 71:1:13.

Version finalised prior to the public consultation process

Section 24

(Restrictive laws)

1. *Restriction of rights, freedoms and guarantees can only be imposed by law in order to safeguard other constitutionally protected rights or interests and in cases clearly provided for by the Constitution.*

2. *Laws restricting rights, freedoms and guarantees have necessarily a general and abstract nature and may not reduce the extent and scope of the essential contents of constitutional provisions and shall not have a retroactive effect.*

Representations and submissions

District consultations: No comments on this section appear in the summary of District consultations prepared by the Systematisation and Harmonisation Committee.

Submissions listed in the Systematisation and Harmonisation Committee's Consultations Report: The UN SRSG and Transitional Administrator recommended that this provision explicitly incorporate requirements of international law by providing that limitations on rights be 'proportionate' and closely tailored to meet the legitimate ends or reason for the limitation. The danger of not doing this was illustrated by giving an example of a potential disproportionate response: a government prohibiting all forms of criticism of political figures or justifying a ban on critical publications by reference to protection of an individual's honour.[118]

---

117 Manuel Tilman's intervention was prompted by the President of the Assembly's suggestion that a jurist provide further explanation. The recording available to the author cut off in the midst of Manuel Tilman's speech. The author's and contemporary monitors' notes also include reference to João Carrascalão querying the rationale for inclusion of the section.

118 The suggestion was made in the comments attached to the letter from the UN SRSG and Transitional Administrator to heads of the political parties, 22 February 2002.

The Minister for Foreign Affairs suggested amending sub-s (1) so that limitations imposed by law needed to be in conformity with international law regarding human rights.[119]

The Asia Foundation similarly recommended adding that restrictions must be 'justifiable in a democratic society, necessary and proportional to the objectives to be achieved'.[120]

Other submissions made during the process: Several organisations made further comments about the phrasing of this provision. The Timor Lorosa'e Journalists' Association (TLJA) in their submission of 7 March 2002 considered that sub-s (1) should more clearly state in what circumstances freedoms and guarantees could be restricted in order to avoid abuse.[121] The Human Rights Unit of UNTAET encouraged revision of the sub-s (2) to provide that limitations needed to be 'proportionate and closely tailored to meeting the legitimate ends under (1)'.[122]

The East Timor Study Group queried the need for this section in the Constitution.[123]

---

119   Letter from the Minister of State and for Foreign Affairs and Cooperation, Dr José Ramos Horta, to the President of the Constituent Assembly, 25 February 2002.

120   The Asia Foundation, 'Comments and Suggested Amendments to East Timor's Draft Constitution of 9/2/02', undated, but attached to a cover letter to the President of the Constituent Assembly dated 8 March 2002, 2.

121   Timor Lorosa'e Journalists' Association, 'Submission on Freedom of Expression', 7 March 2002.

122   Human Rights Unit, UNTAET, 'Thematic Committee One's Proposals for the Protection of Human Rights in the Constitution: An analysis by the HRU', 14 November 2001, 6; and 'Summary of select technical comments concerning the East Timorese draft Constitution and its treatment of human rights', December 2001, 3.

123   East Timor Study Group (ETSG), 'Debate on the Draft Constitution: Positive and Negative Implications for the Future of East Timor', 20 February 2002, 7 [Tetum]. Note that the Systematisation and Harmonisation Committee made reference to receiving a submission from the ETSG, which appears to be this report. However, no recommendations from the ETSG were included in the table of sections and suggestions. The International Commission of Jurists were also critical of this provision, describing it as 'meaningless' and 'unenforceable': 'Commentary on the Draft Constitution Proposed for East Timor by the Constituent Assembly', undated, 5.

Section 25
(State of exception)

1. Suspension of the exercise of fundamental rights, freedoms and guarantees shall only take place if a state of siege or a state of emergency has been declared as provided for by the Constitution.

2. A state of siege or a state of emergency shall only be declared in case of effective or impending aggression by a foreign force, of serious disturbance or threat of serious disturbance to the democratic constitutional order, or of public disaster.

3. A declaration of a state of siege or a state of emergency shall be substantiated, specifying rights, freedoms and guarantees the exercise of which is to be suspended.

4. A suspension shall not last for more than thirty days, without prejudice of possible justified renewal, when strictly necessary, for equal periods of time.

5. In no case shall a declaration of a state of siege affect the right to life, physical integrity, citizenship, non-retroactivity of the criminal law, defence in a criminal case and freedom of conscience and religion, the right not to be subjected to torture, slavery or servitude, the right not to be subjected to cruel, inhuman or degrading treatment or punishment, and the guarantee of non-discrimination.

6. Authorities shall restore constitutional normality as soon as possible.

(Official translation of the final text)

Drafting history

Thematic Committee I text

Section 21
(State of exception)

1. *Suspension of the exercise of fundamental rights, freedoms and guarantees shall only take place if a state of siege or a state of emergency has been declared as provided for by the Constitution.*

2. *A state of siege or a state of emergency shall only be declared in case of effective or impending aggression by a foreign force, of serious disturbance or threat of serious disturbance to the democratic constitutional order, or of public disaster.*

3. *A declaration of a state of siege or a state of emergency shall be substantiated, specifying rights, freedoms and guarantees the exercise of which is to be suspended.*

4. *A suspension shall not last for more than thirty days without prejudice, when strictly necessary, of possible renewal for equal periods of time.*

5. *In no case shall a declaration of a state of siege affect the right to life, physical integrity, citizenship, non-retroactivity of the criminal law, defence in a criminal case <u>and freedom of conscience and religion.</u>*

6. *Authorities shall restore constitutional normality as soon as possible.*

Commentary: This provision was based on art 21 of the FRETILIN Project, with the addition in sub-s (5)'s reference to 'freedom of conscience and religion' approved unanimously (20:0:0). The section was also approved unanimously in a vote of 20:0:0.

Systematisation and Harmonisation Committee draft text used in the plenary debate

Section 24

(State of exception)

1. *Suspension of the exercise of fundamental rights, freedoms and guarantees shall only take place if a state of siege or a state of emergency has been declared as provided for by the Constitution.*

2. *A state of siege or a state of emergency shall only be declared in case of effective or impending aggression by a foreign force, of serious disturbance or threat of serious disturbance to the democratic constitutional order, or of public disaster.*

3. *A declaration of a state of siege or a state of emergency shall be substantiated, specifying rights, freedoms and guarantees the exercise of which is to be suspended.*

4. *A suspension shall not last for more than thirty days, without prejudice, when strictly necessary, of possible renewal for equal periods of time.*

5. *In no case shall a declaration of a state of siege affect the right to life, physical integrity, citizenship, non-retroactivity of the criminal law, defence in a criminal case and freedom of conscience and religion.*

6. *Authorities shall restore constitutional normality as soon as possible.*

Plenary debate (18 December 2001)

Jacob Xavier (PPT) was critical of the fact that the text had been taken verbatim from the Portuguese Constitution. António Ximenes (PDC) questioned the interpretation of sub-s (2) in the Bahasa text. Rui Meneses da Costa (PD) asked whether a state of siege was the same or different to a state of emergency. Vicente Guterres (UDC/PDC), Secretary of the Systematisation and Harmonisation Committee, defended the text. He argued that it was not a problem to adopt provisions from the Portuguese Constitution since it and other comparable documents reflected a rich heritage. In his understanding, a state of emergency related to situations of public calamity. Subsection (2) outlined the situations in which such states could be declared.

Voting on the section during the plenary session

The section passed: 80:1:4.

Version finalised prior to the public consultation process

Section 25
(State of exception)

1. *Suspension of the exercise of fundamental rights, freedoms and guarantees shall only take place if a state of siege or a state of emergency has been declared as provided for by the Constitution.*

2. *A state of siege or a state of emergency shall only be declared in case of effective or impending aggression by a foreign force, of serious disturbance or threat of serious disturbance to the democratic constitutional order, or of public disaster.*

3. *A declaration of a state of siege or a state of emergency shall be substantiated, specifying rights, freedoms and guarantees the exercise of which is to be suspended.*

4. *A suspension shall not last for more than thirty days, without prejudice of possible justified renewal, when strictly necessary, for equal periods of time.*

5. *In no case shall a declaration of a state of siege affect the right to life, physical integrity, citizenship, non-retroactivity of the criminal law, defence in a criminal case and freedom of conscience and religion.*

6. *Authorities shall restore constitutional normality as soon as possible.*

Commentary: In this text, only minor changes were made on a stylistic base (for example, the ordering of phrases). The only substantive change related to sub-s (4)'s reference to renewal of a suspension of rights, adding in a reference to 'justified' renewal.[124]

Representations and submissions

District consultations: No comments on this section appear in the summary of District consultations prepared by the Systematisation and Harmonisation Committee.

Submissions listed in the Systematisation and Harmonisation Committee's Consultations Report: The major external representations focused on ensuring greater compliance between this section and the equivalent article in the International Covenant on Civil and Political Rights (ICCPR) – in terms of the range of non-derogable rights, and the preconditions and process for a state of emergency to be properly declared.

The SRSG and Transitional Administrator suggested that s 25 be amended to prevent abuse of the state of emergency provision. He recommended broadening the listed non-derogable rights to include rights of non-discrimination, and freedom from torture or cruel and unusual punishment. Further detail was also requested in relation to the process to be followed in declaring a state of emergency. It was important that derogation be limited to the extent necessary to respond to the state of siege or emergency. The emergency might, for instance, be limited to a particular geographical area. The UN SRSG and Transitional Administrator also recommended that the declaration of a state of emergency should be subject to review by the Supreme Court.[125]

The Minister for Foreign Affairs placed similar reliance on the scheme provided for under art 4 of the ICCPR.[126] After explaining that scheme, the Minister proposed adding to the list of non-derogable rights the right to be free from torture, slavery or servitude, the right not to be subject to cruel, inhuman or degrading treatment or punishment, the right of non-discrimination, and freedom of thought. He also recommended that State measures abrogating rights be limited to those strictly required by the exigencies of the situation.

The Asia Foundation considered it would be sufficient to refer to a 'state of emergency' alone (that it was not necessary to have a state of siege as well), but that if each were kept, it was important to recognise rights as non-derogable for

---

124 The Portuguese text changed from *'de eventual renovação'* to *'de eventual renovação fundamentada'*.
125 Comments attached to the letter from the UN SRSG and Transitional Administrator to heads of the political parties, 22 February 2002.
126 Letter from the Minister of State and for Foreign Affairs and Cooperation, Dr José Ramos Horta, to the President of the Constituent Assembly, 25 February 2002.

each type of situation.[127] The Asia Foundation also focused on the list of non-derogable rights, suggesting the addition of the right to be free from torture and cruel, inhuman or degrading treatment or punishment, freedom from slavery or servitude, and the right of non-discrimination. Furthermore, it recommended explicit recognition of derogations needing to be reasonably justifiable in a democratic society, necessary and proportional to the objectives to be achieved.[128] The Asia Foundation also noted the difficulties of understanding the procedure for declaring a state of emergency or state of siege under the Constitution given the respective roles of the President, the Parliament and the Government and suggested a single section be drafted clearly stating the role of each organ and the chronological steps that needed to be taken in making the declaration.[129] In a separate submission, The Asia Foundation also noted the lack of a definition of 'state of siege'.[130]

Other submissions made during the process: Additional submissions were made during the constitutional process, though the substance was similar to those quoted by the Systematisation and Harmonisation Committee. Common to many was the call to broaden the list of non-derogable rights. Yayasan HAK,[131] the Church-Constitution Working Group,[132] and the Human Rights Unit of UNTAET, for instance, all proposed adding in references to freedom from torture and cruel, inhuman or degrading treatment or punishment. The most extensive suggestions came from the Human Rights Unit of UNTAET which also recommended inclusion of non-discrimination, freedom from slavery or servitude, freedom of thought and the right to recognition as a person before the law as non-derogable rights.[133]

Some concern was expressed concerning the language used to describe situations of 'state of siege or state of emergency'. The Timor Lorosa'e Journalists' Association, for instance, considered the reference to a serious disturbance or threat of such to be too broad, preferring the language employed in the ICCPR of a public emergency threatening the life of the nation.[134] The Human Rights Unit of UNTAET advocated consistency in the use of language concerning a state of

---

127 The Asia Foundation, 'Comments and Suggested Amendments to East Timor's Draft Constitution of 9/2/02', undated, but attached to a cover letter to the President of the Constituent Assembly dated 8 March 2002, 3.

128 Ibid.

129 Ibid. 4.

130 The Asia Foundation, 'Discussion Paper on Draft of East Timorese Constitution', March 2002, 4.

131 Yayasan HAK, 'Draft Proposals for the Constitution of East Timor', received by the Assembly on 15 March 2002, 6 [Bahasa Indonesian].

132 Letter from the Centre for Peace and Development to the President of the Constituent Assembly, January 2002, received by the Assembly on 23 January 2002. This letter contained the submission of the Church-Constitution Working Group.

133 Human Rights Unit, 'Summary of select technical comments concerning the East Timorese draft Constitution and its treatment of human rights', December 2001, 4.

134 Timor Lorosa'e Journalists' Association, 'Submission on Freedom of Expression', 7 March 2002.

siege or a state of emergency, and more specific procedures as to how and by whom the declaration was to be made. A public declaration of how the rights were to be derogated was needed. The Human Rights Unit also recommended that any derogation of rights should be limited to the extent necessary to respond to the state of siege/emergency.[135] Yayasan HAK suggested stipulating that a declaration of state of siege/emergency only be made where the declaration was necessary to restore peace and order.[136] The Church-Constitution Working Group recommended limiting any suspension of rights to 15 days.[137]

Post-consultation plenary debate

The Systematisation and Harmonisation Committee recommended *adding the following rights to the list of non-derogable rights: the right not to be subjected to torture, slavery or servitude, the right not to be subjected to cruel, inhuman or degrading treatment or punishment, and the guarantee of non-discrimination.*

These grounds were added by virtue of a joint proposal of FRETILIN, PST, PDC, PD, ASDT, PSD, Ind, PPT, PNT, PL, KOTA, UDC/PDC[138] and adopted by the Plenary on 15 March 2002 as part of a package of agreed amendments.

---

135   Human Rights Unit, UNTAET, 'Thematic Committee One's Proposals for the Protection of Human Rights in the Constitution: An analysis by the HRU', 14 November 2001, 7; 'Summary of select technical comments concerning the East Timorese draft Constitution and its treatment of human rights', December 2001, 4.

136   This suggestion was incorporated within the draft Bill of Rights within Yayasan HAK, 'Civil and Political, Economic, Social and Cultural rights', undated, but received by the Assembly on 22 October 2001, art 41.

137   The Church-Constitution Working Group recognised the equivalent provision in the Portuguese Constitution, art 19(5), which restricted the period of suspension to 15 days 'or, where the declaration resulted from a declaration of war, for the period laid down by law, whilst allowing for the period to be renewed from time to time subject to the same time limits': Letter from the Centre for Peace and Development, to the President of the Constituent Assembly, January 2002, received by the Assembly on 23 January 2002.

138   As indicated on the draft text produced by the Systematisation and Harmonisation Committee on 14 March 2002.

Section 26
(Access to courts)

1. Access to courts is guaranteed to all for the defence of their legally protected rights and interests.

2. Justice shall not be denied for insufficient economic means.

(Official translation of the final text)

Drafting history

Thematic Committee I text

Section 21A
(Access to courts)

1. *Access to courts is guaranteed to all for the defence of their legally protected rights and interests.*

2. *Justice shall not be denied for insufficient economic means.*

(Identical to final)

Commentary: This provision was based on art 25 of the PSD Project, albeit with an amended title. The heading in the PSD Project had been 'Judicial protection'. The section was approved in a vote of 19:0:2.

Systematisation and Harmonisation Committee draft text used in the plenary debate

Section 25
(Access to courts)

1. *Access to courts is guaranteed to all for the defence of their legally protected rights and interests.*

2. *Justice shall not be denied for insufficient economic means.*

Plenary debate (18 December 2001)

This section prompted no interventions during the plenary session. In his declaration of vote, Mariano Sabino Lopes (PD) noted the need for the State to provide assistance [legal aid] for those without means.

Voting on the section during the plenary session

The section passed: 82:1:2.

Version finalised prior to the public consultation process

Section 26
(Access to courts)

1. *Access to courts is guaranteed to all for the defence of their legally protected rights and interests.*

2. *Justice shall not be denied for insufficient economic means.*

Representations and submissions

District consultations: No comments on this section appear in the summary of District consultations prepared by the Systematisation and Harmonisation Committee.

Submissions listed in the Systematisation and Harmonisation Committee's Consultations Report: The Asia Foundation suggested adding a new subsection requiring the State to provide a lawyer to a person accused of a crime who could not afford a lawyer if she/he was liable to a prison term of six months or more. They also supported inclusion of an obligation on the State to establish an independent commission to ensure the effective provision of legal aid in East Timor.[139] In a second set of comments, The Asia Foundation submission explained that it would only be through an independent institution or commission that the public would have confidence in the competence and independence of legal aid.[140]

Other submissions made during the process: The Human Rights Unit, UNTAET, proposed making explicit reference to human rights as one type of rights and interests for which access to courts was to be guaranteed.[141]

---

139   The Asia Foundation, 'Comments and Suggested Amendments to East Timor's Draft Constitution of 9/2/02', undated, but attached to a cover letter to the President of the Constituent Assembly dated 8 March 2002, 4.

140   The Asia Foundation, 'Discussion Paper on Draft of East Timorese Constitution', March 2002, 4.

141   Human Rights Unit, UNTAET, 'Summary of select technical comments concerning the East Timorese draft Constitution and its treatment of human rights', December 2001, 4.

Section 27
(Ombudsman)

1. The Ombudsman shall be an independent organ in charge of examining and seeking to settle citizens' complaints against public bodies, certifying the conformity of the acts with the law, preventing and initiating the whole process to remedy injustice.[142]

2. Citizens may present complaints concerning acts or omissions on the part of public bodies to the Ombudsman, who shall undertake a review, without power of decision, and shall forward recommendations to the competent organs as deemed necessary.

3. The Ombudsman shall be appointed by the National Parliament through absolute majority votes of its members for a term of office of four years.

4. The activity [of] the Ombudsman shall be independent from any means of grace and legal remedies as laid down in the Constitution and the law.

5. Administrative organs and public servants shall have the duty to collaborate with the Ombudsman.

(Official translation of the final text)

Drafting history

Thematic Committee IV text

There was no equivalent provision to s 27 in the draft text produced by Thematic Committee I despite it having before it at least one written proposal on a national human rights institution submitted by the Working Group on Future Human Rights Institutions (see further under 'Representations and submissions' below). Instead, the draft text came from Thematic Committee IV

---

142 The contemporary Assembly English translation used a different tense to the official translation, referring to the function of the Ombudsman to 'examine and seek ... certify ... prevent and initiate' in sub-s (1). The Portuguese text remained consistent from the text of the proposal put forward in the Plenary (complete with handwritten additions) to the final version and thus the form of the official translation of the final text has been preferred.

(the committee looking at Fundamental Principles, Final and Transitional Arrangements, and Amendments) as a suggestion to be considered by Thematic Committee I. The draft text proposed read:

Section ...
(Ombudsman [*Provedor de Justiça/Inspector-Geral*])

1. *Citizens may present complaints concerning acts or omissions on the part of public bodies to the Ombudsman/Inspector-General, who shall undertake a review, without power of decision, and shall forward recommendations to the competent organs as deemed necessary to prevent or remedy injustice.*

2. *The Ombudsman/Inspector-General may request the Supreme Court of Justice to declare the unconstitutionality of legal rulings issued by organs of the State.*

3. *The Ombudsman/Inspector-General shall be an independent organ; the Ombudsman/Inspector-General shall be appointed by the National Parliament for a term established by law*

4. *The organs and personnel of the Public Service shall cooperate with the Ombudsman/Inspector-General in the discharge of the Ombudsman's responsibilities.*[143]

Systematisation and Harmonisation Committee draft text used in the plenary debate

Section 26
(Ombudsman [*Provedor de Justiça*])[144]

1. *Citizens may present complaints concerning acts or omissions on the part of public bodies to the Ombudsman, who shall undertake a review, without power of decision, and shall forward recommendations to the competent organs as deemed necessary to prevent or remedy injustice.*

2. *The Ombudsman may request the Supreme Court of Justice to declare the unconstitutionality of legal rulings issued by organs of the State.*

---

143   Note that this translation has been streamlined according to the official translations. Any differences between this translation and the translation of the Portuguese Constitution (containing virtually identical provisions in arts 23(1), (3) and (4)) are purely stylistic.

144   The Portuguese text used the title '*Provedor de Justiça*', although in the English Assembly version the term was shortened to Ombudsman. Here both titles are presented each text in order to provide the fuller understanding of what was debated.

3. *The Ombudsman shall be an independent organ; the Ombudsman shall be appointed by the National Parliament for a term established by law.*[145]

4. *The organs and personnel of the Public Service shall cooperate with the Ombudsman in the discharge of the Ombudsman's responsibilities.*

Commentary: This text was identical to that proposed by Thematic Committee IV with the exception of omitting any reference to the dual title 'Inspector-General'.

The Bench of the Systematisation and Harmonisation Committee recommended a section to read:

1. *Citizens may present complaints concerning acts or omissions, corruption or illegal administrative acts to the Ombudsman, who shall undertake a review, without power of decision, and shall forward recommendations to the competent organs as deemed necessary to prevent or remedy injustice.*

2. *The activity of the Ombudsman shall be independent from any means of grace or legal remedies as laid down in the law.*[146]

3. *The Ombudsman shall be appointed [elected] by the National Parliament.*

In making these drafting suggestions, the Systematisation and Harmonisation Committee would have had available to it a proposal advanced by Isabel Ferreira (the Chief Minister's Adviser on Human Rights) and Maria Domingas Alves (the Chief Minister's Adviser on the Promotion of Equality), the details of which are included below under the heading 'Other submissions'. The Chief Minister's Advisers' proposal was read out to the Plenary of the Assembly on 23 November 2001. It thus postdates the thematic committee's deliberations, but coincides with the time of the Systematisation and Harmonisation Committee's deliberations.[147] The text recommended by the Systematisation and Harmonisation Committee was virtually identical to three of the five subsections in that proposal. The only notable differences were that the Systematisation and Harmonisation clause included a reference to corruption and illegal administrative acts as part of the jurisdiction of the Provedor, and did not include the advisers' suggested recognition of an individual's fundamental right to seek a remedy.

---

145 The Assembly's English translation of the Systematisation and Harmonisation Committee's text referred to the Warden of Justice. However, the Portuguese version referred in sub-s (3) to the Provedor, and thus has been presented here.

146 The English Assembly text referred to the 'actions' of the Ombudsman. However, as the Portuguese term *'actividade'* is translated in the final text as 'activity', the latter term has been used here.

147 Thematic Committee IV's report was date-stamped 6 November 2001 and the Plenary did not commence debate on this topic until mid-December 2001. The Systematisation and Harmonisation Committee's draft was produced in late November.

Plenary debate (18 December 2001)

An alternative text for this section was put forward by Jacob Fernandes (FRETILIN) and supported by 15 FRETILIN members. The version which was finalised after discussion with Mari Alkatiri (FRETILIN)[148] read:

Section 26
(Ombudsman [*Provedor de Direitos Humanos e Justiça*])

1. *The Ombudsman shall be an independent organ in charge of examining and seeking to settle citizens' complaints against public bodies, certifying the conformity of the acts with the law, preventing and initiating the whole process to remedy injustice.*

2. *Citizens may present complaints concerning acts or omissions on the part of public bodies to the Ombudsman, who shall undertake a review, without power of decision, and shall forward recommendations to the competent organs as deemed necessary.*

3. *The Ombudsman shall be appointed[149] by the National Parliament through absolute majority votes of its members (for a term of office of four years)*.*

4. *The activity of the Ombudsman shall be independent from any means of grace and legal remedies as laid down in the Constitution and the law.*

5. *Administrative organs and public servants[150] shall have the duty to collaborate with the Ombudsman.[151]*

*Bracketed text added during the debate

The written text of the proposal explained its importance in terms of cementing a culture of respect for human rights and justice, an outcome which all craved within Timor-Leste. The proposal was said to be a Timorese version of the institution born in Nordic countries, known as the Ombudsman. The final proposal considered in the plenary included an amendment from Mari Alkatiri to stipulate that the Provedor's term would be limited to four years.

---

148 Mari Alkatiri was elected as a member of the Constituent Assembly, but was also the Chief Minister of the Second Transitional Government of East Timor.

149 The term in Portuguese appearing in the typed amendment was *'designado'*, which was the same term as used by Thematic Committee IV, but differed from the term *'eleito'* contained in the recommended text of the Systematisation and Harmonisation Committee and subsequently used in the text.

150 The Portuguese text changed from *'Os órgãos e agentes da Administração Publica'* to *'Os órgãos e os agentes da administração'*.

151 The signatories to the proposal were Jacob Fernandes (FRETILIN), Ana Pessoa (FRETILIN), Lourdes Alves (FRETILIN), José dos Reis (FRETILIN), Adaljiza Magno (FRETILIN), Joaquim Barros Soares (FRETILIN), Norberto Santo (FRETILIN), Francisco Branco (FRETILIN), Januário Soares (FRETILIN), Elias Freitas (FRETILIN), Constância de Jesus (FRETILIN), Gregório Saldanha (FRETILIN), Jerónimo da Silva (FRETILIN), and further members whose signatures are unclear.

Discussion

Debate in the plenary focused on (i) the heading for the section; (ii) the extent of independence of the Provedor; and (iii) the adequacy of powers given to the Provedor.

Some members queried the new heading introduced in the FRETILIN proposal ('Provedor for Human Rights and Justice'). A number of speakers saw the term 'justice' as itself embracing the concept of human rights. Cipriana Pereira (FRETILIN) expressed a preference for the original heading of a 'Provedor for Justice'. She stressed that the Provedor should not only consider human rights violations, but also other elements of KKN (an acronym corresponding to the Indonesian phrase '*korupsi, kolusi, nepotisme*', meaning 'corruption, collusion and nepotism'). Leandro Isac (PSD), agreed with Cipriana Pereira, and regarded the reference to both 'justice' and 'human rights' in the heading as confusing, whilst Jacob Xavier (PPT) asked for clarification of the term 'justice'.

In favour of narrowing the scope of the provision was João Carrascalão (UDT), who considered it preferable for the body to deal with human rights violations alone. As drafted, he considered that the provision mixed up an Ombudsman and a human rights body. An Ombudsman had the function of protecting people against the State, whereas a human rights body would have a broader role, since human rights violations were committed not only by the State. Merging the two bodies, Carrascalão argued, risked altering the function of the Ombudsman. Rui Meneses da Costa (PD) was concerned that there was insufficient clarity about the budget for the Provedor, and how this body would work with the proposed Administrative Court. Manuel Tilman (KOTA) queried whether the proposal involved some duplication with State bodies considering human rights. He also saw a contradiction between the terms of sub-s (1) and sub-s (2): whereas sub-s (1) made reference to the Provedor having the function of remedying injustice, sub-s (2) excluded any decision-making power.[152]

Speaking in support of the provision, Mari Alkatiri (FRETILIN) characterised the provision as clear in its ambit. Timor needed an independent mechanism to defend human rights. Ana Pessoa (FRETILIN) explained that the model followed the tradition of Nordic countries developed over many years. While the emphasis was on human rights, this would not close the door to citizens raising concerns about public administration. Nor would it replace other mechanisms such as the courts and the General Prosecutor. However, it would give citizens a more direct and less formal way of raising their complaints. The wording used in this proposal was preferable to that of the original which Pessoa described as being borrowed from the Portuguese Constitution, since this proposal was

---

152 A similar contradiction was seen by João Carrascalão (UDT) and Clementino Amaral (KOTA).

more tailored to the Timorese situation.[153] Pessoa also explained that while the State would have its own mechanisms for controlling its own organs (to prevent human rights violations), the Ombudsman would be an additional guarantee. People would be able to appeal to an independent institution when concerned about violation of their rights. No contradiction existed as between sub-ss (1) and (2). The Ombudsman would check facts reported to him/her, make a conclusion as to conformity of those acts with the constitution, inform the citizen of his/her findings and reasons, and make recommendations to the bodies involved. The reports of the Ombudsman could also play a preventive role in deterring future violations as bodies looked to the reasoning in the Ombudsman's reports. The Ombudsman was not designed to replace other organs of the State and so did not have decision-making powers. However, weight and legitimacy to the Ombudsman and his/her recommendations would flow from the Ombudsman being chosen by an absolute majority of the Parliament.

Eusébio Guterres (PD) called for the tenure of the Ombudsman to be clarified to provide for a long term of office. Mari Alkatiri (FRETILIN) responded that the provision already said that the organ was to be independent and could take its decisions without any (external) influence. Alkatiri explained that the Ombudsman would have a term of four years and be voted in by an absolute majority of Parliament. (The stipulation of four years was added into the proposal during the plenary session.) In relation to Leandro Isac (PSD) noting earlier that the proposal no longer included a power for the Provedor to approach the Supreme Court, Alkatiri considered it unnecessary to specifically mention this power in this context, given that the Provedor could apply to the Supreme Court for a review of constitutionality under what became s 150.

Voting on the section during the plenary session

The section was approved: 65:8:13.

Those voting against the section included João Carrascalão (UDT), who explained that he thought human rights should be dealt with separately, and Cipriana Pereira (FRETILIN) who supported the creation of a 'Provedor for Justice'.

---

153 Comparing the original text included in the Systematisation and Harmonisation Committee's text (reflecting Committee IV's suggestion), with the Portuguese Constitution, it is apparent that sub-ss (1), (3) and (4) are virtually identical to provisions arts 23(1), (3) and (4) of the Portuguese Constitution. Subsection (2) suggested by the Systematisation and Harmonisation Committee is identical to art 23(2) of the Portuguese Constitution.

Version finalised prior to the public consultation process

Section 27
(Ombudsman [*Provedor de Direitos Humanos e Justiça*])

1. *The Ombudsman shall be an independent organ in charge of examining and seeking to settle citizens' complaints against public bodies, certifying the conformity of the acts with the law, preventing and initiating the whole process to remedy injustice.*

2. *Citizens may present complaints concerning acts or omissions on the part of public bodies to the Ombudsman, who shall undertake a review, without power of decision, and shall forward recommendations to the competent organs as deemed necessary.*

3. *The Ombudsman shall be appointed by the National Parliament through absolute majority votes of its members for a term of office of four years.*

4. *The activity of the Ombudsman shall be independent from any means of grace and legal remedies as laid down in the Constitution and the law.*

5. *Administrative organs and public servants shall have the duty to collaborate with the Ombudsman.*

(Identical to final)

Whilst the English translation remained consistent, the term 'elected (*'eleito'*) was substituted for the term 'appointed' (*'designado'*) in sub-s (3) of this section.

Representations and submissions

District consultations: There was comparatively little discussion of this section in District consultation reports. In the report of Baucau, a suggestion was made to eliminate sub-s (2) (which concerned the complaints function of the Provedor) without further elaboration.

Submissions listed in the Systematisation and Harmonisation Committee's Consultations Report: The UN SRSG and Transitional Administrator recommended adding a new subsection recognising the broader responsibilities of the Office of Provedor.[154] Specifically, additional functions might include:

- responding to systemic abuses;
- investigating human rights violations in the private sector;
- scrutinising government policies for compliance with human rights standards;

---

154 Comments attached to the letter from the UN SRSG and Transitional Administrator to heads of the political parties, 22 February 2002.

- instituting inquiries into human rights violations of its own accord;
- advising the government on human rights issues; and
- undertaking public education on human rights issues.

Alternatively, the SRSG suggested that the provision could allow a later law to vest 'further functions relating to the protection and promotion of human rights according to international human rights standards'. Other topics commented upon included the desirability of including a definition of 'human rights' for the purpose of the Provedor in the Constitution or in a later law, by reference to international human rights law.[155] In discussing an individual's right to a remedy, the SRSG also suggested it was preferable for s 27 to specifically mention 'human rights'.

The Minister for Foreign Affairs noted the importance of explicitly providing for measures of reparation for violation of human rights from the court.[156] Reference was made back to art 8 of the UDHR and support given for an amended subsection stating that:

> The activity of the Ombudsman [the Provedor for Human Rights and Justice] shall not prejudice and shall be independent from the right of all persons to seek remedies for the violation of their human rights through the national Courts and from any other means of grace and legal remedies as laid down in the Constitution and the law.

The Vice-Minister for Justice, Domingos Maria Sarmento, sought clarification as to whether the President or the Parliament had the responsibility for the Provedor, and likewise the power of dismissal. In the event of the Provedor committing any irregularities or criminal acts, the Vice-Minister also queried how such a case would be processed and whether she/he would be entitled to the immunity enjoyed by other organs of State.[157]

The Asia Foundation made a number of suggestions concerning the powers and functions of the Provedor's office to make clear:

- that complaints could be made by all persons;
- that the Provedor could commence investigations on his/her own initiative;
- that the Provedor would administer a code of conduct for leaders to be provided for by law;

---

155   Ibid.
156   Letter from the Minister of State and for Foreign Affairs and Cooperation, Dr José Ramos Horta, to the President of the Constituent Assembly, 25 February 2002.
157   Letter from the Vice-Minister for Justice, Domingos Maria Sarmento, to the President of the Constituent Assembly, 2 March 2002 [Portuguese].

- that the Provedor had power to recommend prosecutions for criminal acts discovered in its investigations, for breaches of the leadership code and also to initiate court proceedings for enforcement of human rights; and

- that detailed roles and powers of the Provedor would be set out in later legislation.[158]

In their second submission, The Asia Foundation suggested there might be advantages in separating the justice and human rights roles.[159]

Other submissions made during the process: Several interlocutors advanced specific proposals concerning the establishment of a national human rights mechanism. The Chief Minister's Adviser on Human Rights, Isabel Ferreira, and the Chief Minister's Adviser on the Promotion of Equality, Maria Domingos Alves, submitted a draft provision for a Provedor's office, entitled '*Provedor de Assistencia para Direitos Humanos e Justiça*'.[160] It read:

1. Citizens may present complaints concerning acts or omissions, to the Ombudsman of Assistance for Human Rights and Justice, who shall undertake a review, without power of decision, and shall forward recommendations to the competent organs as deemed necessary to prevent or remedy injustice, which is a fundamental right of the complainant.

2. The activities of the Ombudsman of Assistance for Human Rights and Justice shall be independent from any means of grace or legal remedies as laid down in the Constitution and the law.

3. The Ombudsman of Assistance for Human Rights and Justice shall be an independent organ; the Ombudsman shall be appointed by the National Parliament [Assembly of the Republic] for a term established by law.

4. The organs and personnel of the Public Service shall cooperate with the Ombudsman of Assistance for Human Rights and Justice in the discharge of the Ombudsman['s] mission.

5. The Ombudsman shall be elected by the National Parliament.

---

158 The Asia Foundation, 'Comments and Suggested Amendments to East Timor's Draft Constitution of 9/2/02', undated, but attached to a cover letter to the President of the Constituent Assembly dated 8 March 2002, 4.

159 The Asia Foundation, 'Discussion Paper on Draft of East Timorese Constitution', March 2002, 5.

160 Letter from the Chief Minister's Adviser on Human Rights, Isabel Ferreira, and the Chief Minister's Adviser on the Promotion of Equality, Maria Domingas Alves, to the President of the Constituent Assembly, 21 November 2001, received by the Constituent Assembly on 23 November 2001. [Portuguese]

The Working Group on Future Human Rights Institutions advanced a submission to the Thematic Committee in October 2001 with draft text covering a National Human Rights Commission.[161] It read:

National Human Rights Commission

1.1 An independent National Commission on Human Rights shall be established.

1.2 All organs of the State shall respect the independence of the Commission and the right and duty of the Commission to carry out its functions to promote and protect the human rights of East Timorese people.

1.3 The manner of the establishment, operation and functioning of the National Commission on Human Rights shall be the subject of legislation. Such legislation in particular is to take into account the need for:

(a) The Commission to have the competency and responsibility to:

  i. investigate complaints of human rights violations when requested or on its own initiative;

  ii. to seek remedies for individuals and groups whose rights have been violated;

  iii. to undertake inquiries into human rights matters;

  iv. make recommendations to government concerning the protection and promotion of human rights; and

  v. to undertake public education campaigns concerning human rights.

(b) The Commission to enjoy adequate financial and legal independence to fulfil its mandate;

(c) Commissioners and members of the Commission to be persons of high moral character and proven integrity; and

---

161 The Working Group on Human Rights Institutions/Human Rights Unit, UNTAET, 'Submission of the Working Group on Future Human Rights Institutions to the Constituent Assembly', 30 October 2001. This text was also incorporated in the Human Rights Unit, UNTAET's comments on the draft text to the Systematisation and Harmonisation Committee.

> (d) Civil society to be involved in discussions concerning the structure of the Commission and appointment of Commissioners.

> 1.4 Parliament shall be under an obligation to allocate adequate funds for the operation of the Commission. The Commission shall, however, retain the power to manage its funds and operations.

In addition to outlining more detailed functions and an independent budget for the national human rights institution, this proposal gave the body jurisdiction to hear complaints of violations from all individuals and groups. The High Commissioner for Human Rights, in her submission to the Constituent Assembly in December 2001, underlined the importance of East Timor constitutionally entrenching a national human rights institution, established in accordance with UN standards, to promote and protect human rights. She recommended including a provision within the Constitution committing the State to establish an independent national institution to promote and protect human rights within three years.[162]

The International Commission of Jurists was critical of the fact that the section did not require authorities to comply with recommendations of the Ombudsman, and contained no guarantees of the pay, qualifications, term and employment conditions of the office holder such as to ensure independence of the Ombudsman.[163]

---

162   Letter from the UN High Commissioner for Human Rights to the President of the Constituent Assembly, 19 December 2001. To similar effect was the call by the Human Rights Unit, UNTAET, for the State to commit itself 'to establish an independent national institution to promote and protect human rights within 3 years of independence': 'Summary of select technical comments concerning the East Timorese draft Constitution and its treatment of human rights', December 2001, 5.

163   International Commission of Jurists (Australian Section), 'Commentary on the Draft Constitution Proposed for East Timor by the Constituent Assembly', undated, 6.

Section 28
(Right to resistance and self-defence)

1. Every citizen has the right to disobey and to resist illegal orders or orders that affect their fundamental rights, freedoms and guarantees.

2. The right to self-defence is guaranteed to all, in accordance with the law.

(Official translation of the final text)

Drafting history

Thematic Committee I text

Section 22

(The right to disobey illegal orders <u>and the right to self-defence</u>)

1. *Every citizen has the right to disobey illegal orders or orders that affect their rights, freedoms and guarantees.*

2. *<u>The right to resist and the right to self-defence is guaranteed to all.</u>*[164]

Commentary: Subsection (1) was based on art 22 of the FRETILIN Project. It was approved in a vote of 16:2:2.

Subsection (2) came from art 14(2) of the KOTA project. It was approved in a vote of 16:2:2. The title was amended as a result of the inclusion of this second subsection.

Lú Olo is recorded as having suggested a merged provision, though this was not subject to a vote.

---

164 In the final translation, the term *'legítima defesa'* was translated as 'self-defence' rather than 'legitimate defence', and the term *'ofendam'* in sub-s (1) as 'affect' rather than 'offend'.

Systematisation and Harmonisation Committee draft text used in the plenary debate

Section 27
(Right to resistance and self-defence)

1. *Every citizen has the right to disobey and to resist illegal orders or orders that affect their rights, freedoms and guarantees.*

2. *The right to self-defence is also guaranteed to all, in accordance with the law.*[165]

Commentary: Several changes appeared in this draft text. First, in the heading, the 'right to resistance' was substituted for the 'right to disobey illegal orders'. Secondly, the right to resist was moved from sub-s (2) up into sub-s (1). Thirdly, sub-s (2) of this text now included the phrase 'in accordance with the law'. The identical change was listed as a suggestion of Lú Olo recorded in Annex II of Thematic Committee I's report.

In addition, the Bench of the Systematisation and Harmonisation Committee also recommended adding 'fundamental' before 'rights, freedoms and guarantees'.

Plenary debate (18 December 2001)

Discussion in the plenary focused around the implications of a right to self-defence.[166] Eusébio Guterres (PD) considered that the section was ambiguous and requested further explanation from the Systematisation and Harmonisation Committee. Manuel Tilman (KOTA), Rapporteur of that committee, explained that the law needed to provide for the right of self-defence. If a thief attempted to kill a person, that person should be able to defend him/herself. Speaker Lú Olo spoke in support of the section, viewing it as applying not only to acts of physical defence, but also to situations requiring protection against illegal or unconstitutional acts. Concern about the breadth of the provision was voiced by João Carrascalão (UDT). Using the same example, he asked: if a person came into a house and was killed by the houseowner, who would prove that the person was attempting to kill someone as opposed to just intending to steal? In his opinion, the section was dangerous as it would open the door to persons killing each other. Jacob Xavier (PPT) also considered that the term 'self-defence' was capable of many interpretations. Vicente Faria (FRETILIN), Rapporteur of Thematic Committee I, raised concerns as to the

---

165 The Assembly English translation used the phrase 'as provided for by law'. The Portuguese version remained *'nos termos da lei'* from this version through to the final; thus the translation for the final version has been preferred.

166 The following summary draws upon the information contained in a contemporary monitoring report by The Asia Foundation in relation to the intervention of Eusébio Guterres and the first intervention of Manuel Tilman (given a break in the recording at this time).

modifications in wording undertaken by the Systematisation and Harmonisation Committee. He indicated his preference for the original wording. No additional amendment proposals were put to the Plenary, however.

Voting on the section during the plenary session

The Systematisation and Harmonisation Committee's *recommended addition of the word 'fundamental' to sub-s (1) was approved: 54:7:22.*[167]

The section as a whole passed: 80:0:3.

Version finalised prior to the public consultation process

Section 28
(Right to resistance and self-defence)

1. *Every citizen has the right to disobey and to resist illegal orders or orders that affect their fundamental rights, freedoms and guarantees.*

2. *The right to self-defence is guaranteed to all, in accordance with the law.*

(Identical to final)[168]

Representations and submissions

District consultations: No comments on this section appear in the summary of District consultations prepared by the Systematisation and Harmonisation Committee.

Submissions listed in the Systematisation and Harmonisation Committee's Consultations Report: None listed.

Other submissions made during the process: In responding to the Thematic Committee text, the Human Rights Unit of UNTAET queried how sub-s (1) would be interpreted, suggesting that it might be preferable to adopt language such as 'persons have a defence to any action taken by government in respect of failure

---

167   One document in the Assembly records lists the vote in favour as 57; however, the vote as read out during the session was 54.
168   The change made in this text was removing the word 'also' from sub-s (2). The final text of the Constitution did include one further grammatical correction to the opening words of sub-s (1).

to obey an order which was illegal or which was contrary to their rights, freedoms or guarantees'.[169] In their draft Bill of Rights, Yayasan HAK included a right 'not to respect orders which are in contravention of their constitutional rights'.[170]

---

169   Human Rights Unit, UNTAET, 'Thematic Committee One's Proposals for the Protection of Human Rights in the Constitution: An analysis by the HRU', 14 November 2001, 7. The International Commission of Jurists also criticised sub-s (1) as 'too vague', and suggested sub-s (2) be dealt with in ordinary law: 'Commentary on the Draft Constitution Proposed for East Timor by the Constituent Assembly', undated, 6.
170   Yayasan HAK, 'Civil and Political, Economic, Social and Cultural Rights', undated, but received by the Assembly on 22 October 2001, art 42.

Title II: Personal Rights, Freedoms and Guarantees (Sections 29–49)

Section 29
(Right to life)

1. Human life is inviolable.

2. The State shall recognise and guarantee the right to life.

3. There shall be no death penalty in the Democratic Republic of East Timor.

(Official translation of the final text)

Drafting history

Thematic Committee I text

Section 23

(Right to life)

1. *Human life is inviolable.*

2. *The State shall recognise and respect the right to life.*

3. *There shall be no death penalty in the Democratic Republic of East Timor.*

Commentary: Subsection (1) came from art 29 of the PSD Project which was initially rejected (in a vote of 5:8:6), but later approved unanimously as part of the committee's general revisions.

Subsections (2) and (3) originated from art 23 of the FRETILIN project and were approved in a vote of 15:2:2.

An additional proposal to add a reference to the State's duty to protect the right to life in sub-s (2) came from Joaquim dos Santos (FRETILIN). However, no vote was taken on this proposal.

Systematisation and Harmonisation Committee draft text used in the plenary debate

Section 28
(Right to life)

1. *Human life is inviolable.*

2. *The State shall recognise and guarantee the right to life.*[1]

3. *There shall be no death penalty in the Democratic Republic of East Timor.*

(Identical to final)

Commentary: In this draft text, the term 'guarantee' was substituted for 'respect' in sub-s (2).

Plenary debate (18 December 2001)

Subsection (1)'s general statement that human life was inviolable served as the focus for much of the debate on this provision.[2] João Carrascalão (UDT) considered sub-s (1) was redundant given the inclusion of sub-s (2). He was concerned that it also gave rise to potential conflicts with freedom of religion. Some religions, for instance, did not permit their adherents to have blood transfusions. João Carrascalão (UDT) urged caution in relation to the terms of sub-s (1), reminding members of the separation of church and State. Rui António da Cruz (FRETILIN) similarly feared sub-s (1) was too broad and might contradict other fundamental rights and liberties. Manuel Tilman (KOTA) defended the section, stating that the Constitution should consecrate the principle that life was inviolable. Religious institutions had to act in conformity with the Constitution. In response to Carrascalão's example, Tilman stated that every effort must be taken to ensure people did not die.

The issue of 'when life starts' was raised by Jacob Xavier (PPT), who highlighted the association of the 'right to life' with issues of women and abortion. The right to life was described as a 'heavy subject' needing close consideration. Eusébio Guterres (PD) characterised this as a legal issue. If a mother was going to die because of the foetus, the mother had the [prevailing] right to life. Speaking in support of the subsection, Clementino Amaral (KOTA) noted that a guarantee of the inviolability of life was contained in numerous Constitutions and the

---

1   The English Assembly translation of this text translated '*reconhece*' as 'ensure', rather than 'recognise'. However, in keeping with the final translation, the term 'recognise' has been preferred here.

2   Vicente Faria (FRETILIN) queried whether sub-s (1) came from Thematic Committee I. Manuel Tilman (KOTA) highlighted its inclusion in the committee's report.

UDHR.[3] Even countries that allowed abortion and euthanasia, like Holland, recognised the inviolability of life in their Constitutions. For Amaral, sub-s (1) remained important to signify that someone could not kill another person.

In relation to sub-s (2), there was discussion of the fact that the Bahasa version used the term 'respecting' the right to life, whereas the Portuguese version referred to 'recognising' the right.[4] The issue was viewed as one of translation, rather than intent, however, with Lú Olo noting after the vote that he considered 'respect' to be included within the Portuguese text.

Mariano Sabino Lopes (PD) and others proposed an amendment so that sub-s (1) would read: 'Everyone has the right to life'.[5] The proposal also included amending sub-s (2) to provide for respect for the right to life and, seemingly, protection from arbitrary deprivation of life.[6] This proposal failed in a vote of 31:16:35. Given that abstention was the most popular voting option in relation to this amendment, there would appear to have been considerable uncertainty remaining around the issues raised.

Voting on the section during the plenary session

The section was passed: 68:2:13.

Version finalised prior to the public consultation process

Section 29

(Right to life)

1. *Human life is inviolable.*

2. *The State shall recognise and guarantee the right to life.*

3. *There shall be no death penalty in the Democratic Republic of East Timor.*

Representations and submissions

District consultations: The section did not attract particular attention within the Districts. In Oecusse, however, the consultation summary report noted a view that the Constitution should condemn acts of witchcraft and domestic violence.

---

3   In fact the UDHR protects the 'right to life' and does not make reference to 'inviolability' of life.

4   Leandro Isac (PSD).

5   Other proponents were Paulo Sarmento (PD), Eusébio Guterres (PD), and Aquilino Guterres (PD).

6   Note that the recording at this point is broken and differing translations of the proposal (originally made in Bahasa Indonesian) were provided in the contemporaneous translation and later review.

Submissions listed in the Systematisation and Harmonisation Committee's Consultations Report: The Vice-Minister for Justice suggested merging s 29(3) concerning the death penalty and s 32 (Limits on sentences).[7]

The East Timor Study Group (whose report was referred to in the Systematisation and Harmonisation Committee report, but not extracted in relation to individual sections) noted that according to Catholic doctrine, life began at conception. It thus perceived a need to have a precise definition of when life began for the purpose of the Constitution.[8]

---

7   Letter from the Vice-Minister for Justice, Domingos Maria Sarmento, to the President of the Constituent Assembly, 2 March 2002 [Portuguese].

8   East Timor Study Group, 'Debate on the Draft Constitution: Positive and Negative Implications for the Future of East Timor', 20 February 2002, 11 [Tetum].

Section 30
(Right to personal freedom, security and integrity)

1. Everyone has the right to personal freedom, security and integrity.

2. No one shall be arrested or detained, except under the terms clearly provided for by applicable law, and the order of arrest or detention should always be presented for consideration by the competent judge within the legal timeframe.

3. Every individual who loses his or her freedom shall be immediately informed, in a clear and precise manner, of the reasons for his or her arrest or detention as well as of his or her rights, and allowed to contact a lawyer, directly or through a relative or a trusted person.

4. No one shall be subjected to torture and cruel, inhuman or degrading treatment.

(Official translation of the final text)

Drafting history

Thematic Committee I text

Section 24
(Right to freedom, security and integrity)

1. *Everyone has the right to freedom, integrity and physical security.*

2. *No one shall be arrested or detained except in cases clearly provided for by law.*

3. *Every citizen who loses his or her freedom, shall be immediately informed, in a clear and precise manner, of the reasons for his or her arrest or detention.*

4. *No one shall be subjected to torture and cruel, inhuman or degrading treatment.*

Commentary: This section was based on art 24 of the FRETILIN Project. It was adopted in a vote of 17:0:2.

Systematisation and Harmonisation Committee draft text used in the plenary debate

Section 29
(Right to freedom, security and integrity)

1. *Everyone has the right to personal freedom, security and integrity.*

2. *No one shall be arrested or detained, except in cases clearly provided for by applicable law.*

3. *Every citizen who loses his or her freedom shall be immediately informed, in a clear and precise manner, of the reasons for his or her arrest or detention, and allowed to contact a lawyer, directly or through a relative or a trusted person.*

4. *No one shall be subjected to torture and cruel, inhuman or degrading treatment.*

Commentary: Comparing the text of Thematic Committee I to that of the Systematisation and Harmonisation Committee reveals several changes. Firstly, in relation to the guarantees in sub-s (1), the wording was changed from 'freedom, integrity and physical security' to 'personal freedom, security and integrity'. Secondly, the qualifier 'applicable' was added before law in sub-s (2). Most substantively, sub-s (3) was extended to include the right to contact a lawyer. No explanation was provided for these changes in the written text submitted to the Plenary.

Plenary debate (18 December 2001)

The appropriate limits to authorities' powers of detention provoked particular comment in the plenary session. Jacob Xavier (PPT) put forward a detailed proposal suggested by Professor Jorge Carlos Fonseca which, *inter alia*, limited the period an individual could be detained before being brought before a competent judge to 48–72 hours. At this point, the judge would have to either order the release of the individual, authorise pre-trial detention or make an order regarding other constraints adequate for the case. The judge was also to be informed of the causes for the detention, and to be obliged to communicate such reasons to the detainee, interrogate him/her and hear him/her in the presence of his/her chosen lawyer. The detainee was to be guaranteed the opportunity to defend him/herself. In this suggested amendment, pre-trial detention was to be regarded as exceptional and of a 'subsidiary nature'. It was not to be maintained where there was an alternative adequate and sufficient measure (such as bail or another more favourable measure). Pre-trial detention was also to be made subject to a maximum time period provided for in law, but in any case not more than 36 months from the moment of detention or arrest. The proposal did not receive detailed consideration in the context of this section, but a similarly worded amendment was subsequently advanced by Manuel Tilman (see discussion of s 29A below).

Lucia Lobato (PSD) suggested a reformulation of sub-s (2) to give greater protection to citizens. Her preference was to replace the reference to persons being able to be arrested or detained in cases provided by 'applicable law' with wording providing that only courts could authorise the arrest/detention of a person.[9] Manuel Tilman (KOTA), Rapporteur of the Systematisation and Harmonisation Committee, explained that under the draft text, persons would only be able to be detained where this was provided for in a previously promulgated law. Although Indonesian law had been different, the Timorese Parliament would now make laws for the nation. Under the existing UNTAET regulation, persons could only be held for 72 hours before being presented to the court. Thus the subsection referred to detention needing to be authorised by 'applicable law'. However, Tilman acknowledged concerns regarding arrest and detention arising from the experience of the last 24 years and suggested further explanation be provided by members of FRETILIN or the thematic committee that had proposed the text.

João Carrascalão (UDT) sought clarification of sub-s (1). Given that the Assembly had already approved a right of self-defence, what would be the situation if someone used a knife to defend themselves? What was 'integrity'? Was it moral and physical integrity? What about a right to privacy? In Carrascalão's view, there were many issues left unanswered by this section.

Subsection (4) elicited particular interest. Concerns were expressed about the need to prevent torture and ill-treatment of individuals. Armando da Silva (PL) noted the reality that torture and ill-treatment often occurred, referring to law enforcement officials[10] arresting people and ill-treating them. Jacob Xavier (PPT) emphasised the importance of ensuring persons were not beaten when they were arrested by police, in practice, as well as in theory. Lú Olo (FRETILIN) referred also to the problems of police beating individuals upon arrest, whilst noting that the Constitution was looking forward to the future rather than backwards.

Voting on the section during the plenary session

The section passed: 72:1:9.

---

9   Concern about the existing phrase that arrest or detention be 'clearly provided for by applicable law' was echoed by Rui Meneses (PD), who emphasised that it should be the court determining whether there was consistency with the law.

10   Reference to da Silva's intervention appears in The Asia Foundation monitoring notes.

Version finalised prior to the public consultation process

Section 30

(Right to personal freedom, security and integrity)

1. *Everyone has the right to personal freedom, security and integrity.*

2. *No one shall be arrested or detained, except under the terms clearly provided for by applicable law, and the order of arrest or detention should always be presented for consideration by the competent judge within the legal timeframe.*

3. *Every individual who loses his or her freedom shall be immediately informed, in a clear and precise manner, of the reasons for his or her arrest or detention as well as of his or her rights, and allowed to contact a lawyer, directly or through a relative or a trusted person.*

4. *No one shall be subjected to torture and cruel, inhuman or degrading treatment.*

(Identical to final)

Commentary: This text included additional wording in sub-s (2), namely that the order of arrest or detention be presented before the judge within the legal timeframe. No source was included in the text. It was, however, reminiscent of the discussion surrounding the proposal of Manuel Tilman (KOTA) (draft s 29A). Tilman was also an influential member of the Systematisation and Harmonisation Committee. The right of detainees to be informed of their rights was also inserted into sub-s (3). The other significant change which appears to have been made in this version was to change the phrasing in sub-s (3) to 'every individual' rather than 'every citizen'. This was one of many such alterations made by the Systematisation and Harmonisation Committee, seemingly responding to submissions advocating the enjoyment of rights by all persons. More minor changes were also made: for example, in sub-s (2) in referring to 'under the terms' as opposed to 'in cases' provided for by law.

Representations and submissions

District consultations: No comments on this section appear in the summary of District consultations prepared by the Systematisation and Harmonisation Committee.

Submissions listed in the Systematisation and Harmonisation Committee's Consultations Report*:* The UN SRSG and Transitional Administrator suggested that the section should not only prohibit detentions which were not in accordance with the law, but also ensure that persons were not subject to 'arbitrary detention'. In addition to referring to the importance of speedy access to seeking *habeas corpus*, the SRSG highlighted that detention should ordinarily be reviewed by a court within a short period, recommending 48 hours rather than the eight days provided in the text.[11]

The Asia Foundation proposed that sub-s (2) be revised to state that 'no person shall be subjected to arbitrary arrest or detention and any person arrested or detained shall be brought before a judge no later than 72 hours after arrest or detention'.[12]

Other submissions made during the process: In the draft texts put forward by civil society during the constitutional process, there were more extensive clauses suggested in relation to the rights of arrested and detained persons. Yayasan HAK drafted several clauses on this topic, recognising a number of additional rights for persons arrested or detained, in particular, the right:

- to be brought before a court as soon as reasonably possible;
- to challenge the lawfulness of the detention in person before a court and, if the detention is unlawful, to be released;
- to choose, as well as to consult with, a legal practitioner;
- to be informed of rights in a language that the person understands;
- to conditions of detention that are consistent with human dignity; and
- to communicate with, and be visited by, that person's family

(mirroring much of the language of the ICCPR).[13]

The Human Rights Unit of UNTAET recommended more explicit recognition of the right to be free from arbitrary arrest and detention. An amended s 29(2) was put forward, stating: 'No person may be subject to arbitrary arrest or detention. All arrests and detentions must be authorized under provisions in law.'[14] The HRU also suggested including more detailed rights of criminal procedure, as set out in the ICCPR including the right of legal representation paid for by the State where the interests of justice require it and the person is unable to afford legal representation; and the right to be treated with dignity when imprisoned.[15]

---

11 Comments attached to the letter from the UN SRSG and Transitional Administrator to heads of the political parties, 22 February 2002.

12 The Asia Foundation, 'Comments and Suggested Amendments to East Timor's Draft Constitution of 9/2/02', undated, but attached to a cover letter to the President of the Constituent Assembly dated 8 March 2002, 5.

13 This listing draws upon elements in draft art 8 in Yayasan HAK's Bill of Rights within the submission 'Civil and Political, Economic, Social and Cultural Rights', undated, but received by the Assembly on 22 October 2001, and HAK's submission of March 2002.

14 Human Rights Unit, UNTAET, 'Thematic Committee One's Proposals For the Protection of Human Rights in the Constitution: An analysis by the HRU', 14 November 2001, 8.

15 Ibid 15.

The Church-Constitution Working Group recommended that the right to be informed of the reasons for arrest or detention (s 29(3)) be extended to all persons, together with the right of *habeas corpus*.[16] It was also suggested that s 29(2) provide for freedom from arbitrary arrest or detention. During the drafting process, the Human Rights Unit of UNTAET, and the UN High Commissioner for Human Rights, amongst others, stressed the importance of human rights such as this one applying to all persons, rather than being limited to citizens.[17]

REDE Feto Timor Lorosae proposed that sub-s (1) be extended to include 'psychological integrity' and that a sub-s (5) be added: 'The State must protect women's right to live free from any forms of violence, both private and public.'[18]

The Women's Charter of Rights in East Timor, developed in mid-2001, also included this phrasing.[19]

Proposed section 29A on preventive detention

Manuel Tilman (KOTA) supported a new s 29A concerning 'preventive detention' (pre-trial detention), which was discussed in detail immediately prior to s 31.[20] It provided that arrest and detention needed to be in accordance with law and reviewable by a court. It was in similar terms to Jacob Xavier's earlier proposed amendment to s 29. Specifically, this included the proposal that a person's detention needed to be reviewed by a court within 48–72 hours of arrest, and that a trial had to commence within 36 months. Vicente Guterres (UDC/PDC) recalled that this proposal had been made by the Cape Verde expert (Dr Carlos Jorge Fonseca) in supporting its inclusion in the Constitution. João Carrascalão (UDT) spoke in favour of the proposal whilst noting the need for clarity about what was meant by 'preventive detention'. In his view, this could include situations of persons being detained as suspects in the commission of a crime, as well as situations where persons were detained to provide for their protection/security. A number of members linked their support for this proposal, particularly the time limits on preventive detention, to concern about the lengthy pre-trial detention experienced by those in Becora and Baucau prisons.[21]

---

16 Letter from the Centre for Peace and Development to the President of the Constituent Assembly, January 2002, received by the Assembly on 23 January 2002. This letter contained the submission of the Church-Constitution Working Group.

17 See discussion of this issue under the entry covering 'Section 16' above.

18 Letter from REDE Feto Timor Lorosae to the President of the Constituent Assembly, 31 October 2001.

19 Women's Charter of Rights in East Timor, art 2.

20 The other proponents of this new section were not read out in the recording available to the author. Nor did the recording capture the precise amendment. This summary is based on the author's contemporary notes and the discussion captured in the recording.

21 Quitéria da Costa Gonsalves (UDT) and Mariano Sabino Lopes (PD).

Jacob Fernandes (FRETILIN) spoke against the proposed amendment. In Fernandes' view, while the provision might be suitable for Cape Verde, it did not fit the circumstances of East Timor. In particular, he was concerned that there were insufficient human resources to meet the timing requirements of, for example, bringing a person before a judge within 72 hours.[22] Rui Meneses da Costa (PD) suggested putting the time limits in ordinary law rather than the Constitution, a suggestion with which Lú Olo (FRETILIN) agreed. Lú Olo also highlighted the existence of sections dealing with the application of criminal law and *habeas corpus*.

The proposed s 29A failed: 27:41:15.

---

22   António Ximenes (PDC) also expressed concern that in serious cases, such as people planning a revolt, the police needed more than 72 hours to conduct an investigation to look for proof of the crime.

Section 31
(Application of criminal law)

1. No one shall be subjected to trial, except in accordance with the law.

2. No one shall be tried and convicted for an act that does not qualify in the law as a criminal offence at the moment it was committed, nor endure security measures the provisions of which are not clearly established in previous law.

3. Penalties or security measures not clearly provided for by law at the moment the criminal offence was committed shall not be enforced.

4. No one shall be tried and convicted for the same criminal offence more than once.

5. Criminal law shall not be enforced retroactively, except if the new law is in favour of the accused.

6. Anyone who has been unjustly convicted has the right to a fair compensation in accordance with the law.

(Official translation of the final text)

Drafting history

Thematic Committee I text

Section 25
(Application of criminal law)

1. *No one shall be arrested or subjected to trial, except in accordance with the law.*

2. *No one shall be tried and convicted for an act that did not qualify in the law as a criminal offence at the moment it was committed.*

3. *Penalties not clearly provided for by law at the moment the criminal offence was committed shall not be enforced.*

4. *No one shall be tried and convicted for the same criminal offence more than once.*

5. *Criminal law shall not be enforced retroactively, except if the new law is in favour of the accused.*

6. *Citizens who have been unjustly convicted have the right to a fair compensation and to a review of the sentence, in accordance with the law.*

Commentary: This section was based on art 25 of the FRETILIN Project. It was adopted in a vote of 18:0:1.

Systematisation and Harmonisation Committee draft text used in the plenary debate

Section 30
(Application of criminal law)

1. *No one shall be arrested or subjected to trial, except in accordance with the law.*

2. *No one shall be tried and convicted for an act that does not qualify in the law as a criminal offence at the moment it was committed.*[23]

3. *Penalties or security measures not clearly provided for by law at the moment the criminal offence was committed shall not be enforced.*

4. *No one shall be tried and convicted for the same criminal offence more than once.*

5. *Criminal law shall not be enforced retroactively, except if the new law is in favour of the accused.*

6. *Citizens who have been unjustly convicted have the right to a fair compensation and to a review of the sentence in accordance with the law.*

Commentary: The Systematisation and Harmonisation Committee added the term 'security measures' into sub-s (3). Other minor grammatical changes were made at this point.

Plenary debate (18 December 2001)

Minimal discussion of this section took place in the plenary session. António Ximenes (PDC) sought an explanation of sub-s (4). The concept of double jeopardy was outlined by Vicente Guterres (UDC/PDC), Secretary of the Systematisation and Harmonisation Committee.

---

23 The Assembly English translation of this text did not include the phrase 'in the law', but the Portuguese version included the phrase *'na lei'*. The Systematisation and Harmonisation Committee also changed the tense of this clause from the past to the present.

Voting on the section during the plenary session

The section passed: 76:0:6.

Version finalised prior to the public consultation process

Section 31
(Application of criminal law)

1. *No one shall be subjected to trial, except in accordance with the law.*

2. *No one shall be tried and convicted for an act that does not qualify in the law as a criminal offence at the moment it was committed, nor endure security measures the provisions of which are not clearly established in previous law.*

3. *Penalties or security measures not clearly provided for by law at the moment the criminal offence was committed shall not be enforced.*

4. *No one shall be tried and convicted for the same criminal offence more than once.*

5. *Criminal law shall not be enforced retroactively, except if the new law is in favour of the accused.*

6. *Anyone who has been unjustly convicted has the right to a fair compensation in accordance with the law.*

(Identical to final)

Commentary: In this version, several amendments were made. Subsection (1) was shortened to refer to persons subjected to trial alone (removing the reference to arrest). Subsection (2) was broadened out to include a reference to security measures, presumably to make sub-s (2) consistent with sub-s (3). This amendment was bolded in the text distributed. Another amendment (not highlighted) was to expand the coverage of sub-s (6) to apply to all persons (rather than be limited in its application to citizens). In their summary of methodology, the Systematisation and Harmonisation Committee noted their policy to substitute the broader term 'individual' or 'person' for 'citizen' wherever possible, a move which was in accord with many submissions to the Assembly. Subsection (6)'s reference to a review of sentence was also deleted.

Representations and submissions

District consultations: Little comment on this section appeared in the reports of the District consultations. In the Los Palos report, a suggestion was made to eliminate the provision, and instead deal with the subject in the ordinary law. In Oecussi, there was also a suggestion that the section should be widened to deal with the application of the civil code and customary law.

Submissions listed in the Systematisation and Harmonisation Committee's Consultations Report: The Vice-Minister for Justice, Domingos Maria Sarmento, suggested the need for revision of sub-s (6). He queried whether a person unjustly imprisoned by being in preventive detention [ordered] by a judge because of police investigation was eligible for fair compensation according to law.[24]

---

24   Letter from the Vice-Minister for Justice, Domingos Maria Sarmento, to the President of the Constituent Assembly, 2 March 2002 [Portuguese].

Section 32
(Limits on sentences and security measures)

1. There shall be no life imprisonment nor sentences or security measures lasting for unlimited or indefinite period of time in the Democratic Republic of East Timor.

2. In case of danger as a result of mental illness, security measures may be extended successively[25] by judicial decision.

3. Criminal liability is not transmissible.

4. Persons who are subjected, on conviction, to a sentence or a security measure involving loss of freedom remain entitled to their fundamental rights, subject to the limitations that necessarily derive from that conviction and from the requirements for its enforcement.

(Official translation of the final text)

Drafting history

Thematic Committee I text

Section 26
(Limits on sentences and security measures)

1. *There shall be no life imprisonment or security measures lasting for unlimited or indefinite period of time in the Democratic Republic of East Timor.*

2. *In case of danger as a result of mental disturbance, security measures may be extended successively by judicial decision.*

3. *Criminal liability is not transmissible.*

4. *Persons who are subjected, on conviction, to a sentence or a security measure involving loss of freedom remain entitled to their fundamental rights, subject to the limitations that necessarily derive from that conviction and from the requirements for its enforcement.*

---

25 All contemporary Assembly English translations referred to measures being 'successively extended', whilst the official translation uses the phrase 'extended successively'. The Portuguese phrase remained '*ser sucessivamente prorrogadas*' throughout.

Commentary: Subsections (1) and (2) were based on art 26 of the FRETILIN Project, with the addition of 'security measures' in the heading.

Subsection (3) was based on art 47(3) of the PSD Project. It was adopted unanimously: 20:0:0.

Subsection (4) was based on art 47(5) of the PSD Project. It was adopted unanimously: 20:0:0.[26]

Another PSD proposal to include wording that 'No penalty should involve loss of any civic, professional or political rights' was rejected in a vote of 2:11:7.

The heading represented a mixture of those appearing in the FRETILIN and PSD Projects.

Systematisation and Harmonisation Committee draft text used in the plenary debate

Section 31

(Limits on sentences and security measures)

1. *There shall be no life imprisonment or security measures lasting for unlimited or indefinite period of time in the Democratic Republic of East Timor.*

2. *In case of danger as a result of mental illness,[27] security measures may be extended successively by judicial decision.*

3. *Criminal liability is not transmissible.*

4. *Persons who are subjected, on conviction, to a sentence or a security measure involving loss of freedom remain entitled to their fundamental rights, subject to the limitations that necessarily derive from that conviction and from the requirements for its enforcement.*

Plenary debate (18 December 2001)

Discussion in the plenary session focused on two topics: (i) the length of sentences and (ii) clarification of the non-transmissibility of criminal liability. Jacob Xavier (PPT) considered life imprisonment was appropriate for cases in which one person killed another. There was a need for justice for the community, a desire which had been expressed during consultations of the Constitutional Commissions. In voicing some support for Jacob Xavier's perspective, António Ximenes (PDC) added that the law should also make provision for repeat offenders. João Carrascalão (UDT) agreed there should be no life imprisonment,

---

26 A minor alteration was made to this clause after the vote for grammatical reasons.
27 The term used in the Portuguese version was *'anomalia psiquica'*, substituting for Thematic Committee I's term *'demência mental'*. It appears as 'mental illness' in the Assembly and official translations.

but felt the system should allow for cumulative sentences. Thus, there should be a difference in the sentencing between a person convicted of killing one person, and another who committed multiple murders, or also committed other crimes such as rape.

Lú Olo (FRETILIN) requested an explanation of sub-s (3)'s statement that criminal liability was not transmissible. Manuel Tilman (KOTA), Rapporteur of the Systematisation and Harmonisation Committee, explained that sub-s (3) meant that crimes were not transmissible to others such as daughters or sons.

Voting on the section during the plenary session

The section passed: 77:1:4.[28]

Version finalised prior to the public consultation process

Section 32
(Limits on sentences and security measures)

1. *There shall be no life imprisonment nor sentences or security measures lasting for unlimited or indefinite period of time in the Democratic Republic of East Timor.*

2. *In case of danger as a result of mental illness, security measures may be extended successively by judicial decision.*

3. *Criminal liability is not transmissible.*

4. *Persons who are subjected, on conviction, to a sentence or a security measure involving loss of freedom remain entitled to their fundamental rights, subject to the limitations that necessarily derive from that conviction and from the requirements for its enforcement.*

(Identical to final)

Commentary: A reference to 'sentences' was added into sub-s (1) in this text, without any specific explanation.

Representations and submissions

District consultations: In one district, Liquiça, the suggestion was made that Timor adopt the death penalty.

---

28   One document from the Assembly lists the vote as 77:1:9. However, other Assembly records and the recording of the plenary session present the vote as 77:1:4. This is also consistent with the numbers present in the Constituent Assembly at the time.

Submissions listed in the Systematisation and Harmonisation Committee's Consultations Report: None listed.

Other submissions made during the process: The Human Rights Unit of UNTAET suggested deleting the reference to prolonging security measures 'in case of danger from mental disturbance' and replacing it with a prohibition on arbitrary and unreasonable security measures, leaving the details of procedure to later law.[29] It also proposed recognising more explicitly the rights of prisoners to be treated humanely and with dignity.

Yayasan HAK advocated limiting the reference to mental illness to cases to proven mental illness.[30]

---

29   Human Rights Unit, UNTAET, 'Thematic Committee One's Proposals For the Protection of Human Rights in the Constitution: An analysis by the HRU', 14 November 2001, 8, 15.

30   Article 10 of the draft Bill of Rights within Yayasan HAK, 'Civil and Political, Economic, Social and Cultural Rights', undated, but received by the Assembly on 22 October 2001.

Section 33
(Habeas corpus)

1. Everyone who illegally loses his or her freedom has the right to apply for *habeas corpus*.

2. An application for *habeas corpus* shall be made by the detainee or by any other person in the exercise of his or her civil rights, in accordance with the law.

3. The court shall rule on the application for *habeas corpus* within 8 days at a hearing in the presence of both parties.

(Official translation of the final text)

Drafting history

Thematic Committee I text

Section 27
(Habeas corpus)

1. *Every citizen has the right to apply for habeas corpus.*

2. *An application for habeas corpus shall be made by the detainee or by any citizen in the exercise of his or her civil rights, in accordance with the law.*

3. *The court shall rule on the application for habeas corpus within 8 days.*

Commentary: This provision was based on art 27 of the FRETILIN Project. It was approved unanimously: 21:0:0.

Systematisation and Harmonisation Committee draft text used in the plenary debate

Section 32
(Habeas corpus)

1. *Every citizen has the right to apply for habeas corpus.*

2. *An application for habeas corpus shall be made by the detainee or by any citizen in the exercise of his or her civil rights, in accordance with the law.*

3. *The court shall rule on the application for habeas corpus within 8 days at a hearing in the presence of both parties.*

Commentary: The Systematisation and Harmonisation Committee added in the extra words in sub-s (3), that a hearing be conducted in the presence of both parties.[31] No specific explanation was provided in the written text provided by the committee to the Plenary.

Plenary debate (19 December 2001)

There was little discussion of this section. Rui Meneses (PD) suggested that it would be useful for relevant Assembly members to provide a concrete example of situations giving rise to *habeas corpus* for those not familiar with the concept. Manuel Tilman (KOTA), Rapporteur of the Systematisation and Harmonisation Committee, explained the need for a court procedure to deal with illegal detentions. Where, for instance, there was an accident leading to death and a person who simply witnessed the accident was arrested, that person needed to be able to have a lawyer put a case to the court that the arrest was illegal and request that the person be released. The eight-day time period was necessary to permit the police, the Minister and the court to examine the case. Jacob Xavier (PPT) queried the relationship between preventive detention and *habeas corpus*. Manuel Tilman explained that a person being held in preventive detention might bring a *habeas corpus* action if she/he was being held illegally.

Voting on the section during the plenary session

The section passed: 79:1:2.

Version finalised prior to the public consultation process

Section 33
(Habeas corpus)

1. *Everyone who illegally loses his or her freedom has the right to apply for habeas corpus.*

2. *An application for habeas corpus shall be made by the detainee or by any other person in the exercise of his or her civil rights, in accordance with the law.*

3. *The court shall rule on the application for habeas corpus within 8 days at a hearing in the presence of both parties.*

(Identical to final)

---

31 The Portuguese term used was '*em audiência contraditória*' which was interpreted in the final official version as 'at a hearng in the presence of both parties'.

Commentary: In this text, citizen-specific references had been replaced by references to 'everyone' and 'any other person'. Subsection (1) was also altered to refer specifically to 'everyone who illegally loses his or her freedom'. Several external interlocutors had made representations supporting the enjoyment of rights by all persons, and the Systematisation and Harmonisation Committee explained in their methodology that they had attempted to broaden references (from 'citizen' to 'individual' or 'person') whenever possible.

Representations and submissions

District consultations: Limited feedback was received on this section. The summary of the Dili consultation contained a suggestion to reduce the time (for ruling on an application) from eight days to 24 hours. It also recommended substituting an appropriate Tetum or Portuguese term for '*habeas corpus*'.

Submissions listed in the Systematisation and Harmonisation Committee's Consultations Report: The UN SRSG and Transitional Administrator underlined the importance of speedy access for persons in detention to apply for *habeas corpus*.[32]

Other submissions made during the process: In comments to the Systematisation and Harmonisation Committee, the Human Rights Unit of UNTAET proposed that courts be required to make a decision on a *habeas corpus* application within 48 or 72 hours, at a hearing in the presence of both parties.[33] During the drafting process, the Human Rights Unit of UNTAET, and the UN High Commissioner for Human Rights, amongst others, stressed the importance of human rights such as this one applying to all persons, rather than being limited to citizens. The International Commission of Jurists suggested deleting the words 'in the exercise of his/her civil rights' in sub-s (2), and feared inclusion of the phrase 'in accordance with the law' in the same subsection rendered any constitutional protection illusory.[34]

Post-consultation plenary debate

The Systematisation and Harmonisation Committee recommended reconsideration of the eight-day period (to lower the period).[35] However, this recommendation was not the subject of consensus and no change was made by the Assembly.

---

32 Comments attached to the letter from the UN SRSG and Transitional Administrator to heads of the political parties, 22 February 2002.

33 Human Rights Unit, UNTAET, 'Thematic Committee One's Proposals For the Protection of Human Rights in the Constitution: An analysis by the HRU', 14 November 2001, 8.

34 International Commission of Jurists (Australian Section), 'Commentary on the Draft Constitution Proposed for East Timor by the Constituent Assembly', undated, 8. The ICJ also considered the time limit in sub-s (3) to be superflous and artificial.

35 Amongst the Constituent Assembly's documentation, the author found a document entitled 'PSD Proposals' which appeared to contain their views relevant to the post-consultation debates. This document contained a proposal to reduce the relevant period to three days.

Section 34
(Guarantees in criminal proceedings)

1. Anyone charged with an offence is presumed innocent until convicted.[36]

2. An accused person has the right to select, and be assisted by, a lawyer at all stages of the proceedings and the law shall determine the circumstances for which the presence of the lawyer is mandatory.

3. Every individual is guaranteed the inviolable right of hearing and defence in criminal proceedings.

4. Evidence is of no effect if obtained by torture, coercion, infringement of the physical or moral integrity of the individual, or wrongful interference with private life, the home, correspondence or other forms of communication.

(Official translation of the final text)

Drafting history

Thematic Committee I text

Section 28
(Guarantees in criminal proceedings)

1. *Anyone charged with an offence is presumed innocent until convicted.*

2. *An accused person has the right to select, and be assisted by, a lawyer at all stages of the proceedings and the law shall determine the circumstances for which the presence of the lawyer is mandatory.*

3. *Evidence is of no effect if obtained by torture, coercion, infringement of the physical or moral integrity of the individual, or wrongful interference with correspondence or telecommunications.*

Commentary: This provision was based on art 28 of the FRETILIN Project (entitled 'Presumption of innocence'). The heading accepted by the committee came from art 49 of the PSD Project, after consideration of a range of options.

---

36 Contemporary Assembly translations used the term 'everyone' in sub-s (1). However, the official translation uses the term 'anyone' and has thus been preferred here. The Portuguese term used was '*todo*'.

The heading was approved in a vote of 7:6:8. The section with its heading was approved in a vote of 19:0:2.

Systematisation and Harmonisation Committee draft text used in the plenary debate

Section 33

(Guarantees in criminal proceedings)

1. *Anyone charged with an offence is presumed innocent until convicted.*

2. *An accused person has the right to select, and be assisted by, a lawyer at all stages of the proceedings and the law shall determine the circumstances for which the presence of the lawyer is mandatory.*

3. *Evidence is of no effect if obtained by torture, coercion, infringement of the physical or moral integrity of the individual, or wrongful interference with private life, the home, correspondence or telecommunications.*

Commentary: This version added in references to 'private life', and 'the home' in sub-s (3). No explanation was provided in the written text submitted to the Plenary.

The Bench of the Systematisation and Harmonisation Committee recommended an additional guarantee stating: 'The right of hearing and defence in criminal proceedings is inviolable and shall be guaranteed to any accused person.'

Plenary debate (19 December 2001)

Discussion centred on sub-s (3)'s exclusion of evidence obtained. Quitéria da Costa (UDT) asked for a concrete example of the type of situation which would trigger the exclusion. Manuel Tilman (KOTA), Rapporteur of the Systematisation and Harmonisation Committee, referred to the case of forced confessions. During Indonesian times, some persons had been beaten until they confessed. This section embodied a commitment not to permit use of a confession obtained in such circumstances; that is, where there had been torture or the threat of torture.

Vicente Guterres (UDC/PDC) noted that while there might be exceptional circumstances where interference with a person's private life or home might be warranted (for example, in terrorism or espionage cases), such interference needed to be in accordance with the law and have court authorisation.

Voting on the section during the plenary session

There was a positive vote for the Systematisation and Harmonisation Committee's suggested amendment (having a new subsection on the right of hearing and defence), in addition to the vote on the section.

The Systematisation and Harmonisation Committee suggested amendment passed: 55:4:23.[37]

The section passed: 80:0:2.

Version finalised prior to the public consultation process

Section 34
(Guarantees in criminal proceedings)

1. *Anyone charged with an offence is presumed innocent until convicted.*

2. *An accused person has the right to select, and be assisted by, a lawyer at all stages of the proceedings and the law shall determine the circumstances for which the presence of the lawyer is mandatory.*

3. *Every individual is guaranteed the inviolable right of hearing and defence in criminal proceedings.*

4. *Evidence is of no effect if obtained by torture, coercion, infringement of the physical or moral integrity of the individual, or wrongful interference with private life, the home, correspondence or other forms of communication.*

(Identical to final)

Commentary: In this text, the phrase 'other forms of communication' was substituted for 'telecommunications'. The text of the Systematisation and Harmonisation Committee-sponsored amendment (adopted during the plenary session) was also altered slightly in form.

Representations and submissions

District consultations: According to the Systematisation and Harmonisation Committee's summary report, only one District consultation included any comment about this section. In Oecussi, it was suggested that the perpetrators of crimes should not have access to legal aid.

Submissions listed in the Systematisation and Harmonisation Committee's Consultations Report: None listed.

Other submissions made during the process: Several submissions advocated the inclusion of more detailed fair trial rights. In the the initial stages of the

---

37   Some Assembly records show a vote of 55:9:23. However, a vote of 55:4:23 was captured on the recording in Portuguese.

process, Yayasan HAK put forward a detailed listing of rights which should apply to persons being tried. In addition to those in the draft clause, they included rights to:

- have adequate time and facilities to prepare a defence;
- have sufficient detail of the charge so as to be able to answer it;
- a public trial before an ordinary court;
- have the trial begin and conclude without unreasonable delay;
- be present when tried;
- be silent and not to testify during proceedings;
- not to be compelled to give self-incriminating evidence;
- be tried in a language that the accused person understands or, if that is not practicable, to have the proceedings interpreted in that language; and
- appeal to, or have review by, a higher court.[38]

Similarly, the Timor Lorosa'e Journalists' Association proposed a more extensive listing which included the rights to:

- be informed of the supporting evidence against the person; and
- be represented by counsel at all stages of the proceeding without delay;

as well as general fair trial rights, such as the right to:

- a fair and public trial by an independent and impartial court or tribunal,
- examine prosecution witnesses and the right not to have evidence introduced at trial unless it has been disclosed to the accused and he or she has the opportunity to rebut it;
- be tried within the shortest period of time that is compatible with the defence guarantees; and
- appeal to an independent court or tribunal with power to review the decision on law and facts and set it aside.[39]

Whilst not putting forward an alternative text, The Asia Foundation queried the effect of the exclusionary rule concerning evidence in sub-s (4). They suggested modifying the rule, so that the total exclusion did not apply to the category of 'improper interference'.[40]

---

38 Yayasan HAK, 'Civil and Political, Economic, Social and Cultural Rights', undated, but received by the Assembly on 22 October 2001, art 9.

39 See Timor Lorosa'e Journalists' Association/Internews, 'Submission to the Constituent Assembly on Articles in the FRETILIN Draft Constitution of May 2001 concerning freedom of expression', undated, but with a handwritten note indicating it was distributed to Assembly members on 26 November 2001.

40 The Asia Foundation, 'Discussion Paper on Draft of East Timorese Constitution', March 2002, 5. Whilst not putting forward alternative drafting proposals, the International Commission of Jurists also commented on this

Section 35
(Extradition and expulsion)

1. Extradition shall only take place following a court decision.

2. Extradition on political grounds is prohibited.

3. Extradition in respect of offences punishable, under the law of the requesting State, by death penalty or life imprisonment or whenever there are grounds to assume that the person to be extradited may be subjected to torture and inhuman, degrading and cruel treatment, shall not be permitted.

4. An East Timorese national shall not be expelled or expatriated from the national territory.

(Official translation of the final text)

Drafting history

Thematic Committee I text

Section 29
(Extradition)

1. *Extradition shall only take place following a court decision.*

2. *Extradition on political grounds is prohibited.*

3. *An East Timorese national shall not be expelled or expatriated from the national territory.*[41]

Commentary: This section was based on art 29 of the FRETILIN Project. It was adopted in a vote of 19:0:1. A PSD proposal to have the heading changed to 'Expulsion and extradition' was rejected in a vote of 5:12:3.

---

section, concluding that sub-s (2) did not provide for substantive protection (given the reference to law defining the circumstances where the presence of a lawyer was mandatory), and that the phrasing of sub-s (3) was too vague: 'Commentary on the Draft Constitution Proposed for East Timor by the Constituent Assembly', undated, 8.

41 In this and all subsequent drafts of this section, the Portuguese version referred to '*O cidadão timorense*', which might be translated as 'A Timorese citizen'. However, the official translation of the final text refers to 'An East Timorese national', thus the language has been preferred here.

Systematisation and Harmonisation Committee draft text used in the plenary debate

Section 34

(Extradition)

1. *Extradition shall only take place following a court decision.*

2. *Extradition on political grounds is prohibited.*

3. *Extradition in respect of offences punishable, under the law of the requesting State, by death penalty or life imprisonment or whenever there are grounds to assume that the person to be extradited may be subjected to torture and inhuman, degrading and cruel treatment, shall not be permitted.*

4. *An East Timorese national shall not be expelled or expatriated from the national territory.*

Commentary: Subsection (3) was added to this version by the Systematisation and Harmonisation Committee. No explanation was provided in the written text produced by the committee.[42]

Plenary debate (19 December 2001)

Debate in the plenary session focused in particular on (i) the heading, (ii) the extradition of persons with dual nationalities and (iii) the potential consequences for Timor of adopting this clause.

Manuel Tilman (KOTA) suggested including 'expulsion' in the heading of the section, a move argued against by Rui António (FRETILIN). Manuel Tilman (KOTA) also proposed a new sub-s (5) stipulating that a court order was required for the expulsion of anyone who had properly entered or was properly present in East Timor, those holding a residence permit or asylum seekers awaiting the determination of their asylum applications.[43] Indicating support for this idea, Jacob Xavier (PPT) wanted to ensure that expulsion took place where the police had evidence of criminality, referring to the example of a foreigner convicted of drug offences. Rather than having a separate vote on the heading and the extra subsection, there appears to have been only one vote concerning both aspects of Tilman's proposal. It failed in a close vote of 31:34:18.[44]

---

42 The PSD Project contained a shorter provision dealing with some of the circumstances mentioned in sub-s (3), namely the death penalty or other penalties that resulted in irreversible harm to a person's physical integrity: art 50(4).

43 The proposal as read out was identical to the first sentence of art 33(2) of the Portuguese Constitution.

44 Whilst there is a gap in the recording at the end of this debate, contemporary notes of the author and another monitor reflect only one vote occurring. The President of the Assembly referred to both the heading

In relation to the ban on extradition of Timorese nationals, the case of persons with dual nationalities was raised by Rui Meneses da Costa (PD). If a person had two nationalities, such as Timorese and Portuguese, Rui Meneses asked, would she/he enjoy protection from extradition even where she/he had committed a crime in Portugal and then fled to Timor? This concern was echoed by Mariano Sabino Lopes (PD), who preferred the matter to be dealt with in ordinary law. Francisco Xavier Do Amaral (ASDT) also supported leaving the subject in general to ordinary law rather than the Constitution, perceiving that it would be better to make decisions once there was further data on persons present in East Timor.

Questions were also raised as to the significance of the clause for Timorese extradition requests. António Ximenes (PDC) prefaced his remarks by noting that sometimes 'politics can create crimes'. In Timor, for instance, because of the politics of the time, crimes were committed. He queried the impact of the clause on a person who had committed a crime such as murder, and then left the country. Would Timor be able to ask for that person to be handed back? The particular example given was of Abilio Osório Soares, the former Governor of East Timor, who had been indicted in Timor for international crimes committed in 1999, but who remained in Indonesia. Ximenes was mindful of creating conditions for him to return to answer for his crimes.

Manuel Tilman (KOTA), Rapporteur of the Systematisation and Harmonisation Committee, provided an explanation of the extradition process. If a person committed a crime elsewhere and then the person came to East Timor, that person could be sent back to face trial on the request of the other State. If there was a treaty obligation to extradite, the person should be sent back. If not, there would be no obligation on East Timor to extradite the person. One needed to consider, however, the type of crime and penalty. For instance, in Malaysia, even small drug offences attracted the death penalty. In such cases, persons would not be sent back to Malaysia, but could be tried by Timorese courts to determine, for instance, if they were drug traffickers. In response to queries concerning the meaning of 'political motives', Tilman explained that if a person left a country for political reasons, she/he should not be sent back. Such a rule was motivated by international solidarity with those suffering political persecution. Tilman conceded that the definition of 'political motives' could be subjective, but identified the key feature as a person being engaged politically against a government. Some concern was expressed by individual members that the terms of s 34(3) were too wide and might, for instance, encourage criminals to come to East Timor because they would not be extradited from the territory.[45]

---

and the proposal prior to the vote on the amendment. In the lead-up to the vote, an unnamed speaker made a point of order suggesting there would be no need to consider changing the heading if the subsection was not adopted.

45   Adaljiza Magno (FRETILIN).

Several speakers also urged caution in relation to this section on the basis of other countries' experience of the movement of terrorists. Reference was made, for instance, to the reaction of the United States to the presence of Osama bin Laden in Afghanistan.[46]

Joaquim dos Santos (FRETILIN) noted that sub-s (3) of the text did not come from Thematic Committee I, leading to the suggestion of a separate vote on the subsection.[47] This did not eventuate.

Voting on the section during the plenary session

The section passed: 56:4:22.

Amongst those speaking after the vote, Francisco Branco (FRETILIN) expressed concern as to the effect of this clause. Whilst Timor wished to be a country based on human rights, one also needed to recognise the political fragility of the country. Given that neighbouring countries had the death penalty and life imprisonment, Branco feared that the exclusions in this clause would prove problematic for Timor in the future.

Version finalised prior to the public consultation process

Section 35
(Extradition and expulsion)

1. *Extradition shall only take place following a court decision.*

2. *Extradition on political grounds is prohibited.*

3. *Extradition in respect of offences punishable, under the law of the requesting State, by death penalty or life imprisonment or whenever there are grounds to assume that the person to be extradited may be subjected to torture and inhuman, degrading and cruel treatment, shall not be permitted.*

4. *An East Timorese national shall not be expelled or expatriated from the national territory.*

(Identical to final)

Commentary: In this version, the heading was changed to 'Extradition and expulsion', as per the earlier suggestion of Manuel Tilman (KOTA). No explanation was provided for this change, though it had been earlier noted that at least one subsection dealt with matters of expulsion.

---

46   Januario Soares (FRETILIN), Quiteria da Costa (UDT).
47   Joaquim dos Santos (FRETILIN).

Representations and submissions

District consultations: This section received little comment. In Baucau, there was the suggestion to eliminate sub-ss (2), (3) and (4), which would have left only the subsection that extradition was to take place after a court decision.

Submission listed in the Systematisation and Harmonisation Committee's Consultations Report: The Asia Foundation recommended that extradition of nationals be permitted to countries which themselves would extradite their nationals to East Timor, given that the system of extradition was built on reciprocity. This was to avoid the risk of East Timor becoming a haven for criminals and experiencing extradition refusals from other States because of a lack of reciprocity.[48] The Asia Foundation noted practical difficulties in refusing extradition to countries that imposed life sentences, noting the breadth of such countries and questioning whether Timor would have the resources to carry out the investigations and prosecutions needed as a result of refusing extradition. No specific alternative language was included in their commentary.[49]

Other submissions made during the process: The East Timor Study Group expressed concern that Timor might become a 'criminal club' by virtue of this section. It suggested that this section not apply to those involved in terrorism, money laundering and drug trafficking.[50] The International Commission of Jurists considered that if the provision meant a ban on extraditing East Timorese, this would be out of step with international practice.[51]

---

48 The Asia Foundation, 'Comments and Suggested Amendments to East Timor's Draft Constitution', undated, but attached to a cover letter to the President of the Constituent Assembly dated 8 March 2002, 5.
49 Ibid. See too The Asia Foundation, 'Discussion Paper on Draft of East Timorese Constitution', March 2002, 5–6.
50 East Timor Study Group, 'Debate on the Draft Constitution: Positive and Negative Implications for the Future of East Timor', 20 February 2002, 11 [Tetum].
51 International Commission of Jurists (Australian Section), 'Commentary on the Draft Constitution Proposed for East Timor by the Constituent Assembly', undated, 8.

Section 36
(Right to honour and privacy)

Every individual has the right to honour, good name[52] and reputation, protection of his or her public image and privacy of his or her personal and family life.

(Official translation of the final text)

Drafting history

Thematic Committee I text

Section 30
(Right to honour and privacy)

Every citizen has the right to honour, good name and reputation, protection of his or her public image and privacy of his or her personal and family life.

Commentary: This provision was based on art 30 of the FRETILIN Project. It was approved unanimously: 20:0:0.

Systematisation and Harmonisation Committee draft text used in the plenary debate

Section 35
(Right to honour and privacy)

Every citizen has the right to honour, good name and reputation, protection of his or her public image[53] and privacy of his or her personal and family life.

Plenary debate (19 December 2001)

The only substantive point of discussion about this section related to whether it would unduly hinder the expression of critical views concerning public officials. Mariano Sabino Lopes (PD) recalled that in the Indonesian system, ordinary

---

52   Contemporary Assembly translations used the term 'good record', whereas the official translation uses the term 'good name' and thus has been preferred here. The Portuguese term used throughout was '*bom nome*'.
53   Note the Portuguese text had changed from '*imagem pública*' in the Thematic Committee text to '*imagem*' in this text. However, the Assembly translation of the Systematisation and Harmonisation Committee text and the official translation of the final text remained 'public image', so this term has been retained here.

people were not able to criticise the 'top people' even where corruption existed. Manuel Tilman (KOTA), Rapporteur of the Systematisation and Harmonisation Committee, agreed that people must have the ability to comment on public officials. At the same time, people must also treat officials with respect given their functions. All citizens retained a right to privacy. Even important persons like the Prime Minister or the President continued to be normal citizens, enjoying a right to privacy and other fundamental rights.

Voting on the section during the plenary session

The section passed: 74:0:6.

After the vote Mariano Sabino Lopes (PD) explained he had abstained because journalists needed to be able to comment upon public officials.

Version finalised prior to the public consultation process

Section 36
(Right to honour and privacy)

Every individual has the right to honour, good name and reputation, protection of his or her public image and privacy of his or her personal and family life.

(Identical to final)

Commentary: In this version, the provision was altered so that it applied to every individual, rather than every citizen. A number of submissions had been received in relation to ensuring the enjoyment of rights by all persons, and the Systematisation and Harmonisation Committee explained in their methodology that they had attempted to broaden references (from 'citizen' to 'individual' or 'person') whenever possible.

Representations and submissions

District consultations: No comments on this section appear in the summary of District consultations prepared by the Systematisation and Harmonisation Committee.

Submissions listed in the Systematisation and Harmonisation Committee's Consultations Report: None listed.

Other submissions made during the process: The Timor Lorosa'e Journalists' Association was concerned that this section had been placed on an equal footing with freedom of expression, rather than expressed as a ground for restricting this freedom. It recommended that references to 'honour, good record [name] and reputation, protection of his or her public image' be removed.[54] In its earlier critique of the FRETILIN project, TLJA had suggested amending the clause to read: 'Everyone has the right to *the defence of* his or her good name and reputation, the right to the protection of the privacy of his or her personal and family life.'[55]

Yayasan HAK suggested an amendment to provide that defamation not attract criminal liability.[56]

During the drafting process, the Human Rights Unit of UNTAET, and the UN High Commissioner for Human Rights, amongst others, stressed the importance of human rights such as this one applying to all persons, rather than being limited to citizens.[57]

---

54 Timor Lorosa'e Journalists' Association, 'Submission on Freedom of Expression', 7 March 2002. The International Commission of Jurists (Australian Section) also considered the section should be removed because of a lack of precision: 'Commentary on the Draft Constitution Proposed for East Timor by the Constituent Assembly', undated, 8.

55 Timor Lorosa'e Journalists' Association/Internews, 'Submission to the Constituent Assembly on Articles in the FRETILIN Draft Constitution of May 2001 concerning freedom of expression', undated, but with a handwritten note indicating it was distributed to Assembly members on 26 November 2001.

56 Yayasan HAK, 'Civil and Political, Economic, Social and Cultural Rights', undated, but received by the Assembly on 22 October 2001, art 14(2).

57 See for instance, Human Rights Unit, UNTAET, 'Thematic Committee One's Proposals For the Protection of Human Rights in the Constitution: An analysis by the HRU', 14 November 2001, 4–5.

Section 37
(Inviolability of home and correspondence)

1. Any person's home[58] and the privacy of his or her correspondence and other means of private communication are inviolable, except in cases provided for by law as a result of criminal proceedings.

2. A person's home shall not be entered against his or her will, except under the written order of a competent judicial authority and in the cases and manner prescribed by law.

3. Entry into any person's home at night against his or her will is clearly prohibited, except in case of serious threat to life or physical integrity of somebody inside the home.

(Official translation of the final text)

Drafting history

Thematic Committee I text

Section 31
(Inviolability of home and correspondence)

1. *Any person's home and the privacy of his or her correspondence and other means of private communication are inviolable, <u>except in cases provided for by law as a result of criminal proceedings.</u>*

2. *A citizen's home shall not be entered against his or her will, except under the order of a competent judicial authority and in the cases and manner prescribed by law.*

3. *Entry into any citizen's home at night against his or her will is clearly prohibited.*

Commentary: This provision was based on art 31 of the FRETILIN Project with additional wording for sub-s (1) ('except in cases provided for by law as a result of criminal proceedings') proposed by Lú Olo (FRETILIN). The addition was approved in a vote of 15:2:3.

---

58   The Portuguese term used from the Thematic Committee I text through to the final Constitution was 'O *domicilio*' which might be translated as 'one's home/domicile'. However, the official translation of the final text is 'any person's home' and thus it is used throughout this account.

Lucia Lobato (PSD) proposed eliminating sub-s (2). However, this was rejected in a vote of 5:9:4.

The whole section was approved in a vote of 17:0:3.

Systematisation and Harmonisation Committee draft text used in the plenary debate

Section 36
(Inviolability of home and correspondence)

1. *Any person's home and the privacy of his or her correspondence and other means of private communication are inviolable, except in cases provided for by law as a result of criminal proceedings.*

2. *A citizen's home shall not be entered against his or her will except under the order of a competent judicial authority and in the cases and manner prescribed by law.*

3. *Entry into any citizen's home at night against his or her will is clearly prohibited.*

Plenary debate (19 December 2001)

Discussion in the plenary session focused primarily on the extent of power authorities should have to enter homes without permission. Rui Meneses da Costa (PD) was pleased to see that the section spoke of entry to homes in broad terms, since in Indonesian times police entered homes in a variety of situations, not simply to conduct arrests. Armando da Silva (PL), Quitéria da Costa (UDT), and Clementino Amaral (KOTA) thought the power of entry should be exercisable only if the authorities had a written order. One of the most vocal critics of sub-s (2) was Leandro Isac (PSD), who considered the subsection was not strong enough and did not provide for 'inviolability' of the home. He recommended that entry to a home be permitted only with a court order and, further, that any reference to entry being permissible in cases 'prescribed by law' be omitted.

Lú Olo (FRETILIN) supported inclusion of the phrase 'in the cases and [in the] manner prescribed by law' in sub-s (2), noting that experts had written the text, and there might be some cases where quick intervention was needed: for example, in responding to domestic violence. The ambit of situations requiring immediate action could be defined by law. Manuel Tilman (KOTA) underlined the fact that sub-s (2) only applied where entry was without consent. If the police were invited guests, there would be no problem. If the entry was non-consensual, a judge's order would normally be needed. Without a warrant, police could only surround the house. Clementino Amaral (KOTA) supported the subsection as written, because police needed to be able to enter and arrest a person in some circumstances; for example, where a criminal has attempted to kill another person and then proceeds to hide in a house. Armando da Silva (PL) highlighted the importance of differentiating between cases in which written authorisation would be required, versus those where urgent intervention was needed. Eusébio Guterres (PD) suggested a further section be included dealing with the police's powers of arrest which stipulated their powers when pursuing offenders.

The interrelationship between sub-ss (2) and (3) attracted some attention. Jacob Fernandes (FRETILIN) highlighted the potential contradiction between the two clauses. Fernandes considered it unsatisfactory if the clause meant that a police officer who was chasing someone from the scene of a crime was not able to perform his/her duty to arrest if the person entered a home at night. Mario Carrascalão (PSD) similarly highlighted the necessity for prompt police action in certain cases, asking: if a person was going to shoot the President, did the police have to wait until the morning to enter a home to undertake the arrest? Pedro Gomes (ASDT) considered that the ordinary law should deal with the subject of police powers of entry. Lú Olo considered that sub-s (2)'s reference to cases 'prescribed by law' would allow for exceptional circumstances where quick intervention was required.

Experiences during Indonesian times were at the forefront of members' minds during this dicussion. Mario Carrascalão (PSD), for instance, reported that during Indonesian times authorities just arrived. They did not follow rules or regulations. One only found out later that people had been arrested, and that after their arrest they had been tortured or beaten. Clementino Amaral (KOTA) noted that the Indonesian law required authorisation for entry into homes but, in practice, that had not occurred. The level of sensitivity around this topic was reflected in the Assembly's decision to hold a roll-call vote on sub-s (3).

The proposal to add the term *'written'* in sub-s (2) advanced by Quitéria da Costa (UDT)[59] *passed in a vote: 56:6:20.*

Voting on the section during the plenary session

Sections 36 (1) and (2) passed: 79:0:3.

Section 36 (3) was the subject of a roll-call vote: It passed 63:4:14.

Section 36 as a whole passed: 73:0:7.

---

59   Other signatories included Manuel Tilman (KOTA), Clementino Amaral (KOTA) and Pedro da Costa (PST).

Version finalised prior to the public consultation process

Section 37

(Inviolability of home and correspondence)

1. *Any person's home and the privacy of his or her correspondence and other means of private communication are inviolable, except in cases provided for by law as a result of criminal proceedings.*

2. *A person's home shall not be entered against his or her will, except under the written order of a competent judicial authority and in the cases and manner prescribed by law.*

3. *Entry into any person's home at night against his or her will is clearly prohibited, except in case of serious threat to life or physical integrity of somebody inside the home.*

(Identical to final)

Commentary: Several changes to the text appeared at this point. Firstly, sub-ss (2) and (3) were broadened out to refer to 'a person's home', rather than a 'citizen's home'. In their summary of methodology, the Systematisation and Harmonisation Committee noted their policy to substitute the broader term 'individual' or 'person' for 'citizen' wherever possible, a move which was in accord with many submissions to the Assembly. The other alteration was adding an exemption to sub-s (3) ('except in cases of serious threat to life or physical integrity of somebody inside the home'). The text explained that this was done on the basis of the recommendation of the Centre for Peace and Development's submission. (See further below.)

Representations and submissions

District consultations: The Systematisation and Harmonisation Committee summary of District consultations reports record only one comment on this section. In Los Palos, a suggestion was made to eliminate the provision and regulate the subject in ordinary law.

Submissions listed in the Systematisation and Harmonisation Committee's Consultations Report: None listed.

Other submissions made during the process: Ensuring police had the authority to enter premises in order to protect life, including at night, was a matter agitated in several external submissions. The Church-Constitution Working Group recommended that the clause be amended so as to ensure that police might enter a house at night to attend any situation of domestic violence being perpetrated by the householder.[60] Recognising that Assembly members were anxious to avoid the invasion of homes 'which was common during Indonesian times', the Church-Constitution Working Group expressed fear that the draft was so broad, it would 'permit violent wrongdoers to hide behind their doors, immune from legal restraint.' It went on to say: 'Our Constitution must not act as an impediment to efforts directing at stopping domestic violence.' REDE Feto Timor Lorosae suggested adding a caveat to sub-s (2), excluding 'cases where it is necessary to protect the rights or interests of a person, as expressed in the Constitution'.[61] The International Commission of Jurists voiced concern that sub-s (1) and sub-s (2) allowed later laws to circumscribe any guarantees, whilst characterising sub-s (3) as an unwarranted restriction on lawful apprehensions which should be deleted.[62]

The Human Rights Unit of UNTAET proposed merging and clarifying the text to ensure that law enforcement officials could enter a house when necessary to protect the safety of any of the inhabitants. A modified text was suggested which read:

> A person's home shall not be entered against his or her will, except under the order of a competent judicial authority and in the cases and in the manner prescribed by law. In general such searches should be conducted during the day time, unless a search at night is necessitated for the protection of any individual in the house, or the overriding interests of justice.[63]

During the drafting process, the Human Rights Unit of UNTAET and the UN High Commissioner for Human Rights, amongst others, stressed the importance of human rights such as this one applying to all persons, rather than being limited to citizens.[64]

---

60   Letter from the Centre for Peace and Development to the President of the Constituent Assembly, January 2002, received by the Assembly on 23 January 2002. This letter contained the joint Catholic/Protestant submission of the Church-Constitution Working Group.

61   Letter from REDE Feto Timor Lorosae to the President of the Constituent Assembly, 31 October 2001.

62   International Commission of Jurists (Australian Section), 'Commentary on the Draft Constitution Proposed for East Timor by the Constituent Assembly', undated, 8–9.

63   See, for instance, Human Rights Unit, UNTAET, 'Thematic Committee One's Proposals For the Protection of Human Rights in the Constitution: An analysis by the HRU', 14 November 2001, 9.

64   Ibid 4–5.

Section 38
(Protection of personal data)

1. Every citizen has the right to access personal data stored in a computer system or entered into mechanical or manual records regarding him or her, and he or she may require correction and up-date [updating] thereof and shall have the right to demand the purpose of such data.

2. The law shall determine the concept of personal data, as well as the conditions applicable to the processing thereof.

3. The processing of personal data on private life, political and philosophical convictions, religious faith, party or trade union membership and ethnical [ethnic] origin, without the consent of the interested person, is prohibited.

(Official translation of the final text)[65]

Drafting history

Thematic Committee I text

Section 32
(Protection of personal data)

1. *Every citizen has the right to access personal data stored in a computer system or entered into mechanical or manual records regarding him or her, and he or she may require correction and up-date [updating] thereof and shall have the right to demand the purpose of such data.*

2. *The law shall determine the concept of personal data, as well as the conditions applicable to the processing thereof.*

3. *The processing of personal data on private life, political, philosophical or religious convictions, or party or trade union membership is expressly prohibited in every case.*

---

65 Unfortunately, the official translation incorrectly omitted sub-s (1)'s reference to the right to require correction and updating. However, as the final Portuguese text retained this phrasing, it has been reproduced here. The contemporary Assembly English translation included the phrasing 'right to know their purpose' rather than 'right to demand the purpose of such data', the phrasing of the official translation.

Commentary: This section was a joint proposal picking up parts of the FRETILIN Project (art 32), the PSD Project (art 33) and the KOTA Project (art 27). It was approved unanimously in a vote of 20:0:0.

Systematisation and Harmonisation Committee draft text used in the plenary debate

Section 37
(Protection of personal data)

1. *Every citizen has the right to access personal data stored in a computer system or entered into mechanical or manual records regarding him or her, and he or she may require correction and up-date[updating] thereof and shall have the right to demand the purpose of such data.*

2. *The law shall determine the concept of personal data, as well as the conditions applicable to the processing thereof.*

3. *The processing of personal data on private life, political, philosophical or religious convictions, party or trade union membership is expressly prohibited in every case.*[66]

Plenary debate (19 December 2001)

The topic provoking most discussion in relation to this section was the prohibition imposed on the processing of data related to religious convictions. Mario Carrascalão (PSD) queried this prohibition, arguing that religious organisations needed data (for example, the number of adherents) to permit a fair distribution of assistance and funds and to help design programs. Several members of the Systematisation and Harmonisation Committee explained the rationale for the provision. Vicente Guterres (UDC/PDC), Secretary of the Systematisation and Harmonisation Committee, recalled that the prohibition was designed to prevent discrimination. Manuel Tilman (KOTA), Rapporteur of the committee, added that the State did not need to know a person's religion and other personal data. Individuals would give information to organisations that needed it. Mario Carrascalão (PSD) felt that persons were already treated equally, disputing any concern about discrimination. Explaining his support for the provision, Clementino Amaral (KOTA) wished to avoid the situation where a person was denied employment because of his/her religion, or political party membership, noting that not all persons may be as open as Mario Carrascalão. Amaral saw the

---

66   The English Assembly translation referred to 'political party' membership. However, the Portuguese text of this version through to the final version was '*filiação partidária*', so the form of translation used in the final text has been preferred.

provision as necessary so that it would be prohibited to discriminate against persons on the basis of their political opinion or particular faith, whether they be Catholic, Protestant, Buddhist, Muslim or Hindu.

Eusébio Guterres (PD) suggested that sub-s (3) should refer to 'organisation membership', rather than 'trade union membership' on the basis of his understanding of the Portuguese text.

No amendments were put to the text.

Voting on the section during the plenary session

The section passed 75:0:7.

Version finalised prior to the public consultation process

Section 38
(Protection of personal data)

1. *Every citizen has the right to access personal data stored in a computer system or entered into mechanical or manual records regarding him or her, and he or she may require correction and up-date [updating] thereof and shall have the right to demand the purpose of such data.*

2. *The law shall determine the concept of personal data, as well as the conditions applicable to the processing thereof.*

3. *The processing of personal data on private life, political and philosophical convictions, religious faith, party or trade union membership and ethnical [ethnic] origin, without the consent of the interested person, is prohibited.*

(Identical to final)

Commentary: In this version, several amendments were made. In sub-s (3), the term 'ethnic origin' was added (translated in the official text as 'ethnical origin'). In addition, a potential exception was inserted into the text concerning the processing of personal data on particular subject matters. Whereas the text before the Plenary had applied the prohibition 'in every case', this text qualified the prohibition to cases of processing 'without the consent of the interested person'. The 9 February 2002 Portuguese text of the Systematisation and Harmonisation Committee explained that this alteration was recommended by the Centre for Peace and Development (see below).[67] A more technical amendment related to the use of the Portuguese term *'tratamento informatizado'*

---

67   Letter from the Centre for Peace and Development to the President of the Constituent Assembly, January 2002, received by the Assembly on 23 January 2002.

('computerised information') in sub-s (3), although the English translation remained 'processing' in this version and the final official translation. The phrase 'religious faith' was also substituted for 'religious conviction', possibly also as a result of the Centre for Peace and Development's stated preference for the form of the clause in the Portuguese Constitution.

Representations and submissions

District consultations: No comments on this section appear in the summary of District consultations prepared by the Systematisation and Harmonisation Committee.

Submissions listed in the Systematisation and Harmonisation Committee's Consultations Report: None listed.

Other submissions made during the process: A desire to avoid hindering the gathering of information on a consensual basis was evident in several of the submissions to the Assembly. The Church-Constitution Working Group, whose submission was provided under the letterhead of the Centre for Peace and Development, suggested that recourse be had to art 35 of the Portuguese Constitution for the following substitute text:

1. Every citizen shall possess the right to access to all computerised data that concern him, to require that they be corrected and updated, and to be informed of the purpose for which they are intended, all as laid down by law.

2. The law shall define the concept of personal data, together with the terms and conditions applicable to its automatised treatment and its linkage, transmission and use, and shall guarantee its protection, particularly by means of an independent administrative body.

3. Computers shall not be used to treat data concerning philosophical or political convictions, party or trade union affiliations, religious beliefs, private life or ethnic origins, save with the express consent of the data subject, with authorisation provided for by law and with guarantees of non-discrimination, or for the purpose of processing statistical data that cannot be individually identified.

4. Third-party access to personal data shall be prohibited, save in exceptional cases provided for by law.

5. The allocation of a single national number to any citizen shall be prohibited.

6. Everyone shall be guaranteed free access to public-use computer networks, and the law shall define both the rules that shall apply

to cross-border data flows and the appropriate means for protecting personal data and such other data as may justifiably be safeguarded in the national interest.

7. Personal data contained in manual files shall enjoy the same protection as that provided for in the previous paragraphs, as laid down by law.[68]

They feared that the existing draft section was so broad it would prevent the collection of material for the State census or the gathering of data about church parishioners.

In their commentary on the FRETILIN project, the Timor Lorosa'e Journalists' Association proposed an amended text in the following terms: 'Computerized storage shall not be used for information concerning private life, religious beliefs and political convictions, party or trade union affiliations, *without the consent of the individual concerned.*'[69]

The International Commission of Jurists recommended limiting the scope of the section to apply only to government processing of data, and expressed concern that sub-s (2) regarding personal data provided only an illusion of protection.[70]

During the drafting process, the Human Rights Unit of UNTAET, and the UN High Commissioner for Human Rights, amongst others, stressed the importance of human rights such as this one applying to all persons, rather than being limited to citizens.[71]

---

68   Ibid.

69   Timor Lorosa'e Journalists' Association/Internews, 'Submission to the Constituent Assembly on Articles in the FRETILIN Draft Constitution of May 2001 concerning freedom of expression', undated, but with an attached handwritten note indicating that it was sent to members of the Assembly on 26 November 2001.

70   International Commission of Jurists (Australian Section), 'Commentary on the Draft Constitution Proposed for East Timor by the Constituent Assembly', undated, 9.

71   See, for instance, Human Rights Unit, UNTAET, 'Thematic Committee One's Proposals For the Protection of Human Rights in the Constitution: An analysis by the HRU', 14 November 2001, 4–5.

Section 39
(Family, marriage and maternity)

1. The State shall protect the family as the society's basic unit and a condition for the harmonious development of the individual.

2. Everyone has the right to establish and live in a family.

3. Marriage shall be based upon free consent by the parties and on terms of full equality of rights between spouses, in accordance with the law.

4. Maternity shall be dignified and protected, and special protection shall be guaranteed to all women during pregnancy and after delivery and working women shall have the right to be exempted from the workplace for an adequate period before and after delivery, without loss of remuneration or any other benefits, in accordance with the law.

(Official translation of the final text)

Drafting history

Thematic Committee I text

Section 33

(Family, marriage and maternity)

1. *The State shall protect the family as the society's basic unit and a guarantor of the harmonious development of the citizen.*

2. *Everyone has the right to establish and live in a family.*

3. *Marriage shall be based upon free consent by the parties and on terms of full equality of rights between spouses.*

4. *Maternity shall be dignified and protected, <u>and special protection shall be guaranteed to all women during pregnancy and after delivery and working women shall have the right to be exempted from the workplace for an adequate period before and after delivery, without loss of remuneration or any other benefits.</u>*

Commentary: This provision was based on art 33 of the FRETILIN Project, with sub-s (4) extended by a proposal by the Bench through the phrasing from 'and special protection ... benefits'. The addition was approved in a vote of 12:4:4. The whole section was approved in a vote of 15:1:4.

Clementino Amaral (KOTA) proposed an additional subsection which would have provided that mothers who were widowed as a result of the struggle against occupation were entitled to the special protection of the State. It was rejected: 1:11:8.

Systematisation and Harmonisation Committee draft text used in the plenary debate

Section 38
(Family, marriage and maternity)

1. *The State shall protect the family as the society's basic unit and a guarantor of the harmonious development of the citizen.*

2. *Everyone has the right to establish and live in a family.*

3. *Marriage shall be based upon free consent by the parties and on terms of full equality of rights between spouses.*

4. *Maternity shall be dignified and protected, and special protection shall be guaranteed to all women during pregnancy and after delivery and working women shall have the right to be exempted from the workplace for an adequate period before and after delivery, without loss of remuneration or any other benefits in accordance with the law.*

Commentary: The Systematisation and Harmonisation Committee appear to have added the qualifier 'in accordance with the law' to sub-s (4).[72] No explanation was provided in the written text submitted to the Plenary.

Plenary debate (19 December 2001)

The relationship between religious concepts of marriage and the law was a particular topic of discussion in relation to this section. Francisco Jeronimo (FRETILIN) was concerned that the provision dealt mostly with what the society and State wanted in relation to marriage, but did not sufficiently refer to the dictates of religion. Marriage was not only a State issue, but also a religious issue. Subsection (2) seemed very open in its terms. In referring to the right to set up a family, for instance, if persons wanted to establish a family, they might later want to divorce. However, some religions did not permit divorce, so the topic

---

72   This reference did not appear in the English translation of the Systematisation and Harmonisation Committee text, but appears in the Portuguese text.

required further attention. Similarly, some religions accepted polygamy, while others did not. He suggested stipulating that the right to found a family (which he interpreted as marriage) would be qualified by the phrase 'according to the teaching of religion'. A religious concept of marriage was also acknowledged by Norberto Espirito Santo (FRETILIN), who stated that God gave men and women the freedom to live together in marriage. However, according to Santo, if couples stopped liking each other, they had the choice to separate.

Lú Olo (FRETILIN), President of the Assembly, spoke out against any amendment referring to religious precepts of marriage. Marriage had to be a free choice of both the man and the woman. The Constitution already recognised freedom of religion, so there was no need for any further reference here. People could act according to their religion, including in relation to divorce. The ordinary law should define divorce.

Upon request for clarification from Pedro Gomes (ASDT), Manuel Tilman (KOTA), Rapporteur of the Systematisation and Harmonisation Committee, took the floor. In Tilman's opinion, the family referred to in the section was the nuclear family. The State must have a law about the rights of families, and individuals' freedom to choose their spouses. Timor was now in an era of development. It was not like in members' grandparents' time where spouses were chosen for individuals by their parents. Timor was moving into an era of equality of men and women. He foresaw a time when polygamy would end: otherwise if men could have several wives, women could also have several husbands. The law needed to regulate the responsibilities of parents to their children, referring to the problem of men abandoning their children when they formed a new relationship. According to Tilman, the law would also need to define the situations for divorce: for example, where there had been a failure in duties such as fidelity, cohabitation, or providing for the family. Whether one was Christian or Muslim, one had the right to a divorce. There remained a need for the State to define through the law a variety of matters; for example, the custody arrangements for children following a divorce.

Quitéria da Costa (UDT) thought there should be further clarification of the 'adequate period' of maternity leave provided for in sub-s (4). She referred in particular to the period of three months provided for during Indonesian times. The need for special services for mothers after giving birth was also noted.

Mario Carrascalão (PSD) preferred to speak of the family as society's basic 'element', rather than 'unit', viewing 'unit' as having potential political connotations. He also noted that sub-s (3) mentioned free consent for marriage, yet in Timor marriages were sometimes arranged by families. Rather than seeking to defend this practice, he wanted to call attention to the reality.

Lucia Lobato (PSD) proposed an amendment based on text included in the PSD Project text: 'The law shall regulate the requirements for and the effects of marriage and its dissolution by death or divorce, regardless of the form in which it was entered into.'[73] Mariano Sabino Lopes (PD) concurred, reminding members that the Assembly had already accepted the separation of church and State. In his view, the proposal was important since laws were necessary to deal with divorce: for instance, in relation to the distribution of wealth and arrangements in relation to any children. In a point of order before the vote on this proposal, Leandro Isac (PSD) highlighted that this was not a text on the Catholic faith/ divorce *per se*. Instead, the text was saying that the law should regulate affairs at the end of a marriage, whether the end had been brought about by death or divorce. Lú Olo spoke against this amendment citing the 'complexity' of society. He considered it would be preferable to include provisions in the ordinary law. Unfortunately, the recording available to the author did not include the vote on this proposal. However, it is apparent that it failed to garner the requisite majority.

Voting on the section during the plenary session

The section passed: 72:1:9.

Following the vote, João Carrascalão (UDT) expressed discontent that the section made no mention of paternity and only dealt with matters superficially. Armando da Silva (PL) considered that the phrase 'free consent' was vague, and that it was unclear whether it referred to, for example, marriage being free from the State/registry, or free vis-à-vis parents.

Version finalised prior to the public consultation process

Section 39
(Family, marriage and maternity)

1. *The State shall protect the family as the society's basic unit and a condition for the harmonious development of the individual.*

2. *Everyone has the right to establish and live in a family.*

3. *Marriage shall be based upon free consent by the parties and on terms of full equality of rights between spouses, in accordance with the law.*

4. *Maternity shall be dignified and protected, and special protection shall be guaranteed to all women during pregnancy and after delivery and working women shall have the right to be exempted from the workplace*

---

73 The text, drawn from art 36(2) of the PSD Project, was identical to art 36(2) of the Portuguese Constitution. The English translation of the Portuguese Constitution has been used here. An alternative literal translation of the final phrase would be 'irrespective of the form of celebration'.

for an adequate period before and after delivery, without loss of remuneration or any other benefits, in accordance with the law.

(Identical to final)

Commentary: Several amendments were incorporated in this text. The phrase 'condition for the harmonious development of the individual' had been substituted for 'guarantor of the harmonious development of the citizen' in sub-s (1). Subsection (3) also included the qualifier 'in accordance with the law' (bolded in the text distributed).

Representations and submissions

District consultations: This section prompted significant comment in the District consultations. In the Systematisation and Harmonisation Committee's summary report, the recommendation that polygamy and polyandry be prohibited, or put positively, that monogamy in marriage be required in Timor, was raised in five Districts (Baucau, Ermera, Liquiça, Manatuto and Viqueque). Suggestions were made for a clause on divorce in Dili and Ermera, without details of the content of such a clause being provided, whilst in Manatuto a suggestion was made to 'add the possibility of divorce'.[74] The Dili consultations also gave rise to a suggestion to enshrine the rights of women who were abandoned by their husbands. In Los Palos, family was said to be the strong foundation of society.

The most extensive comments on the section emanated from Oecusse. Reference was made to customary norms. According to custom, a local man who married would 'bring' his wife with him, whereas a local woman who married a man from another region, must accompany her husband. The desirability of a minimum age to marry was also referred to, and support was forthcoming for having provisions against artificial birth control and domestic violence. The report on Same District mentioned having not only freedom of choice of spouses, but also freedom of religious faith, and ethnic origin (seemingly a reference to the freedom to choose a partner from a differing ethnic origin). The Viqueque report also noted the importance of recognising a wedding's validity, regardless of its 'type' (that is, the nature of the authority for the wedding).

Submissions listed in the Systematisation and Harmonisation Committee's Consultations Report: None listed.

Other submissions made during the process: REDE Feto Timor Lorosae proposed that the Constitution make specific reference to 'marriage and the

---

74 The Manatuto report also raised the legality of the practice of abortion in certain cases in the context of this section.

dissolution of marriage' being regulated by law.[75] Elaborating further, REDE explained their desire to prevent both men and women becoming victims of polygamy or polyandry, and to avoid discrimination in the enjoyment of goods and property. In relation to the phrase 'motherhood is dignified and protected', REDE suggested that reference also be made to the role and responsibilities of fathers (paternal responsibility). These points were reiterated through the advancement of a specific provision which stated, firstly, that marriage and its dissolution would be regulated by law and, secondly, that motherhood and fatherhood was honoured and protected by the family, State and the community.[76]

The joint Catholic/Protestant submission put forward by the Church-Constitution Working Group proposed an addition to s 38 which would in effect outlaw polygamy and polyandry: 'No married person is permitted remarriage unless a previous marriage has been dissolved.'[77]

The East Timor Study Group noted that the Catholic Church had a particular position on marriage – considering marriage to be sacred and requiring monogamy. It considered that the provision had the potential to be divisive, and recommended the Constitution include an express statement that marriage needed to be monogamous.[78]

Post-consultation plenary debate

On the basis of the District reports, the Systematisation and Harmonisation Committee suggested the Constituent Assembly think about including a prohibition of polygamy and polyandry, ensuring monogamy.[79] No such action was taken by the Plenary of the Assembly.

---

75   Letter from REDE Feto Timor Lorosae to members of the Constitutional Commission 1 'Fundamental Rights, Duties and Freedoms', 22 October 2001 [Portuguese].

76   Letter from REDE Feto Timor Lorosae to the President of the Constituent Assembly, 31 October 2001.

77   Letter from the Centre for Peace and Development to the President of the Constituent Assembly, January 2002, received by the Assembly on 23 January 2002. This letter contained the submission of the Church-Constitution Working Group.

78   East Timor Study Group, 'Debate on the Draft Constitution: Positive and Negative Implications for the Future of East Timor', 20 February 2002 [Tetum].

79   Amongst the documentation of the Constituent Assembly viewed by the author was a document entitled 'PSD Proposals', which appeared to contain their stances on post-consultation issues. This indicated support for adding in a State obligation to prohibit polygamy and polyandry.

Section 40
(Freedom of speech and information)[80]

1. Every person has the right to freedom of speech and the right to inform and be informed impartially.

2. The exercise of freedom of speech and information shall not be limited by any sort of censorship.

3. The exercise of rights and freedoms referred to in this Section shall be regulated by law based on the imperative of respect for the Constitution and the dignity of the human person.

(Official translation of the final text)

___

Drafting history

Thematic Committee I text

Section 34
(Freedom of speech and information)

1. *Every citizen has the right to freedom of speech and freedom of the press and the right to inform and be informed impartially.*

2. *The exercise of freedom of speech and information shall not be limited by any sort of prior censorship.*

3. *The exercise of the right[s] of expression and information shall be regulated by law, offences committed in their exercise will be adjudicated upon by courts of law.*

Commentary: This section was based on art 34 of the FRETILIN Project, with the addition of 'and information' in sub-ss (2) and (3) approved by votes of 13:1:6, and 8:5:4 respectively. The report of Thematic Committee I does not record who authored this proposal. The whole section was approved in a vote of 19:0:1.

___

80 The Portuguese term used was *'liberdade de expressão'*, which might also be translated as 'freedom of expression'.

Systematisation and Harmonisation Committee draft text used in the plenary debate

Section 39

(Freedom of speech and information)

1. *Every citizen has the right to freedom of speech and the right to inform and be informed impartially.*

2. *The exercise of freedom of speech and information shall not be limited by any sort of censorship.*

3. *The exercise of rights and freedoms referred to in this Section shall be regulated by law based on the imperative of respect for the Constitution and the dignity of the human person.*

Commentary: The Systematisation and Harmonisation Committee made several alterations in putting forward this text. Reference to freedom of the press was removed from sub-s (1), presumably as a result of the introduction of a separate section on freedom of the press. Also omitted was the term 'prior' appearing before censorship in sub-s (2). Subsection (3) was substantially altered. Instead of providing that offences committed in the exercise of these freedoms would be adjudicated by the courts, the subsection now provided that regulation of the freedoms would be 'based on the imperative of respect for the Constitution and the dignity of the human person'. No explanation for these changes appeared in the draft text submitted to the Plenary of the Assembly.

Plenary debate (19 December 2001)

Censorship: The extent of permissible censorship in sub-s (3) dominated debate in the plenary session. Leandro Isac (PSD) began the debate by suggesting that there should be, in general, no censorship. However, since journalists sometimes expressed 'untruths' or wrote material causing unrest, there was a need for a system so that misinformation could be corrected. However, it was for the courts to provide remedies where warranted, rather than for people to fear comments and so support censorship. Freedom of speech was one of the freedoms for which Timorese had fought. Isac reminded Assembly members that in the last 24 years, Timorese had had no freedom. A debt was owed to journalists for their work. Isac asked members: 'How many times did they come creeping into the back window to interview us? We need to give them freedom not limitation.' Freedom of the press was also strongly supported by Eusébio Guterres (PD) and Jacob Fernandes (FRETILIN).

Lú Olo sought clarification of the meaning of sub-s (3), suggesting some might see a contradiction between censorship and sub-ss (1) and (2) of the section. He personally saw sub-s (3) as designed to ensure that speech was not used to target the dignity of persons. Eusébio Guterres (PD) thought sub-s (3) should be included in the ordinary law rather than in the Constitution. Vicente Guterres (UDC/PDC), Secretary of the Systematisation and Harmonisation Committee, explained that sub-s (3) was necessary to restrict speech which was either abusive, contrary to the honour of a person, or defamatory.

Lucia Lobato (PSD) suggested deleting sub-s (3), noting the existence of a Code of Ethics for journalists. Other mechanisms could deal with breaches of privacy. Action could be taken, for instance, in the courts. Others who spoke in favour of omitting sub-s (3) included António Ximenes (PDC), who regarded journalists as an important safeguard for society, allowing people to know what was happening in the State and providing access to information. João Carrascalão (UDT) similarly supported elimination of sub-s (3), expressing fear that later laws would violate the Constitution. In support of his position, João Carrascalão quoted from the UDHR's provision on freedom of speech.

Those who defended sub-s (3) included Mari Alkatiri (FRETILIN), who considered the provision as necessary to ensure that people could go to court to protect their rights. Speaking of limitations on rights, Alkatiri stated the view that 'freedoms stop where other freedoms start'. If journalists wrote without investigating or checking their facts, that was not covered by freedom of the press. Francisco Xavier Do Amaral (ASDT) agreed that it was problematic to talk only about rights and not duties. People had obligations not to violate others' rights. There was a need to have some type of law, so you could have justice, and to protect people's rights. Ana Pessoa (FRETILIN) stressed that this section needed to be read in conjunction with other sections of the Constitution. Legislators would not be cutting back on rights when they passed subsequent legislation, but would look to the Constitution to set the parameters for any such law. As a result, she did not share the fear that ordinary laws would violate the Constitution. In her opinion, ss 39 and 40 provided sufficient protections (for speech and the media) and no inconsistency with art 12 of the UDHR arose.

Several alternative texts were advanced in proposals.

Mariano Sabino Lopes (PD) put forward a proposal of the Timor Lorosa'e Journalists' Association:[81]

---

81   Other proponents were Rui Meneses da Costa (PD), Eusébio Guterres (PD), Mario Carrascalão (PSD), Lucia Lobato (PSD) and Clementino Amaral (KOTA). This proposal was originally read out in Bahasa during the plenary session, and later in Portuguese by the Vice-President in the Chair. The Timor Lorosa'e Journalists' Association disseminated a slightly different 'ideal' article in March 2002 (in English). Some of the differences appear due to translation differences. The TLJA ideal article, however, also added wording to sub-s (3) providing that the licensing regime be in force as long as technical limitations necessitated such a scheme and that no other media should be subject to licensing.

1. Every person has the right to freedom of speech and freedom of the press and the right to inform [circulate information] and be informed impartially and without intervention and discrimination.

2. The exercise of freedom of expression, the press and information cannot be limited by censorship.

3. The frequency and permission of broadcasting is to be run by an independent institution which is not discriminatory.

4. The implementation of the rights above only can be limited in relation to propaganda for war, motivations towards violence or advocacy with the intention of racial hatred, ethnicity, gender or religion which can end in violence.

5. No one can be criminalised by penal code because of defamation towards an individual or institution.

This was rejected: 15:53:15.

João Carrascalão (UDT) and others[82] also made a proposal:

1. Everyone shall possess the right to freely express and publicise his thoughts in words, images or by any other means, as well as the right to inform others, inform himself and be informed without hindrance or discrimination.

2. Exercise of the said rights shall not be hindered or limited by any type or form of censorship.

3. … (same)

4. Every person and body corporate shall be equally and effectively guaranteed the right of reply and to make corrections, as well as the right to compensation for damages suffered.[83]

Unfortunately, there was no recording of the vote on this proposed amendment on the tape made available to the author (due to a gap in the recording). However, it is clear that it was rejected.

---

82 Other proponents were Quitéria da Costa (UDT), Clementino Amaral (KOTA), António Ximenes (PDC) and Afonso Noronha (ASDT). Pedro Gomes (ASDT) was read out as a proponent; however, he spoke during the debate to say that he was not a proponent.

83 The text read out was identical to arts 37(1), (2) and (4) of the Portuguese Constitution. The translation used has thus been the English translation of the Portuguese Constitution.

Voting on the section during the plenary session

The section passed: 67:7:9.

Version finalised prior to the public consultation process

Section 40
(Freedom of speech and information)

1. *Every citizen has the right to freedom of speech and the right to inform and be informed impartially.*

2. *The exercise of freedom of speech and information shall not be limited by any sort of censorship.*

3. *The exercise of rights and freedoms referred to in this Section shall be regulated by law based on the imperative of respect for the Constitution and the dignity of the human person.*

Representations and submissions

District consultations: Support for censorship was recorded in the report of the Los Palos consultation.

Submission listed in the Systematisation and Harmonisation Committee's Consultations Report: The Minister for Foreign Affairs and The Asia Foundation recommended that the right apply to all persons.[84]

Other submissions made during the process: The most active group within civil society was the Timor Lorosa'e Journalists' Association (TLJA), which advocated that the section protect the right to seek, impart and receive information by all persons. The TLJA supported either deleting sub-s (3) or replacing it with a narrower clause which outlined the circumstances in which freedom of expression could be limited. The TLJA also strongly pushed for a prohibition on criminal penalties for defamation. At several stages of the process, the TLJA put forward texts for consideration.

The most comprehensive section put forward by the TLJA read:

1. Every person has the right to freedom of expression and freedom of the press, the right to seek, impart and receive information and to form opinions without exemption.

---

84 Letter from the Minister of State and for Foreign Affairs and Cooperation, Dr José Ramos Horta, to the President of the Constituent Assembly, 25 February 2002. This call was made also by a variety of other actors, including the Timor Lorosa'e Journalists' Association, The Asia Foundation and the Human Rights Unit, UNTAET.

2. The exercise of freedom of expression and information may not be limited by any form of prior censorship.

3. This article shall not prevent the establishment by law of a scheme for the licensing of broadcasting enterprises by an independent body applying non-discriminatory criteria, so long as technical limitations necessitate such a scheme. No other media shall be subject to licensing.

4. The exercise of these rights does not extend to:

    (a) Propaganda for war;

    (b) Incitement of imminent violence; or

    (c) Advocacy of hatred that is based on race, ethnicity, gender or religion and that constitutes incitement to cause harm.

5. No one shall be made subject to a criminal penalty on the ground only of having defamed a person or institution.[85]

The TLJA explained that it was motivated by two strong desires: to create a legacy for future generations, and to 'honour the memory of all those journalists who died in East Timor over the past 24 years in the effort to ensure information was free and public'. In their critique of the draft FRETILIN Project article, the TLJA highlighted the test in the ICCPR for permissible limitations on freedom of expression: namely, that the limitation be provided for by law; that it be required for the purpose of safeguarding one of the legitimate interests noted in art 19(3) of the ICCPR (respect for the rights or reputations of others, or protection of national security, or of public order, or morals); and that it be necessary in order to achieve this goal. Furthermore, they highlighted that restrictions in the name of national security should only be imposed if there was a significant risk of serious imminent harm, a close causal link between the risk of harm and the expression, and the expression was made with the intention of causing the harm. In relation to the matter of defamatory speech, the TLJA argued that only civil penalties should be applied. On International Women's Day, the TLJA submitted an additional shorter text. In relation to restrictions, the TLJA alternative subsection stated: 'Restrictions to freedom of expression and information are only applicable in accordance with the laws and international conventions on human rights. No-one should be subject to criminal punishments for having peacefully expressed their opinions.'[86]

---

85 TLJA ideal article on freedom of expression and information, 'Submission on Freedom of Expression', 7 March 2002. See also the equivalent clause in TLJA/Internews, 'Submission to the Constituent Assembly on Articles in the FRETILIN Draft Constitution of May 2001 concerning freedom of expression', undated, but with an attached handwritten note indicating that it was sent to members of the Assembly on 26 November 2001. This latter submission provided the TLJA's detailed reasoning, and contained also a right to access government information.

86 Letter from the TLJA to members of the Assembly on International Women's Day, 8 March 2002.

Article XIX, a London based NGO, also made a submission concerning the draft Constitution which was forwarded to the Assembly by the TLJA.[87] Article XIX supported the application of the right to all persons and full recognition of the right to 'seek, receive and impart information and ideas'. A concern was also evinced to ensure that all expression was protected, that is, to ensure there was no conditionality on the impartiality of expression. World Press Freedom's opinion was also transmitted to the Assembly. Their concerns focused on the limitations permissible under sub-s (3) of the provision and the limitations in s 41's terms. Yayasan HAK's proposals very much echoed the language of the UDHR. Yayasan HAK also suggested specifically excluding speech which incited hatred based on race, ethnicity, gender or religion and incitement to cause harm.[88]

During the drafting process, the Human Rights Unit of UNTAET, and the UN High Commissioner for Human Rights, amongst others, stressed the importance of human rights such as this one applying to all persons, rather than being limited to citizens.[89] Whilst not mentioned in the Systematisation and Harmonisation Committee's Report, the UN SRSG and Transitional Administrator made specific reference to the desirability of this clause being extended to all persons.[90]

Post-consultation plenary debate

The Systematisation and Harmonisation Committee had suggested substituting 'every person' for 'every citizen'.

The language of 'every person', rather than 'every citizen' was substituted in sub-s (1) by consensus by the Plenary.

87　Article XIX, 'Note on the Draft Constitution of the Democratic Republic of East Timor of 9 February 2002: Focus on Provisions Affecting Freedom of Expression', London, February 2002.

88　This wording is taken from the draft Bill of Rights in the Yayasan HAK submission entitled 'Civil and Political, Economic, Social and Cultural Rights', undated, received by the Assembly on 22 October 2001, art 18. A slightly differently worded provision appears in Yayasan HAK, 'Draft Proposals for the Constitution of East Timor', received by the Assembly on 15 March 2002, 6 [Bahasa Indonesian], which stated that freedom of speech did not apply to 'inciting crime or discriminatory hatred on grounds of race, gender or belief'. Whilst not offering a specific drafting suggestion, the International Commission of Jurists considered that the section failed to deal with the limits on speech, such as in relation to addressing slander, defamation and pornography: 'Commentary on the Draft Constitution Proposed for East Timor by the Constituent Assembly', undated, 9.

89　Human Rights Unit, UNTAET, 'Summary of select technical comments concerning the East Timorese draft Constitution and its treatment of human rights', December 2001, 1–2; Letter from the UN High Commissioner for Human Rights to the President of the Constituent Assembly, 19 December 2001.

90　Comments attached to the letter from the UN SRSG and Transitional Administrator to heads of the political parties, 22 February 2002.

Section 41
(Freedom of the press and mass media)

1. Freedom of the press and other mass media is guaranteed.

2. Freedom of the press shall comprise, namely, the freedom of speech and creativity for journalists, the access to information sources, editorial freedom, protection of independence and professional confidentiality, and the right to create newspapers, publications and other means of broadcasting.

3. The monopoly on the mass media shall be prohibited.

4. The State shall guarantee the freedom and independence of the public mass media from political and economic powers.

5. The State shall guarantee the existence of a public radio and television service that is impartial in order to, *inter-alia*, protect and disseminate the culture and the traditional values of the Democratic Republic of East Timor and guarantee opportunities for the expression of different lines of opinion.

6. Radio and television stations shall operate only under a licence, in accordance with the law.

(Official translation of the final text)

Drafting history

Thematic Committee I text

There was no equivalent in the text advanced by Thematic Committee I. Instead, there was only the reference to freedom of the press in the preceding section.

Systematisation and Harmonisation Committee draft text used in the plenary debate

Section 40
(Freedom of the press and mass media)

1. *Freedom of the press and other mass media is guaranteed.*

2. *Freedom of the press shall comprise, namely, the freedom of speech and creativity for journalists, the access to information sources, protection*

of independence and professional confidentiality, and the right to create newspapers, publications and other means of broadcasting.[91]

3. *The State shall guarantee the freedom and independence of the mass media from political and economic powers.*

4. *The State shall guarantee the existence of a public radio and television service that is impartial in order to, inter-alia, protect and disseminate the culture and the traditional values of the Democratic Republic of East Timor and guarantee opportunities for the expression of different lines of opinion.*

5. *Radio and television stations shall operate only under a licence.*

The Bench of the Systematisation and Harmonisation Committee suggested two further amendments:

- an amendment to sub-s (4): so that the banning of newspapers or other publications be only allowed in cases of 'grave breach of the press law'; and

- an amendment to sub-s (5): to add 'and with the intervention of the Higher Authority for Mass Media, its opinion being mandatory'.

Commentary: This clause did not appear either in the draft text produced by Thematic Committee I, or in the other thematic committee reports sighted by the author. Instead, it appears to have been introduced during the deliberations of the Systematisation and Harmonisation Committee at the instigation of Milena Pires (PSD).[92] The Timor Lorosa'e Journalists' Association had also advocated for such a clause, advancing a specific proposal at the public hearing of Thematic Committee I.[93]

Plenary debate (19 December 2001)[94]

As indicated during the debate on freedom of speech, freedom of the press enjoyed significant support in the Assembly. However, debate surrounded whether any further protections for journalists were warranted, and the licensing of stations.

João Carrascalão (UDT) wished to see the section extended in a variety of ways. Journalists needed to have access to all forms of information, to be able to publish and not be forced to disclose the source of their information, and

---

91 The reference to publications is found in the Portuguese version of the text, but not in the English translation.

92 The section was said to be a proposal of Milena Pires (PSD) during discussion of the committee: as per the author's observations of the deliberations of the Systematisation and Harmonisation Committee, 27 November 2001.

93 Unfortunately the records of Thematic Committee I that the author accessed did not include the details of the clause proposed by the TLJA.

94 The vote was not included on the recording accessed by the author.

to enjoy professional independence. They should also be protected from being imprisoned for defamation. Given that they sometimes went into dangerous places, journalists also had the right to ask the State for security. Carrascalão considered it was also important to know who was financing the media, since sometimes media coverage was manipulated, with 'huge consequences'. Those who collaborated with journalists also required protection. Manuel Tilman (KOTA), Rapporteur of the Systematisation and Harmonisation Committee, explained that the section was intended to cover journalists, rather than others.

A number of speakers expressed concern about having a system of official licensing of radio and television stations. Some favoured eliminating the provision,[95] whilst others suggested amending the requirement to ensure there was no discrimination in granting licences.[96] Manuel Tilman (KOTA) responded that licences would obviously come from a governmental authority – such as a High Authority. Lú Olo (FRETILIN) considered that the subsections were sufficient without further amendment.

A variety of proposals were advanced in relation to this section.

A PD proposal called for the regulation of licences (in sub-s (5)) to be carried out by an 'independent Commission' which was to carry out its work 'transparently and openly, and without discrimination'.[97] This was rejected in a vote of 23:36:24.

Armando da Silva (PL), Jacob Xavier (PPT), and António Ximenes (PDC) proposed adding 'education' and 'entertainment' before culture and traditions to sub-s (4). This was rejected in a vote of 35:27.[98]

João Carrascalão (UDT) and others sponsored an extensive amendment providing a range of additional guarantees.[99] The amendment gave protection to those collaborating with journalists, recognised the right of journalists to exercise their functions freely and securely, and their right to access information and protect their sources by maintaining confidentiality. The right to maintain professional independence was mentioned explicitly. The amendment further provided a right to establish newspapers independent of administrative authorisation, and stipulated that journalists were not to be subject to criminal prosecution for defamation if they had no intention to defame. Law was to ensure that the names of the owners of media bodies and the means by which bodies were financed were publicised. This amendment was rejected in a vote of 16:41:26. Mari

---

95 António Ximenes (PDC).
96 Mariano Sabino Lopes (PD).
97 Proposal by Mariano Sabino Lopes (PD), Eusébio Guterres (PD), Aquilino Guterres (PD), and Paulo Alves Sarmento (PD). The proposal was made in Bahasa Indonesian.
98 Unfortunately, the tape was switched off for the final recording of the vote. The figures included here are from the author's contemporary notes of those voting for and against, but do not include the number who abstained.
99 Other signatories were Quitéria Da Costa (UDT), Pedro da Costa (PST) and Clementino Amaral (KOTA).

Alkatiri (FRETILIN) explained his vote against this proposal, querying what the term 'collaborators' meant. He also suggested that some topics of freedom of the press should be dealt with in ordinary law.

Of the Systematisation and Harmonisation Committee's suggested amendments, the change to sub-s (4) (limiting banning of newspapers or other publications to cases of grave breach of the press law) was defeated: 14:39:30.

Voting on the section during the plenary session

The Systematisation and Harmonisation Committee proposal for sub-s (5) (making reference to the role of the Higher Authority) passed: 57:14:11.

The section passed: 75:0:7.

Version finalised prior to the public consultation process

Section 41
(Freedom of the press and mass media)

1. *Freedom of the press and other mass media is guaranteed.*

2. *Freedom of the press shall comprise, namely, the freedom of speech and creativity for journalists, the access to information sources, editorial freedom, protection of independence and professional confidentiality, and the right to create newspapers, publications and other means of broadcasting.*

3. *The monopoly on the mass media shall be prohibited.*

4. *The State shall guarantee the freedom and independence of the public mass media from political and economic powers.*

5. *The State shall guarantee the existence of a public radio and television service that is impartial in order to, inter-alia, protect and disseminate the culture and the traditional values of the Democratic Republic of East Timor and guarantee opportunities for the expression of different lines of opinion.*

6. *Radio and television stations shall operate only under a licence, in accordance with the law.*

(Identical to final)

Commentary: Several further changes to the text appeared in this version. 'Editorial freedom' was added to sub-s (2), along with a qualifier, 'in accordance with the law' in sub-s (6). A new subsection was added – sub-s (3) – which prohibited a mass media monopoly. The committee's text explained that this subsection had been suggested by Timorese journalists.

The amendment previously adopted by the Plenary (referring to the High Authority in sub-s (6)) was not included, presumably as a consequence of the removal of the section about the High Authority by the Systematisation and Harmonisation Committee in this text (see later discussion of s 40A).

Representations and submissions

District consultations: The summary of the Baucau consultation included a suggestion to reformulate the first subsection to read: 'The State guarantees freedom of communication, in accordance with the law.' Another suggestion made was to eliminate sub-ss (2) and (6), and leave the subject matters to the ordinary law.

Submissions listed in the Systematisation and Harmonisation Committee's Consultations Report: None listed.

Other submissions made during the process: The licensing process referred to in sub-s (6) was the primary focus of comment in other submissions. The Timor Lorosa'e Journalists' Association (TLJA) recommended that the section include a guarantee that the licensing process be open, transparent, fair and non-discriminatory.[100] The TLJA put forward an alternative provision which stated:

> For the allocation of frequencies, the state guarantees the establishment by law, of a public body, independent of government with the competence to create an open, fair, transparent and non-discriminatory licensing system for independent news organizations, particularly those that involve the creation of radio and television stations. No other form of communication (print media) should be subject to licenses.

The Asia Foundation also queried whether it might be possible to stipulate that the licensing system must be consistent with the fundamental freedom of the media.[101] The East Timor Study Group suggested that frequencies for radio and television be regulated by an independent committee, rather than the State.[102]

---

100 Timor Lorosa'e Journalists' Association, 'Submission on Freedom of Expression', 7 March 2002.
101 The Asia Foundation, 'Discussion Paper on Draft of East Timorese Constitution', March 2002, 6. The International Commission of Jurists suggested that reference also be made in sub-s (5) to newspapers and the internet: 'Commentary on the Draft Constitution Proposed for East Timor by the Constituent Assembly', undated, 9.
102 East Timor Study Group, 'Debate on the Draft Constitution: Positive and Negative Implications for the Future of East Timor', 20 February 2002, 7 [Tetum].

Proposed Section 40A concerning a High Authority for the Mass Media

The Systematisation and Harmonisation Committee had recommended a further provision be included on a High Authority for the Mass Media. Its text read:

1. The High Authority for Mass Media is an independent body whose objective is to ensure the right of information, freedom of the press and independence of the media from political power and economic power, and the possibility that all different currents of opinion are able to express themselves and confront one another, and the right to broadcasting time [broadcast].

2. The composition, functions and competencies of the High Authority for Mass Media are to be regulated by law, and its President shall be elected by the National Parliament.[103]

The Constituent Assembly records include a shorter form of the section said to have been proposed by José Lobato (FRETILIN) during the plenary session on 20 December 2001. This version provided:

1. The High Authority for Mass Media is an independent body whose objective is to ensure the right of information, freedom of the press and independence of the media.

2. The composition, functions and competence of the High Authority for Mass Media are to be regulated by law.

The Constituent Assembly documentation records this proposal as having been subjected to vote and adopted: 68:3:12.

Plenary debate:[104] The proposal for a High Authority related to a desire for an independent body to make decisions concerning the regulation and licensing of the press. Adérito Soares (FRETILIN) explained there was a desire to protect, rather than limit, freedom of the press and recognised the role of journalists in developing the nation. The most contentious issue related to whether Parliament should have a role in choosing the President of this body (as provided for in the Systematisation and Harmonisation Committee text), or whether it should be left to the members/journalists.[105] Mariano Sabino Lopes (PD) and Eusébio Guterres (PD) spoke in favour of journalists approving their own President,

---

103 This text appeared in the first Portuguese version of the Systematisation and Harmonisation Committee as a proposal from the Bench (e.g. in a copy dated 1 December 2001 held by the author), but did not appear in the Portuguese version available online (dated 7 December 2001) or in the English version of the text. The translation here draws upon elements of the translation of arts 38 and 39 of the Portuguese Constitution.

104 Due to a gap in the recording, the details of this debate are drawn from contemporary notes of the author. The written proposal is retained in the Assembly records.

105 Clementino Amaral (KOTA) also put forward a proposal in this regard, though the recording and Assembly records do not capture its terms.

with Parliament later approving the choice. Francisco Kalbaudi Lay (FRETILIN) sought to distinguish between this High Authority and the professional body of journalists (the latter having the head of the organisation chosen by the group). Francisco Branco (FRETILIN) noted that the High Authority would be different from the Department of Information.

This provision had a short-lived history, however. Its removal was recommended in the text prepared by the Systematisation and Harmonisation Committee and was explained as a request of the TLJA. This was subsequently endorsed by the representatives of the thematic committees and the party benches before the text was submitted to the Assembly on 9 February 2002.

Section 42
(Freedom to assemble and demonstrate)

1. Everyone is guaranteed the freedom to assemble peacefully and unarmed, without a need for prior authorisation.

2. Everyone is recognised the right to demonstrate in accordance with the law.

(Official translation of the final text)

Drafting history

Thematic Committee I text

Section 35
(Freedom to assemble and demonstrate)

1. *Every citizen is guaranteed the freedom to assemble peacefully and unarmed, without prior authorisation.*

2. *Everyone is recognised the right to demonstrate in accordance with the law.*

Commentary: This provision was based on art 35 of the FRETILIN Project. It was approved in a vote of 19:0:1.

Systematisation and Harmonisation Committee draft text used in the plenary debate

Section 41
(Freedom to assemble and demonstrate)

1. *Every citizen is guaranteed the freedom to assemble peacefully and unarmed, without prior authorisation.*[106]

2. *Everyone is recognised the right to demonstrate in accordance with the law.*

---

106   The English Assembly translation incorrectly used the term 'everyone', rather than reflecting the restriction to citizens in the Portuguese text (*'a todo o cidadão'*).

Plenary debate (20 December 2001)

The debate in plenary session centred on several proposals to broaden the rights of peaceful assembly and demonstration. The first came from João Carrascalão (UDT), who proposed an amendment to sub-s (1), so that it would cover the right to assemble 'even in public places'. This was defeated in a vote of 24:29:30.

Limitations on the Right to Demonstrate: Adérito Soares (FRETILIN) proposed deleting the phrase 'in accordance with the law' in sub-s (2) in relation to the right to demonstrate. He was supported in this by Leandro Isac (PSD), Eusébio Guterres (PD) and Lucia Lobato (PSD). Lucia Lobato considered that if there was any damage as a result of a demonstration, the demonstrators could be taken to court. She disagreed with any requirement to give, for instance, 24 hours' notice of a demonstration. Pedro da Costa (PST) supported leaving the regulation of demonstrations to ordinary law. Clementino Amaral (KOTA) considered it acceptable for the right to demonstrate to be limited by applicable law. Demonstrations in front of government buildings, for example, needed to be restricted for security reasons. The proposal to delete 'in accordance with the law' was defeated by 51 votes against and five abstentions.[107]

After this proposal failed, several members voiced their dissatisfaction. Adérito Soares (FRETILIN) recalled that in Indonesian times, there was a requirement for authorisation for demonstrations, which he as an activist had demonstrated against. He feared that the Assembly's clause had the potential to have a similar effect. Leandro Isac (PSD) was highly critical of the vote, saying Timorese would be victims of control by the State and of the law, and that the Assembly was being asked to implement a dictatorship.

Voting on the section during the plenary session

The section passed: 65:13:5.

After the vote for the section as a whole, José Lobato (FRETILIN) said that he understood Adérito Soares' position. However, the Indonesian Constitution did not define how the right of assembly was to be regulated by law, whereas here the Assembly was putting a limit on regulation of the right. There was no need for prior authorisation to demonstrate. Lobato remarked that he would defend freedom, but not without limits. Clementino Amaral (KOTA) also considered that the clause did not require the gaining of prior authorisation for a demonstration, but instead involved giving prior notice to the police.

---

107   The recording provided to the author did not contain this proposal and the ensuing debate and vote. These details are taken from the author's contemporary notes.

Version finalised prior to the public consultation process

Section 42

(Freedom to assemble and demonstrate)

1. *Every citizen is guaranteed the freedom to assemble peacefully and unarmed, without a need for prior authorisation.*

2. *Everyone is recognised the right to demonstrate in accordance with the law.*

Commentary: In this text, a small stylistic change was made, adding in the phrase 'a need for' in sub-s (1).

Representations and submissions

District consultations: The nature of appropriate limits on the freedom to demonstrate was a theme repeated in the District Consulations. In Dili, the suggestion was made to eliminate sub-s (2) or the phrase 'in accordance with the law'. A recommendation to delete 'in accordance with the law' was also made in the Liquiça report.

Submissions listed in the Systematisation and Harmonisation Committee's Consultations Report: In their submissions, the Minister for Foreign Affairs and The Asia Foundation recommended that freedom of assembly be broadened to apply to all persons.[108]

Other submissions made during the process: Two aspects of this section provoked particular comment: (i) the textual limitation on the right to demonstrate; and (ii) the restriction of the coverage of the right to assemble to citizens. The Human Rights Unit of UNTAET expressed concern about the usage of the qualifying phrase 'in accordance with the law' in the second subsection and other provisions of the Constitution. It suggested that the phrase might either be deleted (given the existence of a general limitations clause) or be replaced with a more precisely worded limitation. Otherwise, there would

---

108   Letter from the Minister of State and for Foreign Affairs and Cooperation, Dr José Ramos Horta, to the President of the Constituent Assembly, 25 February 2002; The Asia Foundation, 'Comments and Suggested Amendments to East Timor's Draft Constitution of 9/2/02', undated, but attached to a cover letter to the President of the Constituent Assembly dated 8 March 2002, 5.

be nothing to stop, for example, the Parliament from passing a law limiting demonstrations to two hours on a Saturday afternoon.[109] The East Timor Study Group supported deleting the qualifying phrase.[110]

Both the Human Rights Unit and the UN High Commissioner for Human Rights, amongst others, also stressed the importance of human rights such as this one applying to all persons, rather than being limited to citizens. Whilst not listed in the Systematisation and Harmonisation Committee Report, the UN SRSG and Transitional Administrator also made specific reference to the desirability of this clause being extended to all persons.[111]

Post-consultation plenary debate

The Systematisation and Harmonisation Report suggested substituting 'everyone' for 'every citizen', and deleting 'in accordance with the law'.

Following the consultations, *the text of sub-s (1) was changed by consensus to 'everyone'*. A proposal to delete 'in accordance with the law' was put to the Assembly during the final debates. However, it was rejected in a vote of 16:55:11.

---

109   Human Rights Unit, UNTAET, 'Thematic Committee One's Proposals For the Protection of Human Rights in the Constitution: An analysis by the HRU', 14 November 2001, 10. Concern about the phrase was also voiced by the International Commission of Jurists (Australian Section), 'Commentary on the Draft Constitution Proposed for East Timor by the Constituent Assembly', undated, 10.

110   East Timor Study Group, 'Debate on the Draft Constitution: Positive and Negative Implications for the Future of East Timor', 20 February 2002, 7 [Tetum].

111   Comments attached to the letter from the UN SRSG and Transitional Administrator to heads of the political parties, 22 February 2002.

Section 43
(Freedom of association)

1. Everyone is guaranteed freedom of association provided that the association is not intended to promote violence and is in accordance with the law.

2. No one shall be compelled to join an association or to remain in it against his or her will.

3. The establishment of armed, military or paramilitary associations, including organisations of a racist or xenophobic nature or that promote terrorism, shall be prohibited.

(Official translation of the final text)

Drafting history

Thematic Committee I text

Section 36
(Freedom of association)

1. *Every citizen shall enjoy freedom of association provided that the association is not intended to promote violence and is in accordance with the general law.*

2. *No one shall be compelled to join an association or to remain in it against his or her will.*

3. *The establishment of armed, military or paramilitary associations, including organisations of a fascist, totalitarian, racist or xenophobic nature, shall be prohibited.*

Commentary: This provision was based on art 36 of the FRETILIN Project. The addition of sub-s (3) was approved in a vote of 14:0:6. The committee voted on a text which prohibited armed, military or paramilitary associations and organisations of a fascist or racist nature. The whole section was approved in a vote of 16:0:4.

Some of the wording of sub-s (3) (in particular the reference to organisations of a totalitarian or xenophobic nature) was not subject to a vote, but emanated from a suggestion of the Technical Adviser to the committee, José Manuel Pinto (as listed in Annex II of the committee's report). It was integrated into the final text of the committee. A general footnote appears in Annex III of the report explaining that changes which were not subject to vote were adopted by consensus or integrated in the course of a general revision completed centrally.

Systematisation and Harmonisation Committee draft text used in the plenary debate

Section 42

(Freedom of association)

1. *Every citizen shall enjoy freedom of association provided that the association is not intended to promote violence and is in accordance with the general law.*[112]

2. *No one shall be compelled to join an association or to remain in it against his or her will.*

3. *The establishment of armed, military or paramilitary associations, including organisations of a racist or xenophobic nature or that promote terrorism, shall be prohibited.*[113]

Commentary: In this version of the text, the reference to 'fascist' or 'totalitarian' organisations had been removed, but the prohibition was extended to organisations that 'promote terrorism'. No explanation of this change appeared in the Systematisation and Harmonisation Committee draft text presented to the Assembly.

Plenary debate (20 December 2001)

Whilst specific textual matters were raised in relation to the subsections of this provision, the major point of debate concerned the ambit of prohibited organisations.

In the first subsection, the only issue which provoked discussion was the reference to freedom of association being in accordance with the 'general law' as opposed to 'law'. This aspect was queried by Mario Carrascalão (PSD) and Jacob Xavier (PPT). Manuel Tilman (KOTA) from the Systematisation and Harmonisation Committee, explained that the phrase 'general law' referred to

---

112   The Assembly English translation of this draft text stated 'Everyone shall enjoy the freedom to form associations provided that the associations are not intended ...'. The Portuguese text, however, referred only to citizens, and referred to 'freedom of association'. The translation of the text has been streamlined in line with that of the final text.

113   The translation provided at the time differed in minor respects only from the version presented here which is streamlined according to the translation of the final text. The Portuguese version might be translated more directly to refer to organisations that 'defend ideas or appeal to behaviours of' the prescribed types.

a law applying to all associations. He conceded it might also be possible to say 'law' alone. No amendment was put to change the term, but the draft version which was subsequently circulated referred to 'law' alone.

Relatively little discussion focused on sub-s (2). Mario Carrascalão (PSD) questioned the wording relating to the prohibition of persons being compelled to 'remain in' an organisation against his/her will. If persons remained in an organisation, they were part of the organisation and no one was forcing them to stay. In his first intervention, Carrascalão suggested that it might be preferable to omit this aspect. However, in a second intervention, he emphasised the need for clarity, suggesting it might be more appropriate to refer to persons 'coerced' to stay in an organisation. Vicente Guterres (UDC/PDC) explained that the text was intended to prevent persons being forced to maintain their membership, giving the example of criminal organisations that threatened persons in order to force them to remain members.

Subsection (3)'s listing of prohibited associations attracted more interest. Mario Carrascalão (PSD) queried the terms 'military' and 'paramilitary' groups, asking the difference between the terms. For him, the terms were more associated with, for example, the army. Manuel Tilman (KOTA) (for the Systematisation and Harmonisation Committee) explained that paramilitary groups were not police or military, but were groups who were armed, such as militias. Jacob Xavier (PPT) considered it important to make clear that police had the right to form associations to defend themselves, just as journalists did. Pedro Gomes (ASDT) raised sub-s (3)'s reference to associations holding certain views/ideologies, asking whether CPD-RDTL,[114] for instance, would be covered by this prohibition. Gomes also queried how this provision would be enforced in the future in a case where an association had many members.

Vicente Faria (FRETILIN), Rapporteur of Thematic Committee I, explained that the topic of prohibited organisations was debated strongly in the committee. It was recognised that there were associations such as armed militias that should not exist in Timor. The clause also dealt with organisations that had ideologies different to the people of Timor-Leste; for example, organisations that were interested in terrorism. The text approved by the committee extended to the wording concerning xenophobic organisations, with the further amendment of the text authored by the Systematisation and Harmonisation Committee. Clementino Amaral (KOTA) also responded as a member of Thematic Committee I to explain that police could form an association. However, armed groups were not to be permitted as their behaviour was against the Constitution. Mario

---

114   This reference to RDTL was to the CPD-RDTL (*Conselho Popular pela Defesa de República Democrática de Timor-Leste*) whose aim was to restore the Republic declared in 1975 and saw the transition process and the mechanisms established by UNTAET as illegitimate.

Carrascalão (PSD) queried whether an association of hunters would be classed as an 'armed association'. In this respect, Lú Olo (FRETILIN) voiced his opinion that in relation to hunters and shooters, a general law would be needed to regulate their activities, covering, for example, the extent of permissible killing of animals during the hunting season.

Voting on the section during the plenary session

The section passed: 69:0:12.

Version finalised prior to the public consultation process

Section 43
(Freedom of association)

1. *Every citizen shall enjoy freedom of association provided that the association is not intended to promote violence and is in accordance with the law.*

2. *No one shall be compelled to join an association or to remain in it against his or her will.*

3. *The establishment of armed, military or paramilitary associations, including organisations of a racist or xenophobic nature or that promote terrorism, shall be prohibited.*

Commentary: In this version, the reference to 'general' before 'law' was removed. No explanation was provided; however, this appears likely to be a response to the point raised during the plenary session and part of making consistent all usages of the qualifying phrase 'in accordance with the law'.

Representations and submissions

District consultations: The summary of the Dili consultation included a suggestion to eliminate the reference to 'in accordance with the law' in sub-s (3). However, this phrase does not appear in sub-s (3), and so may have been intended to be a reference to its inclusion in sub-s (1). In Liquiça, a suggestion was made that the provision should be limited to freedom of association.

Submissions listed in the Systematisation and Harmonisation Committee's Consultations Report: The Asia Foundation and the Minister for Foreign Affairs noted that freedom of association should be a right of all persons, not just citizens.[115]

---

115 Letter from the Minister of State and for Foreign Affairs and Cooperation, Dr José Ramos Horta, to the President of the Constituent Assembly, 25 February 2002; The Asia Foundation, 'Comments and Suggested Amendments to East Timor's Draft Constitution of 9/2/02', undated, but attached to a cover letter to the

Other submissions made during the process: The Timor Lorosa'e Journalists' Association in their critique of the FRETILIN Project were concerned about the reference to associations with a 'fascist ideology', supporting either deletion of this phrase or inclusion of a definition of what constituted a 'fascist ideology'.[116] In March 2002, Yayasan HAK suggested amending sub-s (1), so that it excluded only associations 'intended to promote violence or affect other rights and freedoms which are protected by the Constitution'. They also proposed removal of the qualifying phrase 'in accordance with the law'.[117]

During the drafting process, the Human Rights Unit of UNTAET noted with concern the usage of the broad phrase 'in accordance with the law' in several sections of the Constitution, recommending either that the matter be left to the general limitations clause, or that more specifically worded limitations be introduced. In addition, the Human Rights Unit and the UN High Commissioner for Human Rights, amongst others, stressed the importance of human rights such as this one applying to all persons, rather than being limited to citizens.[118] Whilst not listed in the Consultations Report, the UN SRSG and Transitional Administrator also made specific reference to the desirability of this clause being extended to all persons.[119]

Post-consultation plenary debate

By consensus, the Plenary changed the language from 'every citizen' to 'everyone' in sub-s (1) in accordance with the post-consultation recommendation of the Systematisation and Harmonisation Committee. Another change also appeared in the version presented to the Plenary, substituting the language of *'is guaranteed'* for 'shall enjoy' in sub-s (1), presumably for reasons of consistency with other clauses in the Bill of Rights.

President of the Constituent Assembly dated 8 March 2002, 5.

116 Timor Lorosa'e Journalists' Association/Internews, 'Submission to the Constituent Assembly on Articles in the FRETILIN Draft Constitution of May 2001 concerning freedom of expression', undated, with attached handwritten note indicating that it was sent to members of the Assembly on 26 November 2001.

117 Yayasan HAK, 'Draft Proposals for the Constitution of East Timor', received by the Assembly on 15 March 2002, 7 [Bahasa Indonesian].

118 Human Rights Unit, UNTAET, 'Summary of select technical comments concerning the East Timorese draft Constitution and its treatment of human rights', December 2001, 1–2; Letter from the UN High Commissioner for Human Rights to the President of the Constituent Assembly, 19 December 2001.

119 Comments attached to the letter from the UN SRSG and Transitional Administrator to heads of the political parties, 22 February 2002.

Section 44
(Freedom of movement)

1. Every person has the right to move freely and to settle anywhere in the national territory.

2. Every citizen is guaranteed the right to emigrate freely and to return to the country.

(Official translation of the final text)

Drafting history

Thematic Committee I text

Section 37
(Freedom of movement)

1. *Every citizen has the right to move freely and to settle anywhere in the national territory.*

2. *Everyone is guaranteed the right to emigrate freely and to return to the country.*

Commentary: This section was based on art 37 of the FRETILIN Project. It was approved in a vote of 19:0:1.

In Annex I of Thematic Committee I's report, the originally adopted sub-s (2) also included a right to immigrate. It does not appear in the text of Annex III of the committee's report, seemingly as a result of a decision to accept the recommendation of the Technical Adviser to Committee I, José Manuel Pinto.

Systematisation and Harmonisation Committee draft text used in the plenary debate

Section 43
(Freedom of movement)

1. *Every citizen has the right to move freely and to settle anywhere in the national territory.*[120]

---

120 The English Assembly translation wrongly included the term 'everyone', rather than referring to citizens only in sub-s (1). The Portuguese text restricted sub-s (1) to apply to citizens (*'todo o cidadão'*).

2. *Everyone is guaranteed the right to emigrate freely and to return to the country.*

Commentary: The Systematisation and Harmonisation Committee changed the heading to *'liberdade de circulação'* (literally, 'freedom of circulation'), replacing the Thematic Committee's usage of *'liberdade de movimentação'*. The English translation used by the Assembly in this text remained 'freedom of movement'.

Plenary debate (20 December 2001)

The change to the heading by the Systematisation and Harmonisation Committee was the subject of some comment, with a proposal put to change the heading back to 'freedom of movement' (*'liberdade de movimentação'*) advanced by Rui António da Cruz (FRETILIN) and supported by several FRETILIN colleagues.[121] This proposal passed in a vote of 68:0:12. During the debate on the heading, João Carrascalão (UDT) suggested referring in the heading to 'travel and emigration'(*'deslocaçao e emigração'*). 'Migration' was another alternative advanced by Mario Carrascalão (PSD), a term said to have the advantage of covering different types of movement. Vicente Guterres (UDC/PDC) spoke against use of the term 'migration', suggesting that it would not capture the situation of people who were just moving, and not settling, in another location.

The subject of settling within the country (sub-s (1)) was discussed by several speakers. Jacob Xavier (PPT), for instance, regarded it as important to be able to settle anywhere in the country, suggesting the addition of 'without restriction' to sub-s (1). Vicente Guterres (UCD/PDC) sounded a note of caution that one could not have the right to settle anywhere without restriction, because there remained rights of private property to be respected and laws to be obeyed. João Carrascalão (PSD) was in favour of deleting the term 'freely' from sub-s (2).[122] However, no further amendments appear to have been put to the substance of the section.

Voting on the section during the plenary session

The section passed: 76:0:4.

Version finalised prior to the public consultation process

Section 44
(Freedom of movement)

---

121   The other signatories were José Loboto (FRETILIN), Alfredo da Silva (FRETILIN), and Vicente Faria (FRETILIN).

122   The recording for 20 December available to the author has several gaps, so it is unclear as to whether there was a separate vote on João Carrascalao's proposals relating to the heading and sub-s (1).

1. *Every citizen has the right to move freely and to settle anywhere in the national territory.*

2. *Every citizen is guaranteed the right to emigrate freely and to return to the country.*

Commentary: This version changed the opening words of sub-s (2) to 'every citizen' (rather than 'everyone'). No explanation was given, but it can be assumed that this was to recognise the context of emigrating and returning to the country of citizenship. Despite the vote in the plenary session to revert to the heading suggested by the thematic committee, the title in this section remained *'liberdade de circulação'* in this and the final text.

Representations and submissions

District consultations: No comments on this section appear in the summary of District consultations prepared by the Systematisation and Harmonisation Committee.

Submissions listed in the Systematisation and Harmonisation Committee's Consultations Report: The Minister for Foreign Affairs submitted that limiting the scope of sub-s (1) to citizens was contrary to the UDHR.[123] Whilst not listed in the Systematisation and Harmonisation Committee Report, the UN SRSG and Transitional Administrator also made specific reference to the desirability of this clause being extended to all persons.[124]

Other submissions made during the process: The Human Rights Unit and the UN High Commissioner for Human Rights, amongst others, stressed the importance of human rights in general applying to all persons, rather than being limited to citizens.[125]

Post-consultation plenary debate

The Systematisation and Harmonisation Committee suggested changing the scope of the section to apply to all individuals.

Subsection (1) was changed by consensus to 'every person' in accordance with the Systematisation and Harmonisation Committee recommendation.

---

123   Letter from the Minister of State and for Foreign Affairs and Cooperation, Dr José Ramos Horta, to the President of the Constituent Assembly, 25 February 2002.

124   Comments attached to the letter from the UN SRSG and Transitional Administrator to heads of the political parties, 22 February 2002.

125   Human Rights Unit, UNTAET, 'Summary of select technical comments concerning the East Timorese draft Constitution and its treatment of human rights', December 2001, 1–2; Letter from the UN High Commissioner for Human Rights to the President of the Constituent Assembly, 19 December 2001.

Section 45
(Freedom of conscience, religion and worship)

1. Every person is guaranteed the freedom of conscience, religion and worship and the religious denominations are separated from the State.

2. No one shall be persecuted or discriminated against on the basis of his or her religious convictions.

3. The right to be a conscientious objector shall be guaranteed in accordance with the law.

4. Freedom to teach any religion in the framework of the respective religious denomination is guaranteed.

(Official translation of the final text)

Drafting history

Thematic Committee I text

Section 38

(Freedom of conscience, religion and worship)

1. *Every citizen is guaranteed the freedom of conscience, religion and worship.*[126]

2. *No one shall be persecuted or discriminated against on the basis of his or her religious convictions.*

3. *The religious denominations have the right to possess and to acquire assets for the achievement of their objectives.*[127]

4. *The right to be a conscientious objector shall be guaranteed in accordance with the law.*

Commentary: This provision was based on art 38 of the FRETILIN Project, with a consensual alteration to remove the expression 'or disbelief' from sub-s (2). The Annex I text was approved as a whole in a vote of 19:0:1.

---

126 Annex I of the thematic committee report contained a significantly shorter version of sub s (1), focusing on the freedom to practice religion.

127 Annex I of the thematic committee's report included a differently worded sub-s (3) proposed by FRETILIN which stated: 'Religious organisations shall have the right to form and participate in political parties.'

Systematisation and Harmonisation Committee draft text used in the plenary debate

Section 44

(Freedom of conscience, religion and worship)

1. *Every citizen is guaranteed the freedom of conscience, religion and worship.*[128]

2. *No one shall be persecuted or discriminated against on the basis of his or her religious convictions.*

3. *The right to be a conscientious objector shall be guaranteed in accordance with the law.*[129]

Commentary: In this text, the original sub-s (3), concerning the right of religious organisations to possess and acquire assets, was omitted. Instead, it was integrated into s 12 (the provision dealing with the separation of church and State).

Plenary debate (20 December 2001)

Discussion on this section focused primarily on the regulation of religion and religious groups. Adaljiza Magno (FRETILIN) reminded members of their earlier decision to move s 12(4) to this section. Section 12(4) dealt with the right of religious denominations to possess and acquire assets for the achievement of their achievements and had been included by the thematic committee in this section. Manuel Tilman (KOTA) agreed with Magno in this recollection. Some members voiced concern that the contents of s 12(4) had not, however, been discussed on the prior occasion.

Jacob Xavier (PPT) considered that this section raised a potential conflict between the individual, church and State. The draft Constitution discussed marriage and divorce and provided that religions had to conform with the Constitution. However, the Constitution also provided for freedom of conscience and the separation of church and State. In the case of marriage and divorce, if he and his wife were to divorce, the Catholic Church would say that as a matter of canon law, there could be no divorce, whilst the State would maintain this was permissible. There would thus be a conflict between the State and religion.

Quitéria da Costa (UDT), João Carrascalão (UDT), Clementino Amaral (KOTA) and Pedro da Costa (PST) advanced a proposal stating that the section did not

---

128 The English Assembly translation wrongly translated this text as applying to all persons, rather than citizens. The Portuguese version used the language of *'todo o cidadão'*.

129 The English Assembly translation used the phrase 'by law'. The Portuguese text used the phrase *'nos termos da lei'*, which in the final text was translated as 'in accordance with the law'.

allow 'practices that are contrary to public order or morality or that violate fundamental rights of citizens'. In response to a request for clarification from Lú Olo as to the significance of practices contrary to rights, João Carrascalão explained that this was intended to cover, for example, the emergence of sects that kill or injure people. A reference was made to sects in Japan – seemingly a reference to the 1995 Japanese sect attack on the Tokyo subway involving sarin gas. This proposal was narrowly defeated in a vote of 39:14:26.[130]

The topic of conscientious objectors also featured during the plenary session. Lú Olo (FRETILIN) explained that freedom of conscience meant not impairing an individual's conscience, but supporting freedom of conscience. So, for example, if the State required you to be in the army, but your conscience/religion did not permit you to be in the army or to be involved in war, the State had to respect your conscience. Manuel Tilman (KOTA) agreed, extending the example to the situation of a person whose conscience did not permit him/her to be armed, in which case he/she would not have to be a member of the police or the military.[131] Mariano Sabino Lopes (PD) and Rui Meneses da Costa (PD) queried the inclusion of the phrase 'in accordance with the law' in sub-s (3), though no formal amendment to delete the phrase was put.

Voting proceeded on the basis of the section having four subsections – that is, including s 12(4), despite the concerns raised that the substance of s 12(4) had not been properly debated.

Voting on the section during the plenary session

The section passed: 69:0:11.

Version finalised prior to the public consultation process

Section 45
(Freedom of conscience, religion and worship)[132]

1. *Every person is guaranteed the freedom of conscience, religion and worship and the religious denominations are separated from the State.*

2. *No one shall be persecuted or discriminated against on the basis of his or her religious convictions.*

3. *The right to be a conscientious objector shall be guaranteed in accordance with the law.*

---

130   The required number for passage was 40.

131   Tilman also gave the example of a person whose religion did not allow them to deal with blood not being required to work in the hospital.

132   A minor grammatical change was made to the heading in the Portuguese version.

4. *Freedom to teach any religion in the framework of the respective religious denomination is guaranteed.*

(Identical to final)

Commentary: In the version of the Constitution finalised prior to the public consultation process, the relationship between s 12 and this section was again renegotiated. The subsection dealing with religious denominations' right to possess goods which had been moved into this section during the plenary section remained in s 12. Instead, what was previously s 12(1) (recognising the separation of religious denominations and the State) was transferred into the section as part of sub-s (1). Secondly, a new subsection was introduced which guaranteed religious denominations the freedom to teach religion (appearing as sub-s (4)). Both changes resulted from acceptance of recommendations of the Centre for Peace and Development.[133]

This text also broadened sub-s (1) to apply to all persons, rather than citizens. Numerous submissions to the Assembly had supported amending rights so that they applied to all persons. The Systematisation and Harmonisation Committee explained in their methodology that they had attempted to broaden references (from citizen to individual/person) wherever possible.

Representations and submissions

District consultations: In the District consultations, a suggestion to eliminate sub-s (3) emanated from Manatuto. In the Los Palos report, there was a proposal to eliminate the whole section.

Submissions listed in the Systematisation and Harmonisation Committee's Consultations Report: None listed.

Other submissions made during the process: Not surprisingly, the most extensive comments on this section came from religious authorities. The joint Catholic/Protestant submission from the Church-Constitution Working Group (written on letterhead of the Centre for Peace and Development) suggested that s 44(2) be replaced with arts 41(2)–(5) of the Portuguese Constitution. Section 44 would then provide:

---

133   In a document explaining its methodology, the Systematisation and Harmonisation Committee explained that sub-s (4) was a suggestion of the Centre for Peace and Development. Their submission had recommended that the Assembly look to art 41 of the Portuguese Constitution for inspiration, an article which included also the freedom to teach religion for religious denominations: see letter from the Centre for Peace and Development to the President of the Constituent Assembly, January 2002, received by the Assembly on 23 January 2002. In the Portuguese version of the text of 9 February 2002, the Systematisation and Harmonisation Committee acknowledged that the reworking of s 12 was related to the recommendation of the Centre. Although the text of s 45 did not contain a similar comment, it is likely that the changes to s 45 were considered at the same time.

1. Everyone is guaranteed the freedom of conscience, religion and worship.

2. No one shall be persecuted or deprived of rights by reason of his or her convictions or religious observance.

3. No one shall be questioned by any authority about his or her convictions or religious observances, except for the purpose of gathering statistical information that does not identify individuals, nor shall anyone be prejudiced by his or her refusal to reply.

4. Churches and other religious groups shall be independent of the State and are free to determine their own organisation and to perform their own ceremonies and worship.

5. Freedom within a religious group to teach its religion and to use its own media for providing public information about its activities is guaranteed.

6. The right to be a conscientious objector shall be guaranteed by law.[134]

The Church-Constitution Working Group stressed that as leaders of religious groups, they were not seeking any special status. They opposed the establishment of any religion as the official religion and accepted the separation of church and State. At the same time, they indicated an openness to cooperation between religious authorities and the State in providing the necessities for the full flourishing of all persons.[135] Yayasan HAK proposed moving recognition of the separation of church and State to s 12 (Fundamental principles).[136]

During the drafting process, the Human Rights Unit of UNTAET, and the UN High Commissioner for Human Rights, amongst others, stressed the importance of human rights such as this one applying to all persons, rather than being limited to citizens.[137]

The topic of conscientious objectors received little comment, though the International Commission of Jurists suggested that it be dealt with under a section dealing with military matters to make clear the right's limited scope.[138]

---

134 Letter from the Centre for Peace and Development to the President of the Constituent Assembly, January 2002, received by the Assembly on 23 January 2002. This letter contained the submission of the Church-Constitution Working Group. Note the wording presented here is that which appears in the English language version of the submission.

135 Ibid.

136 Yayasan HAK, 'Draft Proposals for the Constitution of East Timor', received by the Assembly on 15 March 2002, 7 [Bahasa Indonesian].

137 Human Rights Unit, UNTAET, 'Summary of select technical comments concerning the East Timorese draft Constitution and its treatment of human rights', December 2001, 1–2; Letter from the UN High Commissioner for Human Rights to the President of the Constituent Assembly, 19 December 2001.

138 International Commission of Jurists (Australian Section), 'Commentary on the Draft Constitution Proposed for East Timor by the Constituent Assembly', undated, 10.

Section 46
(Right to political participation)

1. Every citizen has the right to participate in the political life and in the public affairs of the country, either directly or through democratically elected representatives.

2. Every citizen has the right to establish and to participate in political parties.

3. The establishment and organisation of political parties shall be regulated by law.

(Official translation of the final text)

Drafting history

Thematic Committee I text

Section 39
(Right to political participation)

1. *Every citizen has the right to participate in the political life and in the public affairs of the country, either directly or through democratically elected representatives.*

2. *Every citizen has the right to establish and to participate in political parties.*

3. *The law shall regulate the formation of political parties.*

Commentary: This provision was based on art 39 of the FRETILIN Project. It was approved in a vote of 19:0:1.

Systematisation and Harmonisation Committee draft text used in the plenary debate

Section 45
(Right to political participation)

1. *Every citizen has the right to participate in the political life and in the public affairs of the country, either directly or through democratically elected representatives.*[139]

2. *Every citizen has the right to establish and to participate in political parties.*

3. *The State shall value the contribution of the political parties to the organised expression of the will of the people and to the democratic participation of the citizen in the governance of the country.*

4. *The formation of political parties shall be regulated by law.*[140]

Commentary: A new sub-s (3) was inserted, dealing with the State valuing political parties. During the plenary debate Vicente Guterres (UDC/PDC), Secretary of the Systematisation and Harmonisation Committee, noted that it had been transferred from the then draft s 8(2).

The ordering of words in sub-s (4) was also amended, but without changing the substance of the clause.

Plenary debate (20 December 2001)

In the plenary debate, sub-ss (1) and (4) garnered the most attention, with several proposals aimed at increasing transparency of governmental functions.

In relation to sub-s (1), João Carrascalão (UDT) thought the phrase 'freely elected' was preferable to 'democratically elected'. Further recognition should be given to the right to participate in political life, as well as the right of citizens to obtain information. He considered that the State should be obliged to give citizens information about matters of State, and should operate in a transparent fashion in carrying out political actions. Reflecting these concerns, a proposal was put forward by João Carrascalão (UDT), Quitéria da Costa (UDT), Clementino Amaral (KOTA) and Pedro da Costa (PST) to:

- amend sub-s (1): to substitute 'freely' for 'democratically'; and

---

139   The English Assembly translation wrongly presented sub-ss (1) and (2) as applying to 'everyone'. The Portuguese text restricted enjoyment of the rights to citizens ('*todo o cidadão*').

140   The English Assembly translation used the term 'establishment' rather than 'formation' for the Portuguese term '*formaçao*'.

- add a new sub-s (4) to provide that: 'Every citizen shall possess the right to be given clarifications about the actions of the State and of other public bodies and to be informed by the government and other authorities about the management of public affairs'.[141]

This was rejected in a vote of 22:30:25.

Openness and transparency of the government and people's right to participate was also emphasised by Eusébio Guterres (PD), Mariano Sabino Lopes (PD), Aquilino Guterres (PD), and Paulo Alves Sarmento (PD), who advanced a proposal (in Bahasa) to the effect that everyone was to have the right to participate in decision-making policy in a transparent manner, in the context of drafting government regulations that might affect rights and freedoms enshrined in the Constitution. This was rejected in a vote of 11:45:21.

The necessity of sub-s (4) dealing with the formation of political parties was queried. Rui Meneses da Costa (PD) suggested leaving this subject to s 42 (freedom of association), whilst Armando da Silva (PL) and Quitéria da Costa (UDT) thought the subsection was unnecessary given that political parties were already covered in s 66 (a section entitled 'Political parties and the right of opposition').[142]

Vicente Guterres (UDC/PDC) was one of the speakers who spoke in favour of sub-s (4). He explained that political parties were special associations and had public responsibilities such as running for elections. Given this, there should be a special law concerning political parties.

Voting on the section during the plenary session

The section passed: 69:0:8.

Version finalised prior to the public consultation process

Section 46
(Right to political participation)

1. *Every citizen has the right to participate in the political life and in the public affairs of the country, either directly or through democratically elected representatives.*

---

141   The proposal as read out was identical to art 48(2) of the Portuguese Constitution except that the word 'objective' was omitted before clarifications. The English translation of the Portuguese Constitution has thus been used and adapted here.
142   During the plenary session, a proposal was put to eliminate sub-s (3) (this may have been meant to be sub-s (4) given the comments made by Rui Meneses (PD), Armando da Silva (PL) and Quitéria da Costa (UDT). However, it was not proceeded with since it did not have the requisite four sponsors.

2. *Every citizen has the right to establish and to participate in political parties.*

3. *The establishment and organisation of political parties shall be regulated by law.*

(Identical to final)

Commentary: The subsection which the Systematisation and Harmonisation Committee had previously inserted as sub-s (3) (concerning the State valuing political parties) was removed from this section and moved to s 7 dealing with the multi-party system.[143] The form of the final sub-s (3) was also changed: instead of referring to the 'formation of parties', the subsection now referred to the 'establishment and organisation' of political parties.

Representations and submissions

District consultations: No comments on this section appear in the summary of District consultations prepared by the Systematisation and Harmonisation Committee.

Submissions listed in the Systematisation and Harmonisation Committee's Consultations Report: None listed.

Other submissions made during the process: In its draft Bill of Rights, Yayasan HAK supported also recognising citizens' right to stand for public office and, if elected, to hold office. Reference was included to a duty of the State to promote participatory models of political decision making.[144]

The Timor Lorosa'e Journalists' Association suggested deleting sub-s (4)'s recognition that law would regulate the establishment of political parties, seeing it as vague and potentially damaging to freedoms[145] A similar stance was taken by the International Commission of Jurists.[146] The Human Rights Unit of UNTAET likewise suggested removal of the subsection, and the insertion elsewhere in the Constitution of a power to regulate electoral affairs.[147]

---

143 This change occurred in the Portuguese version of the text, though not in the English Assembly translation. A minor grammatical correction was made to sub-s (2) in the final text.

144 Yayasan HAK, 'Civil and Political, Economic, Social and Cultural Rights', undated, but received by the Assembly on 22 October 2001, art 27.

145 TLJA/Internews, 'Submission to the Constituent Assembly on Articles in the FRETILIN Draft Constitution of May 2001 concerning freedom of expression', undated, but with an attached handwritten note indicating that it was sent to members of the Assembly on 26 November 2001.

146 International Commission of Jurists (Australian Section), 'Commentary on the Draft Constitution Proposed for East Timor by the Constituent Assembly', undated, 10.

147 Human Rights Unit, UNTAET, 'Thematic Committee One's Proposals For the Protection of Human Rights in the Constitution: An analysis by the HRU', 14 November 2001, 11; and 'Summary of select technical comments concerning the East Timorese draft Constitution and its treatment of human rights', December 2001, 6.

The Women's Charter of Rights in East Timor advocated for more explicit wording concerning non-discrimination against women in public and political life, in particular calling for recognition of women's rights to vote and be elected, and to participate in government policy decision-making and politically related organsations.[148]

148   Women's Charter of Rights in East Timor, art 3.

Section 47
(Right to vote)

1. Every citizen over the age of seventeen has the right to vote and to be elected.

2. The exercise of the right to vote is personal and constitutes a civic duty.

(Official translation of the final text)

Drafting history

Thematic Committee I text

Section 40
(Right to vote)

1. *Every citizen over the age of <u>eighteen</u> has the right to vote and to be elected, unless subject to an incapacity provided for under the law.*

2. *The exercise of the right to vote is personal and constitutes a civic duty.*

Commentary: This provision was based on art 40 of the FRETILIN Project. The minimum age of voting was, however, increased from 17 years to 18 years by consensus. A small stylistic change was made to add 'the exercise' in the opening words of sub-s (2). The section was adopted in a vote of 20:0:0.

Systematisation and Harmonisation Committee draft text used in the plenary debate

Section 46
(Right to vote)

1. *Every citizen over the age of seventeen has the right to vote and to be elected.*[149]

2. *The exercise of the right to vote is personal and constitutes a civic duty.*

---

149   The English Assembly translation incorrectly presented the subsection as applying to 'everyone'. The Portuguese text referred only to citizens enjoying the right ('*todo o cidadão*').

Commentary: In this version, the Systematisation and Harmonisation Committee reverted to the age threshold in the FRETILIN draft (17 years) without explanation. The draft text also omitted wording relating to persons who were incapacitated by law from voting or being elected.

Plenary debate (20 December 2001)

Initial debate surrounded the fact that the text being debated by the Plenary set the voting age as 17 years, as opposed to the 18 years threshold set by Thematic Committee I. Manuel Tilman (KOTA), Rapporteur of the Systematisation and Harmonisation Committee, explained that the age was set at 17 years because that is what the President advised (seemingly a reference to the President of the Assembly, Lú Olo).

Some members queried sub-s (2)'s phrasing of the right to vote as a duty. Rui Meneses da Costa (PD), for instance, considered voting to be a right, rather than a duty.[150] Making reference to the experience of the United States of America, where only a small percentage of persons voted, he argued that if he did not want to vote or follow an election, that was also his right. Timor was a nation with a small population, with some living in villages in the mountains, seemingly referring to the practical difficulties which might be encountered in voting.

Manuel Tilman (KOTA) acknowledged that citizens had the right to vote, but regarded them as having also a civic and moral duty to vote. If a person did not vote because of sickness or another reason beyond his/her control, that was acceptable. However, in general, a person who did not vote should be subject to a fine. This perspective was supported by Adaljiza Magno (FRETILIN) who considered that the State must require citizens to participate in the political process. Involvement in the political process was important since that that was the forum in which decisions about the nation were taken. Recognising a duty to vote was vital to ensure that it was not only an elite making decisions for the nation.

Voting on the section during the plenary session

The section passed: 75:2:3.

---

150   Others querying the reference to a duty to vote were Armando da Silva (PL), Mariano Sabino Lopes (PD) and Eusébio Guterres (PD).

Version finalised prior to the public consultation process

Section 47
(Right to vote)

1. *Every citizen over the age of seventeen has the right to vote and to be elected.*

2. *The exercise of the right to vote is personal and constitutes a civic duty.*

(Identical to final)[151]

Representations and submissions

District consultations: According to the Systematisation and Harmonisation Committee's summary report of consultations, this section was raised in only one District. In Oecusse, the suggestion was made that minors who are married should have the right to vote.

Submissions listed in the Systematisation and Harmonisation Committee's Consultations Report: None listed.

Other submissions made during the process: The East Timor Study Group recommended that consideration be given to giving the right to vote to those under 17 years of age if they were married.[152]

---

151 Minor grammatical changes in the Portuguese text result in this text being labelled as the one identical to the final version.

152 East Timor Study Group, 'Debate on the Draft Constitution: Positive and Negative Implications for the Future of East Timor', 20 February 2002, 11 [Tetum].

Section 48
(Right to petition)

Every citizen has the right to submit, individually or jointly with others, petitions, complaints and claims to organs of sovereignty or any authority for the purpose of defending his or her rights, the Constitution, the law or general interests.

(Official translation of the final text)

Drafting history

Thematic Committee I text

Section 41
(Right to petition)

Every citizen has the right to submit, individually or jointly with others, petitions, complaints and claims to organs of sovereignty or any authority for the purpose of defending his or her rights, <u>the Constitution, the law</u> or general interests.

(Identical to final)

Commentary: This section was based on art 41 of the FRETILIN Project. The wording of the FRETILIN Project and the Annex I text and the clause adopted differed in so far as the first two versions did not mention the right to petition for the purpose of defending 'the Constitution' or 'the law'. However, the handwritten proposal in Thematic Committee I's records included this wording.

The section was approved unanimously in a vote of 17:0:0.

Systematisation and Harmonisation Committee draft text used in the plenary debate

Section 47
(Right to petition)

Every citizen has the right to submit, individually or jointly with others, petitions, complaints and claims to organs of sovereignty or any authority for the purpose of defending his or her rights, the Constitution, the law or general interests.[153]

Plenary debate (20 December 2001)

Unfortunately, the recording provided to the author for the afternoon of 20 December 2001 commences only in the midst of the vote for this section.[154] Thus, the extent of debate on the provision is not known. What is apparent from Assembly records is that there were no successful amendments to the section. Issues around citizens' access to seek an 'abstract review of constitutionality' of laws from the Supreme Court were, however, agitated in relation to what was to become s 150 of the Constitution.[155]

Voting on the section during the plenary session

The section passed: 69:0:4.

Version finalised prior to the public consultation process

Section 48
(Right to petition)

Every citizen has the right to submit, individually or jointly with others, petitions, complaints and claims to organs of sovereignty or any authority for the purpose of defending his or her rights, the Constitution, the law or general interests.

---

153   The English translation provided by the Systematisation and Harmonisation Committee incorrectly referred to 'every one', rather than 'every citizen' as provided for in the Portuguese text (*'todo o cidadão'*).
154   The recording commences at 2.43 pm, whereas the afternoon session would normally reconvene at 2.30 pm.
155   In the composite text prepared by the Systematisation and Harmonisation Committee in late November, there was provision for an abstract review of constitutionality of laws to be initiated by groups of 2,000 citizens or any nation-wide association provided that the application was made for the purpose of defending constitutionally protected interests that transcended the corporate interest of the association or the sum of the applicants' interests: draft s 118(3)(i). This was one of the provisions that was omitted during the plenary debate of the section.

Representations and submissions

District consultations: No comments on this section appear in the summary of District consultations prepared by the Systematisation and Harmonisation Committee.

Submissions listed in the Systematisation and Harmonisation Committee's Consultations Report: The UN SRSG/Transitional Administrator suggested that the Constitution make reference to the right of persons to a remedy for violation of their human rights.[156]

Other submissions made during the process: Inclusion of this clause in the draft Constitution served to catalyse calls for a more robust 'enforcement of rights' clause. In particular, several submissions sought explicit recognition of the right to a remedy for human rights violations. The UN High Commissioner for Human Rights, for instance spoke of the right of every individual to seek and be granted a remedy for violation of his or her human rights. She stressed that there needed to be an accessible mechanism through which individuals could seek effective redress, and referred to the central importance of the courts in this process.[157]

Yayasan HAK also included in their draft Bill of Rights a clause concerning enforcement of rights:

> [I]n the event of an alleged infringement or threat to a right in the Bill of Rights, anyone acting in their own interest, or on behalf of another person who cannot act in their own name, or in the interest of a group of persons, or in the public interest, or an association acting in the interest of its members, may approach a competent court to claim appropriate relief.[158]

The Haburas Foundation suggested a clause dealing with the enforcement of rights, reading:

> Everyone has the right to approach the Supreme Court in order to claim that a right or a State duty set out in this Constitution has been, is being, or is threatened to be violated or contravened. Where the claim is successful, the Supreme Court may grant such remedy as it sees fit.[159]

---

156   Comments attached to the letter from the UN SRSG and Transitional Administrator to heads of the political parties, 22 February 2001.

157   Letter from the UN High Commissioner for Human Rights to the President of the Constituent Assembly, 19 December 2001.

158   Yayasan HAK, 'Civil and Political, Economic, Social and Cultural Rights', undated, but received by the Assembly on 22 October 2001, art 43.

159   Haburas Foundation, 'Environment and the Constitution Position Paper', undated, received by the Assembly on 22 October 2001, 3.

The Asia Foundation recommended that a new provision be inserted 'giving the courts power to hear cases concerning enforcement of rights, and powers to make whatever orders are necessary to do justice in the particular case where a breach of rights is proved, including the power to award compensation'.[160] Whilst recognising the origins of the Assembly's draft clause in the Portuguese Constitution, The Asia Foundation characterised it as 'rather vague', asking whether a petition needed to be read or heard, and whether the Ombudsman would consider any failures to receive petitions.[161]

In addition to supporting explicit recognition of the right to seek a remedy for violations of constitutionally guaranteed human rights, the UN Transitional Administrator also suggested amending (then) draft s 150 concerning persons entitled to bring an action to the Supreme Court to challenge constitutionality, to extend the power to groups previously included by Thematic Committee III and the Systematisation and Harmonisation Committee, such as the Jurists Association, national associations and groups of over 2,000 citizens.[162] The Asia Foundation drew attention to the lack of an equivalent provision to the *actio popularis'* in the Portuguese Constitution, recognising the right of individuals to access the courts to protect rights and to claim damages.[163]

---

160 The Asia Foundation, 'Comments and Suggested Amendments to East Timor's Draft Constitution of 9/02/2002', undated but with a cover letter to the President of the Constituent Assembly dated 8 March 2002, 2.
161 The Asia Foundation, 'Discussion Paper on Draft of East Timorese Constitution', March 2002, 6.
162 Comments attached to the letter from the UN SRSG and Transitional Administrator to heads of the political parties, 22 February 2002.
163 The Asia Foundation, 'Discussion Paper on Draft of East Timorese Constitution', March 2002, 6.

Section 49
(Defence of sovereignty)

1. Every citizen has the right and the duty to contribute towards the defence of independence, sovereignty and territorial integrity of the country.

2. Serving in the army shall take place in accordance with the law.

(Official translation of the final text)

Drafting history

Thematic Committee I text

Section 42
(Defence of sovereignty)

1. *Every citizen has the right and the duty to contribute towards the defence of independence, sovereignty and territorial integrity of the country.*

2. *Serving in the army [military service] shall be for a limited period and in accordance with terms fixed by law.*[164]

Commentary: This provision was based on art 42 of the FRETILIN Project. Each subsection was voted on separately, presumably because of the perceived importance and sensitivity of the subject matters. Subsection (1) was approved unanimously (19:0:0), with sub-s (2) and the overall section being passed by large majorities (16:0:3 and 18:0:1 respectively).

Systematisation and Harmonisation Committee draft text used in the plenary debate

Section 48
(Defence of sovereignty)

1. *Every citizen has the right and the duty to contribute towards the defence of independence, sovereignty and territorial integrity of the country.*[165]

---

164   The Portuguese text refers to '*serviço militar*' which might be more literally translated as 'military service'. However, in the official translation of the final text, the phrase used is 'serving in the army'; hence this phrase has been preferred here.

165   The English Assembly text wrongly used the term 'everyone' in this subsection. The Portuguese version said 'every citizen' ('*todo o cidadão*').

2. *Serving in the army shall take place in accordance with terms fixed by law.*[166]

Commentary: In this text, the Systematisation and Harmonisation Committee omitted reference to service being for a limited period. No explanation was provided for this change in the written text provided to the Plenary.

Plenary debate (20 December 2001)

Besides concern about the Bahasa translation provided to Assembly members, the major debate on this section related to the topic of military service. Mario Carrascalão (PSD) regarded the provision as out of context in a part of the Constitution dealing with the rights of individuals. Since the composition of the army was not known, such a clause should not be included in the text. Carrascalão also disagreed with the title, regarding it as creating confusion between the role of the army and that of citizens. Armando da Silva (PL) queried the nature of the obligation to join the military, asking what the consequences would be if someone refused. In da Silva's view, one should only be obliged to join the military when the State was in danger. This obligation should be for a limited time only and based on law. In those circumstances, the populace should defend the nation by whatever means at hand. One needed, however, to consider people's condition, without just forcing people to join the military.

Quitéria da Costa (UDT) spoke in support of the section. She considered that every citizen had an obligation to protect/defend the nation. In Indonesian times, university students had military obligations, so that if the State was in danger, they could be called upon to defend the nation. Manuel Tilman (KOTA), Rapporteur of the Systematisation and Harmonisation Committee, explained that the text did not speak of compulsory service, but that a law would define the circumstances of who was or was not to be involved in military service.

Vicente Guterres (UDC/PDC) supported the professionalism of the armed force and for military service to be for a limited time only. There was some discussion of the text's omission of a temporal qualification on military service.

No amendments, however, were put to the Plenary.

Voting on the section during the plenary session

The section passed: 72:0:6.

---

166   The Assembly English translation of the text differed slightly in its translation of the Portuguese phrase *'nos termos fixados na lei'*.

Version finalised prior to the public consultation process

Section 49
(Defence of sovereignty)

1. *Every citizen has the right and the duty to contribute towards the defence of independence, sovereignty and territorial integrity of the country.*

2. *Serving in the army shall take place in accordance with the law.*

(Identical to final)

Commentary: Minor stylistic changes were apparent in this version – for example, using the phrase ' in accordance with the law', rather than 'in accordance with terms fixed by law'. This was presumably for reasons of consistency with other clauses.

Representations and submissions

District consultations: Two District consultations summaries include comments on this section. In Baucau, it was suggested that the entry age of citizens into military service, whether male or female, be stated in the Constitution. In Los Palos, sub-s (2) was slated for potential elimination.

Submissions listed in the Systematisation and Harmonisation Committee's Consultations Report: None listed.

Title III: Economic, Social and Cultural Rights and Duties (Sections 50–61)

Section 50
(Right to work)

1. Every citizen, regardless of gender, has the right and the duty to work and to choose freely his or her profession.

2. The worker has the right to labour safety and hygiene, remuneration, rest and vacation.

3. Dismissal without just cause or on political, religious and ideological grounds is prohibited.

4. Compulsory work, without prejudice to the cases provided for under penal legislation, is prohibited.

5. The State shall promote the establishment of co-operatives of production and shall lend support to household businesses as sources of employment.

(Official translation of the final text)

Drafting history

Thematic Committee I text

Section 43
(Right to work)

1. *Every citizen has the right and the duty to work and to choose freely his or her profession.*

2. *The worker has the right to labour safety and hygiene, remuneration, rest and vacation.*

3. *Dismissal without just cause or on political and ideological grounds is prohibited.*

4. *Compulsory work is prohibited, except <u>forced</u> work done as per penal legislation.*

5. *The State shall promote the establishment of co-operatives of production and shall lend support to <u>household businesses</u> as sources of employment.*

Commentary: This section is described in Thematic Committee I's report as a consensual proposal, with its 'base' in the FRETILIN Project. The equivalent provision in the FRETILIN Project was art 43. It was adopted unanimously in a vote of 19:0:0.

Systematisation and Harmonisation Committee draft text used in the plenary debate

Section 49
(Right to work)

1. *Every citizen has the right and the duty to work and to choose freely his or her profession.[1]*

2. *The worker has the right to labour safety and hygiene, remuneration, rest and vacation.*

3. *Dismissal without just cause or on political and ideological grounds is prohibited.*

4. *Compulsory work, without prejudice to the cases provided for under penal legislation, is prohibited.*

5. *The State shall promote the establishment of co-operatives of production and shall lend support to household businesses as sources of employment.*

Commentary: In this version, the Systematisation and Harmonisation Committee altered slightly the language of sub-s (4), though without substantial change to the meaning of the clause.

Plenary debate (20 December 2001)

While all the discussion in the plenary session was in favour of this section, several proposals were advanced for additional protections.

Two amendments were successful. Firstly, *religion* was added to the list of prohibited grounds in relation to dismissal. This amendment was urged by Clementino Amaral (KOTA) and the written proposal was supported by KOTA and UDT.[2]

---

1 The Assembly English translation incorrectly included the wording 'everyone' in sub-s (1). However, the Portuguese version referred only to citizens (*'todo o cidadão'*).

2 The proposal was supported by Clementino Amaral (KOTA), Manuel Tilman (KOTA), Quitéria da Costa (UDT) and João Carrascalão (UDT). According to the author's notes, this amendment was passed, with a positive vote of 41. The full voting is not captured on the recordings available to the author.

Secondly, the phrase *'regardless of gender'* was inserted in sub-s (1)'s recognition of the right to work. This motion was put by Adaljiza Magno (FRETILIN), and was supported by a number of FRETILIN colleagues.[3] *It was approved in a vote of 58:3:19.*

Several speakers challenged the inclusion of sub-s (5) concerning the State's promotion of co-operatives. Rui Meneses da Costa (PD), for instance, considered the provision was out of keeping with the remainder of the clause concerning the right to work. Topics such as co-operatives were dealt with elsewhere in the Constitution; for example, in the part dealing with the economy. Furthermore, those who started co-operatives were business owners not workers. João Carrascalão (UDT) considered the section as drafted dealt with too many subject matters and recommended that it be focused on workers' rights alone. An openness to moving the clause to another place in the Constitution and combining it with, for example, a State duty to create employment, was evinced by Manuel Tilman (KOTA). Vicente Guterres (UDC/PDC) spoke in favour of retaining sub-s (5), emphasising the importance of the State's seeking to create jobs, and seeing that co-operatives were one of the ways this could happen.[4]

Broader issues regarding a State's obligations with respect to industrial relations were raised by some speakers. Jacob Xavier (PPT) was concerned about the plight of dismissed workers who had no money to live, recalling the experience of persons dying of starvation in the past. He supported the transfer of workers to other jobs, so that persons would not die of hunger. An imbalance of power existed between employees and employers. Employees were not able able to report employers for misconduct. Armando da Silva (PL) evinced concern for some of the conditions of workers – mentioning security workers being forced to work until 10 pm, in violation of their rights. João Carrascalão (UDT) spoke of the need to protect the rights of both those working for employers and those working for family (for example, persons from the same District who came to live and work with their families).

Who would find workers a job? Who had the duty to create jobs? These were two questions asked by Francisco Xavier do Amaral (ASDT). Clementino Amaral (KOTA) also raised the issue of workers' duties: in addition to workers having rights, such as the right to safety, workers needed to properly exercise their functions. If a person did not finish a job or was absent, which boss would be prepared to accept this? Timorese needed to be well educated so as to be able to

---

3   The motion was supported also by José Reis (FRETILIN), Vicente Faria (FRETILIN), and Maria Perreira (FRETILIN).
4   A similar view was expressed by Francisco Xavier do Amaral (ASDT).

work properly – if not as engineers or scientists, then to be good [productive] on the land. Aquilino Guterres (PD) suggested that the right to choose one's profession should be qualified by the phrase 'according to his/her experiences'.

Francisco Lay (FRETILIN) queried how this section affected those with acquired citizenship given its reference to the right to work being a right of citizens. This was a reference to the fact that draft s 4 at that point prevented acquired citizens from holding military and diplomatic posts. Manuel Tilman (KOTA) felt there was no need to clarify the subsection, and that s 4 dealt with the exceptional cases in which acquired citizens could not work whereas this section provided the general rule.

A range of other proposals were advanced and rejected. Eusébio Guterres (PD) spoke to an amendment which involved deleting the reference to compulsory labour and adding in rights to equal remuneration for men and women, together with rights of professional training and education so that workers would be able to upgrade their skills.[5] This proposal was rejected in a vote of 19:31:29.

Another proposal put by João Carrascalão and others made reference to the State's obligation to promote equal opportunities in the choice of work/profession and access to any public position so as to avoid gender-based limitations. The amendment also provided for explicit recognition of the provision of cultural and technical training and vocational developments for workers. It was defeated in a vote of 24:21:35.[6] A further amendment put forward was to delete sub-s (5) and instead insert wording drawn from art 23(2) of the UDHR providing that: 'Everyone, without discrimination, has the right to equal pay for equal work'.[7] It failed in a vote of 29:15:26. Although raised in oral debates, there was no formal written proposal for the deletion of sub-s (5) alone,[8] so that the Assembly proceeded to vote for the section as a whole.

Voting on the section during the plenary session

The section passed: 63:5:12.[9]

---

5   The amendment was also proposed by Eusébio Guterres (PD), Mariano Sabino Lopes (PD), Aquilino Guterres (PD), Paulo Alves Sarmento (PD), Cipriana Perreira (FRETILIN) and another whose name is unclear from the recording. The proposal was made in Bahasa Indonesian.

6   This amendment was proposed by João Carrascalão (UDT), Quitéria da Costa (UDT), Pedro da Costa (PST), Eusébio Guterres (PD). Unfortunately, the recording picks up only the last one and half subsections of the amendment proposal. Based on the context, this amendment may have also picked up the equivalent content of art 58(2)(a) of the Portuguese Constitution, referring to the State pursuing full employment.

7   This amendment was proposed by Feliciano Fatima (ASDT), Pedro Gomes (ASDT), Afonso Noronho (ASDT) and Jacinta de Andrade (ASDT).

8   A point of order was raised by Rui Meneses (PD) that the proposal for the elimination of sub-s (5) supported by himself and several members was not considered separately. However, the presiding officer noted that the suggestion had not been made in writing as was necessary under the rules.

9   Note the Press Release from 20 December 2001 listed the vote as 58:3:11, but the figure here is that included in the Assembly records.

Version finalised prior to the public consultation process

Section 50
(Right to work)

1. *Every citizen, regardless of gender, has the right and the duty to work and to choose freely his or her profession.*

2. *The worker has the right to labour safety and hygiene, remuneration, rest and vacation.*

3. *Dismissal without just cause or on political, religious and ideological grounds is prohibited.*

4. *Compulsory work, without prejudice to the cases provided for under penal legislation, is prohibited.*

5. *The State shall promote the establishment of co-operatives of production and shall lend support to household businesses as sources of employment.*

(Identical to final)

Representations and submissions

District consultations: No comments on this section appear in the summary of District consultations prepared by the Systematisation and Harmonisation Committee.

Submissions listed in the Systematisation and Harmonisation Committee's Consultations Report: None listed.

Other submissions made during the process: In NGO submissions, calls were made for more detailed inclusion of workers' rights.

Yayasan HAK, for instance, proposed:

- deletion of a 'duty to work';
- a reworking of the recognition of the right to fair and favourable working conditions (with content largely similar to the draft in terms of safe and hygienic working conditions, fair pay and wages, rest, vacation and reasonable working hours);
- a more explicit non-discrimination provision in relation to dismissal covering grounds of race, colour, marital status, gender, ethnic background, sexual orientation or political or religious beliefs;
- adding in prohibitions on slavery and indentured labour and removing the reference to compulsory work sanctioned by penal legislation;
- adding a reference to equal pay for equal work; and

- adding a provision that the State was to determine the minimum working age and to guarantee that no worker should be under this age.[10]

In their submission to Thematic Committee I, REDE Feto Timor Lorosae also suggested explicit recognition of the right to equal pay for equal work for men and women, together with a right of female workers to maternity leave without loss of salary, job or other social benefits.[11] The Women's Charter of Rights in East Timor included similar rights, as well as protection of health and safety at work. An explicit prohibition of dismissal in cases of pregnancy or maternity leave was also included in the Charter.[12]

The Human Rights Unit of UNTAET supported the inclusion of a specific reference to the right of equal remuneration for work of equal value.[13]

---

10   Yayasan HAK, 'Draft Proposals for the Constitution of East Timor', received by the Assembly on 15 March 2002, 7–8 [Bahasa Indonesian].

11   Letter from REDE Feto Timor Lorosae to the President of the Constituent Assembly, 31 October 2001.

12   Women's Charter of Rights in East Timor, art 8.

13   Human Rights Unit, UNTAET, 'Thematic Committee One's Proposals For the Protection of Human Rights in the Constitution: An analysis by the HRU', 14 November 2001, 11.

Section 51
(Right to strike and prohibition of lock-out)

1. Every worker has the right to resort to strike, the exercise of which shall be regulated by law.

2. The law shall determine the conditions under which services are provided, during a strike, that are necessary for the safety and maintenance of equipment and facilities, as well as minimum services that are necessary to meet essential social needs.

3. *Lock-out* is prohibited.

(Official translation of the final text)

Drafting history

Thematic Committee I text

Section 44
(Right to strike and prohibition of lock-out)

1. *Every worker has the right to resort to strike, the exercise of which shall be regulated by law.*

2. *Lock-out is prohibited.*

Commentary: This provision was based on art 44 of the FRETILIN Project. It was approved unanimously in a vote of 19:0:0.

Systematisation and Harmonisation Committee draft text used in the plenary debate

Section 50
(Right to strike and prohibition of lock-out)

1. *Every worker has the right to resort to strike, the exercise of which shall be regulated by law.*

2. *The law shall determine the conditions under which services are provided, during a strike, that are necessary for the safety and maintenance of equipment and facilities, as well as minimum services that are necessary to meet essential social needs.*

3. *Lock-out is prohibited.*

(Identical to final)

Commentary: The Systematisation and Harmonisation Committee text added a new subsection (sub-s (2)) concerning the regulation of strikes affecting essential services. This was attributed to advice coming from experts during the deliberations of the Systematisation and Harmonisation Committee.[14]

Plenary debate (20 December 2001)

In the plenary discussion, it was noted that sub-s (2) had not appeared in Thematic Committee I's text. Manuel Tilman (KOTA), Rapporteur of the Systematisation and Harmonisation Committee, explained that sub-s (2) was felt to be necessary to ensure the maintenance of minimum services. Women in childbirth, for instance, needed to be able to access medical services at all times. Vicente Guterres (UDC/PDC), Secretary of the Systematisation and Harmonisation Committee, explained that workers had a fundamental right to strike, but that one also had to protect the fundamental rights of other citizens: making specific reference to the importance of the health services of doctors and nurses. In relation to the section as a whole, Manuel Tilman (KOTA) explained that workers had a right to defend their rights and that employers could not replace striking workers.

Relatively few queries were raised in relation to this section. Rue Meneses da Costa (PD) asked why it was not joined with the previous section on the rights of workers. Armando da Silva (PL) expressed the opinion that the provision concerning lock-out should be extended to say 'lock-out is prohibited without reasonable cause', but no formal amendment was put to this effect.

Voting on the section during the plenary session

The section passed: 73:0:6.

Version finalised prior to the public consultation process

Section 51
(Right to strike and prohibition of lock-out)

1. *Every worker has the right to resort to strike, the exercise of which shall be regulated by law.*

2. *The law shall determine the conditions under which services are provided, during a strike, that are necessary for the safety and*

---

14   Author's notes of the deliberations of the Systematisation and Harmonisation Committee, 27 November 2001.

maintenance of equipment and facilities, as well as minimum services that are necessary to meet essential social needs.

3.   *Lock-out is prohibited.*

Representations and submissions

District consultations: In only one District consultation were comments included in relation to this section. In the Dili report, a suggestion was recorded to eliminate the phrase 'regulated by law' in sub-s (2) (though the intention may have been to refer to sub-s (1) in which this phrase appeared).

Submissions listed in the Systematisation and Harmonisation Committee's Consultations Report: None listed.

Other submissions made during the process: Several submissions focused on the language of limitation in sub-s (1). Yayasan HAK recommended a broader right to strike without qualification. The Human Rights Unit of UNTAET also expressed concern as to the potential breadth of sub-s (1)'s reference to later laws, recommending that it either be deleted (leaving limitations to be dealt with according to the limitations clause) or be replaced by a more specifically worded limitations clause.[15] The International Commission of Jurists concluded that since the right could be removed or restricted by law, no real guarantee had been provided.[16] In relation to essential services, Yayasan HAK recommended a provision along the lines: 'The State may determine criteria under which members of the military, police force and civil service may exercise their right to strike'.[17]

---

15   Human Rights Unit, UNTAET, 'Thematic Committee One's Proposals for the Protection of Human Rights in the Constitution', 14 November 2001, 10.

16   International Commission of Jurists (Australian Section), 'Commentary on the Draft Constitution Proposed for East Timor by the Constituent Assembly', undated, 10.

17   Yayasan HAK, 'Draft Proposals for the Constitution of East Timor', received by the Assembly on 15 March 2002, 9 [Bahasa Indonesian].

Section 52
(Trade union freedom)

1. Every worker has the right to form or join trade unions and professional associations in defence of his or her rights and interests.

2. Trade union freedom is sub-divided, namely, into freedom of establishment, freedom of membership and freedom of organisation and internal regulation.

3. Trade unions and trade union associations shall be independent of the State and the employers.

(Official translation of the final text)

Drafting history

Thematic Committee I text

Section 45

(Trade union freedom)

1. *Every worker has the right to form or join trade unions and professional associations in defence of his or her <u>rights and</u> interests.*

2. *Trade union freedom is sub-divided, namely, into freedom of establishment, freedom of membership and freedom of organisation and internal regulation.*

3. *Trade unions and trade union associations shall be independent of the State and the employers.*

(Identical to final)

Commentary: This clause was described in Thematic Commission I's report as a consensual proposal, with its base in the FRETILIN Project. In its terms it is virtually identical to the art 45 of the FRETILIN Project, with only one substantive amendment: the inclusion of 'rights' as well as interests in sub-s (1). It was approved unanimously: 19:0:0.

Systematisation and Harmonisation Committee draft text used in the plenary debate

Section 51
(Trade union freedom)

1. *Every worker has the right to form or join trade unions and professional associations in defence of his or her rights and interests.*

2. *Trade union freedom is sub-divided, namely, into freedom of establishment, freedom of membership and freedom of organisation and internal regulation.*

3. *Trade unions and trade union associations shall be independent of the State and the employers.*

Plenary debate (20 December 2001)

Two proposals touching upon the topic of collective bargaining formed the basis of most of the debate concerning this section. Eusébio Guterres (PD) wished to see specific recognition of trade unions' function of carrying out negotiations and engaging in collective bargaining. A proposal to add 'collective bargaining' to the section was sponsored by Eusébio Guterres (PD) and supported by PD colleagues,[18] but was defeated in a close vote (38:4:37). In this vote, the number of abstentions was noticeably very close to the number of members who approved the amendment.

The second proposal was advanced by Manuel Tilman (KOTA) and supported by KOTA and UDT.[19] It provided for recognition of the right of trade unions to participate in the elaboration of legislation concerning employment, and to recognise the right of trade unions to engage in collective bargaining.[20] This amendment provoked some discussion about employers also having rights.[21] The proposal was rejected in a vote of 18:17:35.

Francisco Lay (FRETILIN) spoke in favour of a minimum wage, with employers being able to pay more if workers were productive. No amendment was put to the Assembly.

---

18 Other sponsors of the amendment were Aquilino Guterres (PD), Rui Meneses da Costa (PD), and Mariano Sabino Lopes (PD).

19 The sponsors of the amendment were Manuel Tilman (KOTA), João Carrascalão (UDT), Clementino Amaral (KOTA), and Quitéria da Costa (UDT).

20 Note this summary of the proposal is based upon the author's notes from hearing the recordings at the Parliament in 2007. Unfortunately, the copy of the recording subsequently provided to the author stops before discussion of this section. KOTA's original Project text included an article giving trade unions rights to participate in the elaboration of labor legislation, take part in the management of social security institutions, participate in the control of social/economic plans and the right of collective bargaining.

21 Aliança da Araújo (PNT); Cipriana da Costa Perreira (FRETILIN).

Voting on the section during the plenary session

The section passed: 71:0:9.

Version finalised prior to the public consultation process

Section 52
(Trade union freedom)

1. *Every worker has the right to form or join trade unions and professional associations in defence of his or her rights and interests.*

2. *Trade union freedom is sub-divided, namely, into freedom of establishment, freedom of membership and freedom of organisation and internal regulation.*

3. *Trade unions and trade union associations shall be independent of the State and the employers.*

Representations and submissions

District consultations: In Liquiça, the suggestion was made to add a new section providing protection for teachers/professors.

Submissions listed in the Systematisation and Harmonisation Committee's Consultations Report: None listed.

Other submissions made during the process: Yayasan HAK suggested the phrasing that workers have the right to 'determine their own administration, programs and activities, including (a) Organising, (b) Forming and joining a trade union federation, (c) Representing workers; and (d) Engaging in collective bargaining'.[22] The International Commission of Jurists suggested broadening sub-s (1) to refer to the right to form or join trade unions 'in advance of social issues and the protection of the rights and interests of workers in the workplace', whilst querying the inclusion of sub-s (2).[23]

---

22   Yayasan HAK, 'Draft Proposals for the Constitution of East Timor', received by the Assembly on 15 March 2002, 9 [Bahasa Indonesian].

23   International Commission of Jurists (Australian Section), 'Commentary on the Draft Constitution Proposed for East Timor by the Constituent Assembly', undated, 10.

Section 53
(Consumer rights)

1. Consumers have the right to goods and services of good quality, to truthful information and protection of their health, safety and economic interests, and to reparation for damages.

2. Advertising shall be regulated by law, and all forms of concealed, indirect or misleading advertising are prohibited.

(Official translation of the final text)

Drafting history

Thematic Committee I text

Section 45A
(Consumer rights)

1. *Consumers have the right to goods and services of good quality, to guidance[24] and information and protection of their health, safety and economic interests, and to reparation for damages.*

2. *Advertising shall be regulated by law, and all forms of concealed, indirect or false advertising are prohibited.*

Commentary: This provision was based on art 54 of the PSD Project. It was approved in a vote of 18:0:2.

Systematisation and Harmonisation Committee draft text used in the plenary debate

Section 52
(Consumer rights)

1. *Consumers have the right to goods and services of good quality, to guidance and information, and protection of their health, safety and economic interests, and to reparation for damages.*

---

24 The Portuguese term used in the Thematic Committee and Systematisation and Harmonisation Committee versions was '*formação*'. Literally it might be translated as 'formation' (as elsewhere in the Constitution). The Assembly English translation was 'guidance'. English translations of the comparable provision in the Portuguese Constitution use the term 'training'.

2. *Advertising shall be regulated by law, and all forms of concealed, indirect or misleading advertising are prohibited.*

Commentary: In this text, the Systematisation and Harmonisation Committee changed the reference in sub-s (2) from 'false/malevolent' (*'dolosa'*) to 'misleading' (*'enganosa'*). No explanation for the change was given in the written text presented to the Assembly.

Plenary debate (20 December 2001)

Whilst some members queried the linkage between rights of consumers and sub-s (2) concerning advertisers,[25] most speakers supported this section as written. Vicente Faria (FRETILIN), Rapporteur of Thematic Committee I, explained that the committee saw the section as necessary to protect the health and safety of consumers. This included protection against false advertising; for example, the false advertising of medicines. Mari Alkatiri (FRETILIN) also spoke in favour of the text. Once consumers knew their rights, they would be able to make claims to the relevant structure/authority. Advertising needed to be correct. Pedro Gomes (ASDT) highlighted the importance of buyers selling good, clean food such as fish or meat. The Department of Health needed to ensure that goods which were past their expiry dates were not sold. Ana Pessoa (FRETILIN) referred to the provision's utility in ensuring the wellbeing of consumers.

It was adopted without any amendment.

Voting on the section during the plenary session

The section passed: 74:0:6.

Version finalised prior to the public consultation process

Section 53
(Consumer rights)

1. *Consumers have the right to goods and services of good quality, to truthful information and protection of their health, safety and economic interests, and to reparation for damages.*

2. *Advertising shall be regulated by law, and all forms of concealed, indirect or misleading advertising are prohibited.*

(Identical to final)

---

25 Rui Meneses da Costa (PD).

Commentary: In this text, there was a slight amendment to sub-s (1) to refer to the right to 'truthful information' (*informação verdadeira*), rather than 'guidance and information'. No explanation was given for this change. However, it seems to have been designed to provide greater clarity within the text.

Representations and submissions

District consultations: No comments on this section appear in the summary of District Consultations prepared by the Systematisation and Harmonisation Committee.

Submissions listed in the Systematisation and Harmonisation Committee's Consultations Report: None listed.

Other submissions made during the process: The Regional Office for Asia and the Pacific of Consumers International put forward a more extensive clause which read:

1.1 The rights of a person as a consumer shall be protected by law.

1.2 The law under paragraph 1.1 shall recognise the rights of the consumer to basic goods and services, safety, information, choice, redress, representation, consumer education and a safe and clean environment.

1.3 The law under paragraph 1.1 shall deal with regulating advertising, sale of goods and services, product safety and liability, consumer credit, competition, licensing of business enterprises, consumer redress, provision of public utilities, and any other matters affecting the interests of consumers.

1.4 The law under paragraph 1.1 shall provide for the freedom to form independent organizations to represent the interests of consumers in decision making processes and shall confer them the requisite standing to defend that interest in the courts of the land.

1.5 The State shall designate an authority to develop policies and legislation to protect the interests of consumers, provide for effective redress mechanisms, and enforcement of consumer protections laws.[26]

The International Commission of Jurists queried the inclusion of this section in the Constitution.[27]

---

26 Consumers International, Regional Office for Asia and the Pacific, 'Proposed Constitutional Provision on Consumer Protection for East Timor', undated.

27 International Commission of Jurists (Australian Section), 'Commentary on the Draft Constitution Proposed for East Timor by the Constituent Assembly', undated, 10.

Section 54
(Right to private property)

1. Every individual has the right to private property and can transfer it during his or her lifetime or on death, in accordance with the law.

2. Private property should not be used to the detriment of its social purpose.

3. Requisitioning and expropriation of property for public purposes shall only take place following fair compensation in accordance with the law.

4. Only national citizens have the right to ownership of land.

(Official translation of the final text)

Drafting history

Thematic Committee I text

Section 46
(Right to private property)

1. *Every citizen has the right to private property and can transfer it during his or her lifetime or on death, in accordance with the law.*

2. *Private property should not be used to the detriment of its social purpose.*

3. *Requisitioning and expropriation of property can only take place in accordance with the law.*

4. *Only national citizens have the right to ownership of land.*

Commentary: This provision was based on art 46 of the FRETILIN Project. It was adopted unanimously in a vote of 19:0:0.

PSD proposed a substitute sub-s (3), based on art 58(2) of their project. It provided limitations on the acquisition and expropriation for public use, stipulating that acquisitions and expropriation also needed to be for a public purpose/use, and involve payment of fair compensation. This proposal was rejected in a vote of 6:9:3. A similar recommendation was advanced by the Technical Adviser to the committee (as recorded in Annex II of the committee's report).

Systematisation and Harmonisation Committee draft text used in the plenary debate

Section 53
(Right to private property)

1. *Every citizen has the right to private property and can transfer it during his or her lifetime or on death, in accordance with the law.*[28]

2. *Private property should not be used to the detriment of its social purpose.*

3. *Requisitioning and expropriation of property for public purposes shall only take place in accordance with the law following payment of fair compensation.*[29]

4. *Only national citizens have the right to ownership of land.*

Commentary: In this text, the Systematisation and Harmonisation Committee inserted the requirement that requisitions or expropriation be for a public purpose and that fair compensation be paid. During the committee's deliberations, this additional phrasing was questioned. Manuel Tilman (Rapporteur of the committee) explained that the suggestion had come from Thematic Committee II, and that the addition completed the text.[30]

Plenary debate (21 December 2001)

The right to property led to one of the longer debates on an issue of economic, social or cultural rights. Land rights were regarded as complex and sensitive. Particular reference was made to difficulties associated historically with competing land rights and appropriations of land and the need to find a just solution. Debate continued to revolve around whether there should be a right to fair compensation for those whose land was expropriated.

In an extensive intervention on this topic, Lú Olo (FRETILIN) referred to the different types of title existing in Timor, mentioning specifically those with a formal certificate of land ownership, and those whose title was based on customary law. He addressed the land problems associated with the Indonesian occupation and more recent times. During the war, some people had run away, while others

---

28 The English Assembly translation of this text incorrectly used the word 'everyone' in sub-s (1), rather than referring only to 'citizen', as provided for in the Portuguese text ('*todo o cidadão*').

29 The Portuguese text referred to '*pagamento de justa indemnização*'. The Assembly English translation of this text used the term 'adequate' rather than 'fair' in describing the form of compensation. However, this has been streamlined in accordance with the final translation.

30 Mario Carrascalão (PSD) suggested that the text should bear a note to the effect that the additional text was a result of 'harmonising' the drafts. However, no such note appeared in the draft text: author's observation of the deliberations of the Systematisation and Harmonisation Committee, 27 November 2001.

remained in Timor. Some sold their land to Indonesians. Some had come back and said, 'I was in the Resistance, this is my land', while others claimed their title from the Indonesians. Lú Olo recognised that these were hard issues to resolve, especially in Dili. He agreed with Armando da Silva that some people had come to Dili to take advantage of houses that had been abandoned by Indonesians. However, it was not just private houses that had been occupied in this fashion, but also State-owned houses. Furthermore, the situations in which houses had been taken over were not limited to cases in which people's own house had been burnt. Sometimes the real owner of a house was in Dili, but was afraid to evict persons occupying their property because of the lack of supportive legislation. The absence of a law defining the property of the State was also a real problem. Lú Olo recommended there be a study to examine how to guarantee the right of people to have their property restored, and what type of law should be used to solve the land-related problems. The law would need to distinguish between private property and State property. He suggested an amendment to sub-s (2) to stipulate that the property belonged to someone 'based on the law'.

António Cardoso (FRETILIN) also spoke in favour of having greater definition of property and land rights. Indonesians had built houses in Timor but, after the refugees fled, their houses had been occupied. When houses were burnt by the militias, there was no aid or assistance program for owners from the UN Transitional Administration. A 'profound investigation' was needed so as to avoid confusion [conflict] between peoples. A number of speakers mentioned the situation of Timorese refugees, seemingly a reference to those who remained in West Timor following the events in 1999. Armando da Silva (PL), for instance, referred to the fact that persons had occupied the houses of refugees, and predicted that when the owners returned from West Timor, there would be problems. António Lelan (Independent) mentioned the situation of those who had struggled for independence, but whose land had been taken by others. António Ximenes (PDC) highlighted the social jealousy in Timor arising from the fact that many of those who were fighting in the bush had no land, whereas the rich had land, as did those who obtained land during Indonesian times. In his local area, kings had, in the past, tortured people if they did not give donations to the kings. Now that Timor had independence, it was important to have land reform and avoid social jealousy. Every Timorese citizen should have land. However, people needed to go through a process based on law.

Mention was also made of the issues around customary law and land rights. Januário Soares (FRETILIN) underlined the importance of the section, referring to the problems experienced in the Districts. He felt, however, that the section did not deal with the real problem in Districts like Viqueque and Uatalori, where *liurai* (kings) had people work on their land. People wanted to claim the land as their own, yet there was no clarity as to whether the land belonged to the *liurai* or was collective land. A law was thus needed to deal with rural land issues. Eusébio Guterres (PD) agreed that this was an issue, particularly in relation to delineating communal property, and suggested seeking more advice concerning conflict resolution in rural areas. Jacob Xavier (PPT) spoke in favour of the *liurai*'s rights to the land from customary law. Where a king owns the land, the land is from their ancestors. The people who work the land do not own it, regardless of whether they are paid. If property below the land [minerals and gas] belonged to the State, as had been stated by Vicente Guterres, that fact needed to be in the Constitution, otherwise 'if it is my land, it is my land'.

Lú Olo recognised that land was a sensitive topic with many aspects. Even in the Portuguese times, there had been transfers of land between people and the *liurais*, and it would cause problems if this were to be changed. Mariano Sabino Lopes (PD) spoke in favour of agrarian reform away from the feudal and colonial system, seeing a movement towards the fair division of land as in furtherance of the liberation struggle. The law should determine the extent of land provided to each person. Borders of land were needed in Dili and other towns so that people could build their houses. People also needed land in the mountain areas to farm.

The Systematisation and Harmonisation Committee's action in adding into sub-s (3) a requirement of fair compensation for requisitions and expropriations prompted some reaction. Vicente Faria (FRETILIN), Rapporteur of Thematic Committee I, for instance, noted that the thematic committee had rejected this proposal. Mario Carrascalão (PSD) sought clarification as to which law was going to determine the requisition/expropriation and who was going to determine if the compensation was fair or not. In his view, compensation should be based on current market value, an opinion echoed by Clementino Amaral (KOTA). Amaral also considered it insufficient to allow acquisitions 'in accordance with law', remarking that during the Indonesian and Portuguese times, land had been taken without compensation for public purposes such as hospitals and schools. Vicente Guterres (UDC/PDC), Secretary of the Systematisation and Harmonisation Committee, explained that, according to the subsection, land could only be taken for public purposes, and that there would need to be reimbursement of the owner. Manuel Tilman (KOTA), also speaking for that committee, emphasised that money would have to be paid on requisitioned/appropriated land based on the market value and suggested the operation of a valuation commission.

Jacob Fernandes (FRETILIN) led a proposal to amend sub-s (3) so that it required only that requisitions and appropriations *'be for a public purpose in accordance with the law'* (that is, omitting any reference to the payment of fair compensation).[31]

---

31 Other signatories were, according to the recording, Flávio da Silva (FRETILIN), Francisco Lelan (FRETILIN) and Elizario Ferreira (FRETILIN).

This amendment was passed: 56:12:18.

Amongst those who voted against the deletion of the compensation requirement was Vicente Guterres (UDC/PDC), who was concerned that there was no clear prohibition on the State arbitrarily taking property. Clementino Amaral (KOTA) was worried that the parameters for the State taking land for public purposes would be unclear for the future.

The restriction of the right to own land to national citizens attracted also some attention. Mario Carrascalão (PSD) suggested changing the heading to the 'Right to private property and land' and making a similar change to sub-s (1). The distinction between movable and immovable property needed to be recognised. Whilst foreigners could not own land, they could have other property. He sought clarification on the meaning of 'land' in this prohibition. In a multi-storey house/apartment block, for instance, could foreigners own the second or third levels? Property needed to be defined properly, whether defining property in a vertical or horizontal sense. Given the complexity of the topic, Carrascalão suggested having a commission look at the topic, allowing for specialist advice on the matter, rather than having a general provision in the Constitution. Manuel Tilman suggested that foreigners could buy vertical property, but not horizontal property. Clementino Amaral (KOTA) queried the situation of churches that had come to Timor and other organisations, noting that the Assembly had recognised their ability to function in Timor (through freedom of religion) yet this section would prevent them owning land. Vicente Guterres (UDC/PDC) expressed the view that private property included all property, both movable and immovable.

Voting on the section during the plenary session

The section passed: 69:7:10.

In late January when the Assembly was in the midst of discussing transitional provisions, the Plenary adopted a provision which it envisaged as sub-section (5) of the right to private property. It recognised past illegal appropriation of movable and immovable assets as a crime, to be resolved within terms of the Constitution and the law. In discussions of the Systematisation and Harmonisation Committee following the plenary session, it was agreed that this provision should be located with other transitional arrangements and became s 161.

Version finalised prior to the public consultation process

Section 54
(Right to private property)

1. *Every individual has the right to private property and can transfer it during his or her lifetime or on death, in accordance with the law.*

2. *Private property should not be used to the detriment of its social purpose.*

3. *Requisitioning and expropriation of property for public purposes shall only take place following compensation in accordance with the law.*

4. *Only national citizens have the right to ownership of land.*

Commentary: In this version, the right to private property was extended to 'every individual', rather than limited to citizens. There had been a number of submissions to the Assembly concerning the enjoyment of rights by all individuals, and the committee explained in their methodology that they had attempted to broaden references to 'individuals' or 'persons' wherever possible.

The issue of compensation for expropriations was evidently reagitated within the Systematisation and Harmonisation Committee, with the reintroduction into sub-s (3) of a requirement for the payment of compensation.[32] This change was bolded and a note inserted that the committee was acting on the recommendation of the Centre for Peace and Development. Examining that submission reveals that the committee did not fully implement the suggestion of the Church-Constitution Working Group – since the specific suggestion had been to reinsert a requirement of *fair compensation.*[33]

Representations and submissions

District Consultations: In two Districts, Baucau and Dili, noticeably the two largest cities of Timor, there were suggestions to emphasise that only citizens (and in the case of Baucau, only 'original citizens') had the right to property. Another recommendation was to change the heading to 'the right to use [property]'. In the Liquiça consultation, a desire was expressed for a clear definition with respect to traditional property. The Oecusse report included a proposal to add 'fair' before compensation.

Submissions listed in the Systematisation and Harmonisation Committee's Consultation Report: The UN SRSG and Transitional Administrator noted that an important element of protecting the right to property was preventing any 'arbitrary deprivation' of property. While acknowledging that governments

---

32 The Portuguese phrase introduced at this point was *'têm lugar mediante indemnização'* (literally 'takes place through compensation').
33 Letter from the Centre for Peace and Development to the President of the Constituent Assembly, received by the Assembly on 23 January 2002. This letter contained the submission of the Church-Constitution Working Group. The working group also drew attention to art 94 of the Portuguese Constitution dealing with agrarian reform. The note of the Systematisation and Harmonisation Committee referred to sub-s (4), but the bolded text was in sub-s (3).

could expropriate property with the payment of compensation when needed, stress was placed on the need for due process. He thus recommended explicitly prohibiting arbitrary expropriation.[34]

The Minister for Foreign Affairs accepted that restricting property rights to nationals was not unusual in relation to protecting national interests. However, he expressed concerns that difficulties might arise for the rights of (foreign) spouses, seeing a need to safeguard their rights, for example, when divorcing.[35]

Other submissions made during the process: The circumstances in which expropriation of property could occur and the means of providing compensation to affected persons were the foremost preoccupations in several submissions presented to the Assembly. Yayasan HAK, for example, advanced an alternative sub-s (4) which read:

> Private property may be expropriated according to law which is public in nature:
>
> (a) in the public interest, including under the State commitment to the redistribution of land tenure to guarantee fair access to natural resources for all citizens; and
>
> (b) based upon fair and proportionate compensation, agreed to by the parties affected by the expropriation; or upon a court ruling that has taken into account the relevant circumstances.[36]

The East Timor Study Group queried the meaning of the term 'social purpose', noting the problems experienced in Indonesian times with people being pressured in respect of the usage of their property.[37] The Human Rights Unit of UNTAET, in their comments following Thematic Committee I's report, suggested that further consideration be given to the protection of individuals from acquisitions and appropriations by government.[38] They suggested a rephrasing in terms of protection from 'arbitrary acquisitions and appropriations', and stipulating that any acquisitions and appropriations had to be 'in laws of general application, and for a public purpose'. The Unit also suggested that

---

34   Comments attached to the letter from the UN SRSG and Transitional Administrator to heads of the political parties, 22 February 2002.

35   Letter from the Minister of State and for Foreign Affairs and Cooperation, Dr José Ramos Horta, to the President of the Constituent Assembly, 25 February 2002.

36   Yayasan HAK, 'Draft Proposals for the Constitution of East Timor', received by the Assembly on 15 March 2002, 10 [Bahasa Indonesian]. See too art 33 of the draft Bill of Rights included in Yayasan HAK's submission entitled 'Civil and Political, Economic, Social and Cultural Rights', undated, but received by the Constituent Assembly on 22 October, 2001.

37   East Timor Study Group, 'Debate on the Draft Constitution: Positive and Negative Implications for the Future of East Timor', 20 February 2002, 11 [Tetum].

38   Human Rights Unit, UNTAET, 'Thematic Committee One's Proposals For the Protection of Human Rights in the Constitution: An analysis by the HRU', 14 November 2001, 12.

consideration might also be given to a clause permitting the government to take into account historic dispossession in settling land disputes or instituting land redistributions.[39]

The Church-Constitution Working Group also recommended restoring the requirement of fair/adequate compensation in s 62(2). It also went further, however, in recommending inclusion of a new section dealing with land reform, such as art 94 of the Portuguese Constitution:

> The law shall provide for the alteration of the size of farming units the dimensions of which are excessive from the standpoint of the policy for agriculture; the law shall entitle the owner of estates that are compulsorily acquired to appropriate compensation and to retain an area that is sufficiently large to enable the land to be utilised in a rational and viable way.
>
> Land that is compulsorily acquired shall be handed over, in accordance with the law, either for ownership or holding by small farmers, preferably family farming units or by co-operatives of rural workers or small farmers, or for other forms of land utilisation by workers; these provisions do not prevent the provision of a period of probation, prior to the transfer of full property rights, for the purpose of assessing whether land is being effectively and rationally utilised.[40]

During deliberations of Thematic Committee I, The Asia Foundation submitted a draft property clause for the Assembly's consideration:

1. All citizens shall have the right to acquire, own, occupy, use and dispose of land and all other forms of property individually, or in association with others or on a communal basis and to bequeath their land and other property to their heirs.

2. Property entails obligations. Its use should serve the public good. To this end, the State has the right to regulate the acquisition, ownership, use and disposition of land and other property.

3. No person shall be arbitrarily deprived of his or her land or other property and no person shall be arbitrarily evicted from his or her home.

---

39   Ibid.
40   Letter from the Centre for Peace and Development to the President of the Constituent Assembly, January 2002, received by the Assembly on 23 January 2002. Note that the translation presented here is that contained in the English version of the letter of the Church-Constitution Working Group, and not the official translation of the Portuguese Constitution.

4. The State and any competent organ authorised by law may acquire property in the public interest. The public interest shall be taken to include programmes of land restitution, land redistribution, land regularisation and land tenure reform.

5. No law shall provide for the compulsory acquisition of property without fair compensation and a right of access to a court of law by any person with an interest in that property to determine the necessity for the acquisition of and the compensation offered for that property. Compensation shall reflect a fair balance between the public interest and the interests of those affected by the acquisition.

6. Parliament shall within four years of its first sitting under this Constitution enact laws providing for programmes to increase the number of persons occupying and using land with secure tenure, for the orderly and equitable operation and regulation of a land and housing market, for regulating the uses of land and for the efficient, effective and economic settlement of disputes about land.[41]

The International Commission of Jurists expressed concern that the section did not deal with land rights in Timor, and suggested that the existence of holdings of land under common title or customary title should be acknowledged. The ICJ also considered that sub-s (4) might deal with the situation of corporations, cooperatives and international corporations, such as banks, that would wish to acquire land.[42]

Traditional rights to land and resources were raised by Haburas Foundation in the key articles it disseminated for the purpose of consultation:

1. The State shall recognise and respect traditional rights to own or use land and natural resources.

2. The State shall not disturb or allow disturbance of any traditional rights to own or use land and natural resources unless it has first obtained the prior informed consent of the holders of the traditional rights.[43]

Post-consultation plenary debate

The Systematisation and Harmonisation Committee recommending adding 'fair' before compensation based on feedback from Districts.

The Plenary added the Portuguese term 'justa' ('fair') before 'compensation' by consensus.

---

41 The Asia Foundation, 'Suggested Draft of a Property Clause for the Constitution of East Timor', 29 October 2001.

42 International Commission of Jurists (Australian Section), 'Commentary on the Draft Constitution Proposed for East Timor by the Constituent Assembly', undated, 10–11.

43 Haburas Foundation, 'Environment and the Constitution Draft Position Paper', undated, but circa October 2001, 2–3.

Section 55
(Obligations of the taxpayer)

Every citizen with a certified income has the duty to pay tax in order to contribute to public revenues, in accordance with the law.[44]

(Official translation of the final text)

Drafting history

Thematic Committee I text

There was no equivalent provision in the draft produced by Thematic Committee I.

Systematisation and Harmonisation Committee draft text used in the plenary debate

Nor was there any equivalent provision in the draft text produced by the Systematisation and Harmonisation Committee.

Plenary debate (22 December 2001)

This section was suggested as a new section by Mario Carrascalão (PSD), with cross-party support. Carrascalão explained that the text derived from PSD's draft (prepared by Professor Miranda). Whilst the original PSD text had three subsections, his suggestion was to pick up sub-s (1) concerning the obligation to pay tax in this part, and place elsewhere sub-ss (2) and (3).[45]

There was some suggestion that this section might be better positioned elsewhere. Manuel Tilman (KOTA) for instance, argued against its inclusion in the Bill of Rights, suggesting it might be better located in the fiscal-related chapter of the Constitution. Feliciano Fatima (ASDT) considered the topic might be covered in (draft) s 134 or s 136. Rui Meneses (PD) argued against this, noting that s 136 dealt with the system of taxation, whereas this proposal concerned an individual's duty to pay tax. Jacob Fernandes (FRETILIN), agreed to sponsor the new section as s 53A in the Bill of Rights.

---

44   The contemporary Assembly English translation omitted reference to the last phrase 'in accordance with the law', which was included in the Portuguese version (*'nos termos da lei'*) and was included in the official translation.

45   Subsections (2) and (3) of the PSD text related the payment of taxation to levels of income.

Whether the duty to pay tax applied to all persons attracted some debate. Jacob Xavier (PPT), for instance, considered that it should be only the rich who paid tax. Rui Meneses (PD) took a similar line. Pedro da Costa (PST) reminded members that taxes could not be collected from those without money, but those who were rich had an obligation to contribute through payment of taxation. For Manuel Tilman (KOTA) the relevant threshold was whether a person had income. Mari Alkatiri (FRETILIN), speaking in favour of the section, supported the application of the obligation to all citizens. Income was received not just by rich people: for example, public servants were not rich, but they did have a monthly income. In relation to the placement of the section, in Alkatiri's view, s 53 was the appropriate spot. Details of the taxation system could be regulated in a taxation law.[46]

Vicente Guterres (UDC/PDC) reminded members of the inter-linkages between this obligation and the State's obligation to assist those without money recognised in the right to social security. Several final speakers spoke in favour of the provision on the basis that taxation was necessary to build the country. Eusébio Guterres (PD) thought taxation was important, but what was also needed was transparency and monitoring of the system. Vicente Faria (FRETILIN) considered that taxation could be one of the sources for the State budget, with the system being built slowly so that people could contribute.

The proposal put forward by Mario Carrascalão (PSD), Mari Alkatiri (FRETILIN), Quitéria da Costa (UDT), Vicente Guterres (UDC/PDC), and Jacob Fernandes (FRETILIN) read:

> *Every citizen with a certified income has the duty to pay tax in order to contribute to public revenues.*

Voting on the section during the plenary session

The section passed: 72:2:2.

After the section was adopted, Manuel Tilman (KOTA) repeated his dissatisfaction with the placement of this section in the Bill of Rights, as well as expressing concern at the stronger language used in this section. Whereas other provisions regarding State obligations referred to [services such as education or a national health system which] 'tends to be' free, this section imposed a blanket duty on individuals.

---

46   António Ximenes (PDC), Feliciano Fatima (ASDT), Aliança da Araújo (PNT), and Quitéria da Costa (UDT).

Version finalised prior to the public consultation process

Section 55
(Obligations of the taxpayer)

Every citizen with a certified income has the duty to pay tax in order to contribute to public revenues.

Representations and submissions

District consultations: The summary of the Baucau consultation included the suggestion that 'Public expenses and incomes are to be regulated by law'. Another suggestion was made in the same consultation to eliminate the section.

Submissions listed in the Systematisation and Harmonisation Committee's Consultations Report: None listed.

Other submissions made during the process: Yayasan HAK suggested more particular language around the duty to pay taxes, specifying that 'every citizen with a certified income and every company and business, has the duty to contribute to public revenues'.[47]

Post-consultation plenary debate

During the final plenary debates, two amendments were suggested and put to the vote concerning this section. The first was to add *'in accordance with the law'*, which was *accepted in a vote of 53:7:19*. The second proposal, to add a reference to companies' duty to pay tax, failed by a substantial majority.

---

47 Yayasan HAK, 'Draft Proposals for the Constitution of East Timor', received by the Assembly on 15 March 2002, 10 [Bahasa Indonesian].

Section 56
(Social security and assistance)

1. Every citizen is entitled to social assistance and security in accordance with the law.[48]

2. The State shall promote, in accordance with its national resources, the establishment of a social security system.

3. The State shall support and supervise the activity and functioning of institutions of social solidarity and other non-profit institutions of recognised public interest, in accordance with the law.

(Official translation of the final text)

Drafting history

Thematic Committee I text

Section 47
(Social security and assistance)

1. *Everyone is entitled to social security, in accordance with the law.*

2. *The State shall promote, in accordance with its national resources, the establishment of a social security system.*

3. *The State shall support and supervise the activity and functioning of institutions of social solidarity and other non-profit institutions of recognised public interest, in accordance with the law.*

Commentary: This section was an amalgam of texts drawn from the PSD and FRETILIN projects. Subsection (1) was based upon art 72(1) of the PSD Project. It was approved unanimously in a vote of 20:0:0.

Subsection (2) was based on art 47 of the FRETILIN Project. No separate recording of vote appears for this subsection in the committee's report.

Subsection (3) was based upon art 72(2) of the PSD Project. It was approved in a vote of 19:0:1.The section as a whole was adopted unanimously in a vote of 20:0:0.

---

48   The Portuguese text *'têm direito é'* might also be translated as 'has the right to'. The language 'is entitled to' appears in the official translation of the final text and is thus reproduced here.

Systematisation and Harmonisation Committee draft text used in the plenary debate

Section 54
(Social security and assistance)

1. *Everyone is entitled to social security, in accordance with the law.*

2. *The State shall promote, in accordance with its national resources, the establishment of a social security system.*

3. *The State shall support and supervise the activity and functioning of institutions of social solidarity and other non-profit institutions of recognised public interest, in accordance with the law.*

Plenary debate (21 December 2001)

Debate on this section focused on two aspects in particular: (i) the qualified nature of sub-s (2) in linking performance of the obligation to promote social security to availability of resources; and (ii) the role of the State in supervising non-governmental organisations in sub-s (3).

In relation to sub-s (2), Leandro Isac (PSD) supported deletion of the phrase 'in accordance with its national resources', preferring the State to be clearly obliged to establish a social security system. If one waited for the State to have resources, how would people know when the State had enough resources? The provision of social security was one of the duties of the State. Eusébio Guterres (PD) also considered that the reference to resources as unclear, supporting its deletion, along with Pedro da Costa (PST). Lú Olo (FRETILIN) spoke in favour of the existing phrasing, arguing that while the State had a duty to support social security, such assistance had to be based on its capacity.[49] Vicente Faria (FRETILIN), Rapporteur of Thematic Committee I, suggested that 'national resources' meant not only the resources of the State, but encompassed all the resources of the nation. He also underlined that the State had a responsibility to use its resources for this purpose.

In relation to the substance of social security, Rui Meneses da Costa (PD) and Armando da Silva (PL), amongst others, referred to the utility of adding in a reference to *'social assistance'* to sub-s (1). *A proposal to add this phrase passed: 49:11:23.*[50]

---

49   Other speakers in support of this perspective were Pedro Gomes (ASDT) and Januário Soares (FRETILIN).
50   The proposal was put by Rui Meneses da Costa (PD), Eusébio Guterres (PD), Mariano Sabino Lopes (PD), Elizario Ferreira (FRETILIN), and Cipriana da Costa Pereira (FRETILIN). This same amendment formed the first part of Mario Carrascalão's proposal.

António Lelan (Independent) argued that special consideration needed to be given to the provision of social security for widows. From his perspective, nothing was happening on the ground in the Districts in this regard. No specific amendment was put to the Plenary, however.

An issue of translation also arose in this context. Rui António da Cruz (FRETILIN) noted differences as between the Portuguese and Bahasa texts as to whether the right was to be enjoyed by all citizens or all persons.

In relation to sub-s (3), Mario Carrascalão (PSD) opened the debate concerning the State supervising institutions, referring specifically to the position of the (Catholic) Church. He saw some contradiction between the Constitution setting out the separation of church and State, but then including a provision stating the State would supervise church institutions. His suggestion was to either amend sub-s (3) or to delete it. Elizario Ferreira (FRETILIN) also queried the supervision aspect of the subsection, whilst Jacinta Andrade (ASDT) sought clarification of the intention of the provision. Josefa Soares (FRETILIN) thought it important for the State to support, rather than supervise, other institutions. Armando da Silva also expressed concern about sub-s (3)'s reference to NGOs, whilst conceding that some NGOs were engaged in business rather than social work. Lú Olo (FRETILIN) understood concerns raised about interference with the (Catholic) Church. However, he supported the State coordinating and supervising efforts, noting the number of NGOs working in the field. For Vicente Guterres (UDC/PDC), if the State supported organisations, it also needed to supervise those organisations. In the future, the State would need to prepare a law to facilitate the functioning of non-profit organisations.

Mario Carrascalão (PSD) put forward a proposal to:

1. Add in language concerning social assistance. (There was no separate vote on this, because it had already passed in an earlier amendment.)

2. Eliminate 'in accordance with its national resources'. This proposal was rejected in a vote of 32:34:17.

3. Eliminate the reference to supervising institutions in sub-s (3). This proposal was also rejected in a vote of 19:44:20.[51]

Voting on the section during the plenary session

The section passed: 74:1:8.

---

51 The proposal was supported also by Armindina Gusmão (PSD), Leandro Isac (PSD) and Lucia Lobato (PSD).

Version finalised prior to the public consultation process

Section 56
(Social security and assistance)

1. *Every citizen is entitled to social assistance and security in accordance with the law.*

2. *The State shall promote, in accordance with its national resources, the establishment of a social security system.*

3. *The State shall support and supervise the activity and functioning of institutions of social solidarity and other non-profit institutions of recognised public interest, in accordance with the law.*

(Identical to final)

Commentary: In this text, the right to social assistance and security was narrowed to 'every citizen'. The terms of sub-s (2) were also modified slightly (from '*deve promover*' to '*promove*'), though the official English translation retains the form 'shall promote'. No explanation was provided for these changes.

Representations and submissions

District consultations: No comments on this section appear in the summary of District consultations prepared by the Systematisation and Harmonisation Committee.

Submissions listed in the Systematisation and Harmonisation Committee's Consultations Report: None listed.

Other submissions made during the process: Yayasan HAK suggested narrowing the reference to non-profit institutions by substituting the phrase 'non profit institutions which provide social services' for 'non profit institutions of recognised public interest'.[52] The International Commission of Jurists queried the extent to which sub-s (1) gave rise to real protection, and considered that the sub-s (2) should refer to a State obligation to establish a system of social security.[53]

---

52 Yayasan HAK, 'Draft Proposals for the Constitution of East Timor', received by the Assembly on 15 March 2002, 11 [Bahasa Indonesian].
53 International Commission of Jurists (Australian Section), 'Commentary on the Draft Constitution Proposed for East Timor by the Constituent Assembly', undated, 11.

Section 57
(Health)

1. Everyone has the right to health and medical care, and the duty to protect and promote them.

2. The State shall promote the establishment of a national health service that is universal and general. The national health service shall be free of charge in accordance with the possibilities of the State and in conformity with the law.

3. The national health service shall have, as much as possible, a decentralised [and] participatory management.

(Official translation of the final text)

Drafting history

Thematic Committee I text

Section 48
(Health)

1. *The State shall recognise the right of every citizen to health and medical care.*[54]

2. *The State shall promote the establishment of a national health service that tends to be universal, general and free of charge.*

3. *The national health service shall be, as much as possible, decentralised and participatory.*

Commentary: This provision was based on art 48 of the FRETILIN Project.

There was a proposal advanced by the Bench (the office holders) to eliminate the expression 'as much as possible' in sub-s (3), but this was rejected in a vote of 6:10:3.

---

54 The Portuguese phrasing was '*saúde e à assistência médica e sanitária*', which can be literally translated as 'health and medical and health assistance'. This text remained consistent to the final Constitution and was translated by the Assembly as 'health and medical care'. For the purpose of consistency with this translation, this terminology has been used here. The Portuguese text '*o Estado reconhece*' could also be translated as 'the State recognises'. However, in keeping with the translation favoured by the Assembly in this and other clauses, the formulation of 'the State shall recognise' has been maintained.

KOTA suggested another subsection based on art 49 (3) of their Project, stating: 'The State is responsible to ensure the right to the protection of health, ensuring access for all citizens to preventive medical care, curative and rehabilitative medicine.' This was also rejected in a vote of 5:7:7.

The section was adopted in a vote of 17:0:3.

Systematisation and Harmonisation Committee draft text used in the plenary debate

Section 55
(Health)

1. *The State shall recognise the right of every citizen to health and medical care.*[55]

2. *The State shall promote the establishment of a national health service that tends to be universal, general and free of charge.*

3. *The national health service shall have, as much as possible, a decentralised and participatory management.*

Commentary: In this version, the term 'management' ('*gestão*') was added into sub-s (3), without explanation, but seemingly to make the intended meaning clearer.

Plenary debate (21 December 2001)

The extent to which health services would be provided free of charge was a particular topic of debate in the plenary session, though the discussion also encompassed practical issues in the delivery of healthcare, traditional medicine and preventive medicine. Several amendments to the section were suggested, though ultimately none were adopted.

Some speakers supported deleting the phrasing 'tends to be' free from sub-s (2) on the basis that the health system should be free of charge. Clementino Amaral (KOTA) was the first to speak against this phrase, making reference to the Minister of Health's advocacy of a free health service. Lucia Lobato (PSD) argued that it if was intended that a general health service be free, this should be stated without qualification. Rui Meneses da Costa (PD) feared that sub-s (2) as drafted was lacking in meaning, asking whether it was just rhetoric. A word of caution was sounded by Armando da Silva (PL), who considered that since the country was just being built, some care needed to be taken in considering a free health

---

55   The English Assembly text incorrectly referred to 'everyone' in sub-s (1), rather than reflecting the Portuguese text's reference to citizen ('*cidadão*').

system for all. He strongly supported, however, a free system for the poor. Mari Alkatiri (FRETILIN) recognised that everyone wanted a free health service and that this was part of the dream of fighting for independence. However, this was a goal which needed to be worked towards. It was not desired that poor people pay for healthcare. Nonetheless, Parliament needed to work out who should receive services for free and who paid, otherwise there would be no criteria for free services. Having such criteria was supported by Jacob Xavier (PPT).[56] Mario Carrascalão (PSD) considered that the text should at least be consistent with the phraseology used in previous sections: using 'in accordance with national resources', rather than 'tends to' be free.

Others, including João Carrascalão (UDT) and Aquilino Guterres (PD), wished to strengthen the statement of State responsibility, so that the State not only recognise the right to health, but be obliged to promote it.

During the debate, particular concern was evinced for those living in remote areas. Constância de Jesus (FRETILIN), for instance, spoke of the need to have a system whereby nurses could reach remote places, such as through mobile clinics. She noted the difficulties posed at present due to the lack of transport to access health services. Francisco Branco (FRETILIN) expressed agreement with the decentralised system mentioned in sub-s (3). Madelena da Silva (FRETILIN) raised the utility of a clause dealing with traditional medicine, but did not put forward a specific clause.

Proposals

Clementino Amaral (KOTA), Manuel Tilman (KOTA), Quitéria da Costa (UDT), Pedro da Costa (PST) and Jacob Xavier (PPT) advanced the proposal to remove 'tends to be' from sub-s (1). This was rejected in a vote of 18:41:23.

Mariano Sabino Lopes (PD), Eusébio Guterres (PD), Paulo Alves Sarmento (PD) and Rui Meneses da Costa (PD) put forward a proposal:[57]

1. Every Timor-Leste citizen has the right to acquire [good and qualified] health assistance equally without discrimination.

2. The State has the duty to support the establishment of a national health system which is universal and free which can be enjoyed by every Timor-Leste citizen.

This was rejected in a vote of 17:34:34.

---

56 Support for the existing text was also voiced by Feliciano Fatima (ASDT), Joaquim dos Santos (FRETILIN), and António Lelan (Independent).
57 This proposal was advanced in Bahasa Indonesian, though the presiding Vice-Chair also read it out in Tetum.

João Carrascalão (UDT),[58] Quitéria da Costa (UDT), Pedro da Costa (PST) and Jacinta de Andrade (ASDT) suggested an alternative provision:

1. Everyone shall possess the right to health protection and the duty to defend and promote health.

2. The State has the competency to realise health by taking measures:

   (a) By means of a national health service that shall be universal and general and, with particular regard to the economic and social conditions of the citizens who use it, shall tend to be free of charge;

   (b) By creating economic, social, cultural and environmental conditions that particularly guarantee the protection of childhood, youth and old age; by systematically improving living and working conditions and also promoting physical fitness and sport at school and among the people; and by developing both the people's health and hygiene education and healthy living practices.

3. In order to ensure enjoyment of the right to the protection of health, the State shall be under a primary duty:

   (a) To guarantee access by every citizen, regardless of his economic situation, to preventive, curative and rehabilitative medical care;

   (b) To guarantee a rational and efficient nationwide coverage in terms of healthcare units and human resources;

   (c) To work towards the public funding of the costs of medical care and medicines;

   (d) To regulate and inspect corporate and private forms of medicine and articulate them with the national health service, in such a way as to ensure adequate standards of efficiency and quality in both public and private healthcare institutions;

   (e) To regulate and control the production, distribution, marketing, sale and use of chemical, biological and pharmaceutical products and other means of treatment and diagnosis;

   (f) To establish policies on the prevention and treatment of drug abuse.

---

58 During the debate, João Carrascalão noted the inconsistency between the draft text of this section and other sections in so far as other sections were phrased 'everyone has the right' whereas this section commenced with 'the State shall recognise'.

4. The national health system shall possess a decentralised and participatory management system.[59]

This was rejected in a vote of 20:41:21.

Two proposals were put forward by António Ximenes (PDC), Armando da Silva (PL), Jacob Xavier (PPT) and Ananias Fuka (PPT). The first was to state (in sub-s (2)): 'The State shall promote a national, universal general health system which is free for those who have no capacity.'[60] This was rejected in a vote of 30:28:27.

The second proposal was to include wording that: 'The State implements the right of citizens for health and medical assistance.' This was also rejected by a clear majority vote of 14:48:23.

Some frustration was evinced by Mari Alkatiri (FRETILIN) at the number of amendments put forward. After the vote, Alkatiri queried why the proposals were being put forward at this point, given that the Assembly had spent two months debating the topics.

Voting on the section during the plenary session

The section passed: 69:7:9.

Version finalised prior to the public consultation process

Section 57
(Health)

1. *The State shall recognise the right of every citizen to health and medical care.*

2. *The State shall promote the establishment of a national health service that is universal and general. The national health service shall be free of charge in accordance with the possibilities of the State and in conformity with the law.*

3. *The national health service shall have, as much as possible, a decentralised and participatory management.*[61]

Commentary: This text included some further amendments: in particular, sub-s (2) was amended to substitute the stronger language that the national health service 'shall be free of charge in accordance with the possibilities of the State

---

59 The proposal as read out was identical to art 64 of the Portuguese Constitution, except for the opening words of sub-s (2) of the proposal. The English translation of the Portuguese Constitution has thus been used here as applicable.

60 The amendment was read out in Bahasa Indonesian and later in Tetum.

61 Note that sub-s (2) was written as one sentence in Portuguese, but has been presented in the format used for the official translation of the final version.

and in conformity with the law.'[62] No explanation was provided, but it appears to have been an attempt to respond to concerns voiced during the plenary session, and may have been justified on the basis of making the language of the Constitution consistent.

Representations and submissions

District consultations: Several District consultations raised comments about this section. In Dili, a suggestion was made to include provision concerning traditional medicine (without specifying the shape of the provision). The summary of the Ermera and Viqueque consultations included recommendations that a clause be included banning the use of drugs; while in Liquiça, support was evinced for a duty on each citizen to ensure their health.

Submissions listed in the Systematisation and Harmonisation Committee's Consultations Report: The Minister of Health, Dr Rui Araújo, in a letter submitted during the formal consultation period, noted the number of inquiries he received about citizens' free access to the health system, highlighting the need to 'develop a clear, firm and cohesive political standard for the community, based on clauses set out in the Constitution'. He requested the Constituent Assembly to provide additional clarification of sub-s (2), especially in relation to its reference that the health service be 'according to its possibilities, free of charge under the law'.[63]

Other submissions made during the process: The most active interlocutor with the Assembly in relation to this section was the then Minister for Health, Dr Rui Araújo, who emphasised the need for a free, accessible health system. Early in the process, Dr Araújo submitted draft clauses on the rights and duties of the citizens in relation to health. After a preliminary statement emphasising the right to protection of health and the duty of each citizen to promote and defend his/her health, the proposal continued:

2. The right to protection shall be realized through

   a. A national health service that is universally accessible and free of charge, taking into account the economic and social conditions of the citizens [who use it];

   b. The creation of economic, social, cultural and environmental conditions that guarantee the protection of citizens and

---

62 The Portuguese text of this version (and the final Constitution) referred simply to 'its possibilities' rather than 'possibilities of the State'. The official translation of the final text does include these words, presumably to assist in the understanding of the clause.

63 Letter from the Minister for Health, Dr Rui Araújo, to the President of the Constituent Assembly, 26 February 2002.

the systematic improvement of their living and working conditions, and for the development of both the people's health and hygiene education and healthy living practices.

3. The right to health protection shall be guaranteed by the State having the duty to:

    a. Guarantee access by every citizen to preventive, curative and rehabilitative medical care.

    b. Guarantee a rational and efficient nationwide coverage in terms of healthcare units and human resources.

    c. Work towards the public funding of the costs of medical care and medicines.

    d. Regulate and inspect corporate and private forms of medicine and articulate them with the national health service, in such a way as to ensure adequate standards of efficiency and quality in both public and private healthcare institutions.

    e. Establish policies with an emphasis on primary healthcare especially maternal and infant health.

4. The national health service shall possess a decentralised and participatory management system and shall be guided by the principles of equity, access, efficiency and sustainability.[64]

Both this proposal and João Carrascalão (UDT)'s proposal drew heavily from art 64 of the Portuguese Constitution, though Dr Araújo's text had additional amendments emphasising the need for healthcare to be accessible and equitable.

Yayasan HAK proposed that the right be reframed in terms of an inalienable right, namely that '[e]very citizen has the right to health and medical care'. It also suggested amending the qualification in sub-s (2) to read 'in accordance with the fullest capabilities of the State'.[65] In an earlier submission HAK had suggested also that the State promote the creation of a national health service

---

64 Letter from the Minister for Health, Dr Rui Araújo, to the President of the Constituent Assembly, 29 October 2001 [Portuguese]. Again many elements of this amendment were similar to art 64 of the Portuguese Constitution, and thus its English translation has been used and adapted here.
65 Yayasan HAK, 'Draft Proposals for the Constitution of East Timor', received by the Assembly on 15 March 2002, 11 [Bahasa Indonesian]. At the point at which the text used language of 'tends to be ...', the International Commission of Jurists expressed concern that this rendered any protection nugatory:'Commentary on the Draft Constitution Proposed for East Timor by the Constituent Assembly', undated, 11.

which was available to all and free of charge, and further that the State provide adequate conditions for everyone to have access to sufficient food, water and sanitation.[66]

REDE Feto Timor Lorosae recommended adding a guarantee of reproductive health for women in sub-s (1).[67]

Whilst not specifically referring to the right to health, the SRSG noted that international human rights law provides for the application of human rights to all persons, with distinctions between citizens and non-citizens being made only in relation to political rights and certain economic rights. He thus recommended a review of the rights within the Bill of Rights to accord with this premise.[68]

Post-consultation plenary debate

The Systematisation and Harmonisation Committee recommended altering sub-s (1) to read: '*Everyone has the right to health and medical care and the duty to protect and promote them.*' This change was the subject of a *consensus agreement* in the post-consultation deliberations of the Assembly.

---

66 Yayasan HAK, 'Civil and Political, Economic, Social and Cultural Rights', undated, but received by the Assembly on 22 October 2001, art 36.
67 Letter from REDE Feto Timor Lorosae to the President of the Constituent Assembly, 31 October 2001. This right had also been included in art 4(2) of the Women's Charter of Rights in East Timor.
68 Comments attached to the letter from the UN SRSG and Transitional Administrator, Sergio Vieira de Mello, to heads of the political parties, 22 February 2002.

Section 58
(Housing)

Everyone has the right to a house, both for himself or herself and for his or her family, of adequate size that meets satisfactory standards of hygiene and comfort and preserves personal intimacy and family privacy.

(Official translation of the final text)

Drafting history

Thematic Committee I text

Section 48A
(Housing)

Everyone has the right to a house, both for himself or herself and for his or her family, of adequate size that meets satisfactory standards of hygiene and comfort and preserves personal intimacy and family privacy.

(Identical to final)

Commentary: This provision was based on art 74(1) of the PSD Project. It was approved in a vote of 16:1:4.

This text was adopted following the rejection of a much longer KOTA proposal based upon art 50 of their Project. The KOTA proposal would have explicitly recognised electricity and potable water as part of adequate housing, and placed obligations on the State to plan and implement housing policies and urban planning. Amongst other matters, it would have also required the State to encourage and support local communities in solving their housing problems and establishing housing cooperatives and the self-construction of houses. This formulation was, however, rejected in a vote of 5:10:1.

Systematisation and Harmonisation Committee draft text used in the plenary debate

Section 56

(Housing)

Everyone has the right to a house, both for himself or herself and for his or her family, of adequate size that meets satisfactory standards of hygiene and comfort and preserves personal intimacy and family privacy.

Plenary debate (22 December 2001)

There was no discussion on this section in the plenary session (that is, no one registered to speak on the topic), so it proceeded directly to the vote.

Voting on the section during the plenary session

The section passed 68:0:1.

Version finalised prior to the public consultation process

Section 58

(Housing)

Everyone has the right to a house, both for himself or herself and for his or her family, of adequate size that meets satisfactory standards of hygiene and comfort and preserves personal intimacy and family privacy.

Representations and submissions

District consultations: No comments on this section appear in the summary of District consultations prepared by the Systematisation and Harmonisation Committee.

Submissions listed in the Systematisation and Harmonisation Committee's Consultations Report: The Asia Foundation suggested adding a sentence to the clause in order to avoid the interpretation that the State was obliged to provide a house for everyone. Their suggested text read: 'The State shall formulate policies which respect, protect and, to the extent that its means permit, facilitate the fulfilment of this right.'[69]

---

69   The Asia Foundation, 'Comments and Suggested Amendments to East Timor's Draft Constitution of 9/2/02', undated, but attached to a cover letter to the President of the Constituent Assembly dated 8 March 2002, 5. See, too, The Asia Foundation, 'Discussion Paper on Draft of East Timorese Constitution', March 2002, 7.

Other submissions made during the process: Yayasan HAK's proposal for alternative wording mirrored the phrasing in international treaties by stipulating: 'Everyone has the right to have access to adequate housing.'[70] The International Commission of Jurists queried inclusion of this clause in the Constitution.[71]

---

70   Article 34 in the Bill of Rights included in Yayasan HAK, 'Civil and Political, Economic, Social and Cultural Rights', undated, but received by the Assembly on 22 October 2001, art 34.
71   International Commission of Jurists (Australian Section), 'Commentary on the Draft Constitution Proposed for East Timor by the Constituent Assembly', undated, 11.

Section 59
(Education and culture)

1. The State shall recognise and guarantee that every citizen has the right to education and culture, and it is incumbent upon it to promote the establishment of a public system of universal and compulsory basic education that is free of charge in accordance with its ability and in conformity with the law.[72]

2. Everyone has the right to equal opportunities for education and vocational training.

3. The State shall recognise and supervise private and co-operative education.

4. The State should ensure the access of every citizen, in accordance to their abilities, to the highest levels of education, scientific research and artistic creativity.

5. Everyone has the right to cultural enjoyment and creativity and the duty to preserve, protect and value cultural heritage.

(Official translation of the final text)

Drafting history

Thematic Committee I text

Section 49
(Education and culture)

1. *The State shall recognise that every citizen has the right to education and culture, and it is incumbent upon it to promote the establishment of a public system of universal and compulsory basic education that tends to be free of charge.*

2. *Everyone has the right to equal opportunities for education and vocational training.*

3. *Private and cooperative education shall be supervised by the State.*

---

72 The contemporary Assembly English translation used the phrase 'in accordance with its possibilities', whereas the official translation used the phrase 'in accordance with its ability'. The Portuguese phrase was 'na medida das suas possibilidades'.

4. *Public education shall be secular.*

5. *The State should ensure the access of every citizen, in accordance to their abilities, to the highest levels of education, scientific research and artistic creativity.*

6. *Everyone has the right to cultural enjoyment and creativity and the duty to preserve, protect and value cultural heritage.*

Commentary: This provision was based on art 49 of the FRETILIN Project with three subsections added.

Subsection (2) came from art 81(1) of the PSD proposal. It was approved unanimously in a vote of 18:0:0.

Subsection (5) derived from art 41(3) of KOTA's Project. It was also approved unanimously in a vote of 21:0:0.

Subsection (6) was based on art 82 (1) of the PSD Project. It was approved in a vote of 9:3:7. Alternative formulations covering enjoyment of culture were considered (including one making specific reference to the ancestral traditions of the Timorese people) but not voted upon.

Prior to the adoption of sub-s (5), the section as a whole was approved in a vote of 19:0:1.

Systematisation and Harmonisation Committee draft text used in the plenary debate

Section 57
(Education and culture)

1. *The State shall recognise[73] that every citizen has the right to education and culture, and it is incumbent upon it to promote the establishment of a public system of universal and compulsory basic education that tends to be free of charge.[74]*

2. *Everyone has the right to equal opportunities for education and vocational training.*

3. *Private and cooperative education shall be supervised by the State.*

---

73 The Assembly English translation used the phrase 'The State recognises', which appears literally correct for the Portuguese phrase '*O Estado reconhece*'. However, the phrase 'The State shall recognise' has been preferred given its usage in the official translation of the final text.

74 The Assembly English translation incorrectly translated the initial phrase as 'everyone', whereas the Portuguese version restricted the right to citizens ('*cidadão*'). It also presented the qualifying phrase 'tends to be' as applying to the requirement of compulsory education in sub-s (1). The translation here has been streamlined according to the translation of the final text.

4. *Public education shall be secular [non-denominational].*[75]

5. *The State should ensure the access of every citizen, in accordance to their abilities, to the highest levels of education, scientific research and artistic creativity.*

6. *Everyone has the right to cultural enjoyment and creativity and the duty to preserve, protect and value cultural heritage.*

Commentary: One change was made in the Portuguese text which was not picked up in the English translation: the language of sub-s (1) was made more direct in referring to it being incumbent upon the State to 'establish' the public education system, rather than 'promote its establishment'. This more direct obligation was retained until the final text of the Constitution. However, the official English translation still included the phrase 'promote the establishment of', and it has thus been reproduced here.

Plenary debate (22 December 2001)

As with social security and health, one of the key issues with respect to education was debating in what circumstances education should be free. The draft before the Plenary spoke of a public system of universal basic education that 'tends to be compulsory and free of charge'. Clementino Amaral (KOTA) encouraged deletion of the language 'tends to be' free, referring to the situation of people, especially in rural areas, who needed access to education but lacked money. Others speaking in support of eliminating this language included Vicente Guterres (UDC/PDC), Mario Carrascalão (PSD), Armando Da Silva (PL), Jacob Xavier (PPT), Leandro Isac (PSD), and Pedro da Costa (PST). Francisco Xavier do Amaral (ASDT) recalled that the aim of supporting free basic education had been consistent since 1975 and that the State needed to find a way to provide this. Rosário Corte Real (FRETILIN) similarly wished to see a system where school was free for those who couldn't afford to pay, whilst those who could should be asked to pay. Joaquim dos Santos (FRETILIN) queried whether private schools should be free, and observing more generally that sometimes when people were asked to pay, it created an incentive for their study. Other speakers displayed particular consciousness of resource limitations facing the State. Adaljiza Magno (FRETILIN), for instance, agreed with guaranteeing access to education, whilst also recognising that thought needed to be given to the State budget. José Lobato (FRETILIN) also made reference to the State's financial difficulties, favouring retention of the language of 'tends to be' free.

José Lobato (FRETILIN) also highlighted the need to address cultural issues with respect to education. In some cases people had money for *lisan* (adat or

---

75 The Assembly English translation used the term 'secular'. However, it would be more consistent with translations used elsewhere in the text (for example, s 12) to use the term 'non-denominational'.

custom), but at the same time did not have money for sending their children to school. Or there were children not going to school because their parents had them working. These issues needed to be addressed. Francisco Xavier do Amaral (ASDT) also recognised family responsibilities in this field. He suggested parents who failed to send their children to school might be subject to punishment.

Extending assistance beyond basic education was raised. Francisco Xavier do Amaral (ASDT), for instance, supported providing assistance for bright children to attend high school. Recalling the deprivations in the past (including during Portuguese colonial rule), Amaral gave the example of Turiscai: in 450 years, only two young people had gone to high school. Mariano Sabino Lopes (PD) also spoke in support of State assistance for secondary schools, suggesting that if possible, secondary school should be free, especially in the Districts. Lopes also stressed that education should be linked with places where the students could gain work skills. António Ximenes (PDC) wished to see State assistance for children at least up to the age of 12 years. By 12 years of age, they were assumed to be more independent. According to Ximenes, if children had only basic education, they would not have the capacity for employment upon graduation.

Mario Carrascalão (PSD) emphasised the State's duty to institute measures to create and guarantee access to education. In his view, recognition of a right to education alone was insufficient. Aquilino Guterres (PD) argued that the government needed to think about how to enable access to education by children from rural areas, and the families of Resistance personnel.

Subsection (3)'s reference to the State inspecting private and cooperative education and (original) sub-s (4)'s reference to education being secular/ non-denominational also prompted specific comment. Armando da Silva (PL) expressed doubt as to the concept of the State supervising private/cooperative education. He feared that people might become confused and think that the Assembly was anti-religion (presumably since the provision would impact on Catholic schools in particular). He also queried where there was to be inclusion of the State's policy on literacy and its policy on educating those with disabilities: in this section, or through having another section on these topics?

José Reis (FRETILIN) thought sub-s (3) should be amended so as to refer to the State 'recognising and supervising' private and cooperative education (agreed by Manuel Tilman (KOTA), Pedro da Costa (PST), Mariano Sabino Lopes (PD), and Rui Meneses da Costa (PD)). He suggested eliminating sub-s (4), and was supported in this by Joaquim dos Santos (FRETILIN). António Ximenes (PDC) expressed the concern that if there were no morals taught, the nation would collapse. Manuel Tilman (KOTA) considered that the two subjects of State schools and private schools based on religion should not be mixed in the Constitution.

Quitéria da Costa (UDT) suggested a new subsection dealing with copyright. Her proposal stated that the State had to guarantee and protect copyright, which would be regulated by law. This was supported by Amando da Silva (PL), and José Lobato (FRETILIN), though Lobato favoured it as a separate economic right, rather than as an aspect of the right to education. Rui Meneses da Costa (PD) thought copyright was already covered in sub-s (6), but other speakers disagreed. Whilst failing to garner sufficient support on this occasion, the subject of copyright was resurrected during debates on Part IV of the Constitution (see discussion of s 60).

Proposals

Two proposals which were passed were advanced by José Reis (FRETILIN), Adaljiza Magno (FRETILIN), Armando da Silva (PL), and Joaquim Barros (FRETILIN). The first was to amend sub-s (3) to read: '*The State shall recognise and supervise private and cooperative education*'. *This was accepted in a vote of 70:0:5.* The second proposal was to *eliminate sub-s (4) requiring public education to be secular. It also passed in a vote of 68:4:4.*

There were a range of other proposals which were unsuccessful. The first (whose proponents were not captured in the recording accessed by the author) was to eliminate the phrasing 'tends to be' free from sub-s (1) and instead substituting an obligation on the State to guarantee free basic education. It failed in a vote of 33:29:13.

António Ximenes (PDC), together with Armando da Silva (PL), Ananias Fuka (PPT), and Jacob Xavier (PPT) made a proposal whose phrasing was not entirely clear.[76] It focused on the State providing compulsory schooling for children up to 12 years of age. It failed in a vote of 16:45:15.

Quitéria Da Costa (UDT), Clementino Amaral (KOTA), Manuel Tilman (KOTA) and Pedro da Costa (PST) sought inclusion of a subsection by which the State would guarantee and protect the copyright of every citizens according to the law. It failed in a vote of 14:16:46.

Mariano Sabino Lopes (PD), Eusébio Guterres (PD), Aquilina Guterres (PD), and Paulo Alves Sarmento (PD) put forward the final proposed amendment. It concerned a new sub-s (7) by which the State would 'recognise and guarantee the right to education and culture for every citizen' and be obliged 'to promote basic primary and secondary education which is compulsory, free and just/fair for everyone in Timor Lorosae'.[77] It failed in a vote of 29:20:27.

---

76 The proposal was read out in Bahasa, with the Vice-President providing an informal translation into Tetum. However, some comment about the form of the amendment was made during discussion.

77 This proposal was read out in Bahasa Indonesian during the plenary session.

Voting on the section during the plenary session

The section passed 61:3:11.

Version finalised prior to the public consultation process

Section 59
(Education and culture)

1. *The State shall recognise and guarantee that every citizen has the right to education and culture, and it is incumbent upon it to promote the establishment of a public system of universal and compulsory basic education that is free of charge in accordance with its ability and in conformity with the law.*

2. *Everyone has the right to equal opportunities for education and vocational training.*

3. *The State shall recognise and supervise private and co-operative education.*

4. *The State should ensure the access of every citizen, in accordance to their abilities, to the highest levels of education, scientific research and artistic creativity.*

5. *Everyone has the right to cultural enjoyment and creativity and the duty to preserve, protect and value cultural heritage.*

(Identical to final)

Commentary: In this text, the form of sub-s (1) was changed. The obligation on the State was extended to guaranteeing (as well as recognising) the rights to education and culture. In place of the reference to education tending to be free was phrasing obliging the State to promote basic education that was free of charge 'in accordance with its ability and in conformity with the law'. No explanation was provided for the change, though it may well have been a response to the concerns agitated during the plenary session. A similar change was made to the right to health provision.

Representations and submissions

District consultations: Several District consultation summary reports included references to this section. In Dili, the suggestion was made to remove the limitation of 'in accordance with its ability' in relation to the State's provision of free basic education. In Oecusse, it was said that education must be free, from the SD level (primary school) to SMP (middle high school).[78] In Los Palos, objection was taken to the State conducting audits of private and cooperative education. The preferred language was that the State would recognise and protect such institutions. In relation to cultural rights, in Baucau, a proposal was made to add the statement 'that the State values, recognizes and promotes ritual and cultural activities in accordance with the law'. Another suggestion arising in Baucau was to have a defined limit on *barlaque* (bride price), with the inclusion of the recommendation against this section apparently linked to the section's dealing with cultural matters.

Submissions listed in the Systematisation and Harmonisation Committee's Consultations Report: None listed.

Other submissions made during the process: The majority of submissions concerning this section focused on the extent to which education would be freely available. Yayasan HAK suggested that the section should state that each citizen had the right to education, and that the State should be obliged to use its 'fullest' abilities in implementing the education system.[79] The joint Catholic/ Protestant submission from the Church-Constitution Working Group favoured stipulating that the public system of universal basic education should *be* free and compulsory for all children.[80]

REDE Feto Timor Lorosae advocated that the State 'should guarantee equal access to formal and non-formal education for men and women, adults and children'.[81] This wording was drawn from the Women's Charter of Rights in East Timor. The Charter specifically mandated women to have equal access to scholarship opportunities. It also contained a guarantee of equal access for women and men to programs designed to eradicate illiteracy.

The East Timor Study Group recommended clarifying the extent of free education. It favoured the State providing free education for primary education, and supporting the development of education at different levels.[82] The Group also noted that any reference to supervising private education should not allow intervention in private institutions.[83]

---

78   In the Indonesian education system, *Sekolah Dasar* (SD) is the primary school level of education (generally catering to ages 6–11 years of age), and *Sekolah Menengah Pertama* (SMP) is the middle school level, or lower secondary, which generally caters for children 12–14 years of age.

79   Yayasan HAK, 'Draft Proposals for the Constitution of East Timor', received by the Assembly on 15 March 2002, 12 [Bahasa Indonesian].

80   Letter from the Centre for Peace and Development to the President of the Constituent Assembly, January 2002, received by the Assembly on 23 January 2002. This letter contained the submission of the Church-Constitution Working Group.

81   Letter from REDE Feto Timor Lorosae to the President of the Constituent Assembly, 31 October 2001.

82   East Timor Study Group, 'Debate on the Draft Constitution: Positive and Negative Implications for the Future of East Timor', 20 February 2002, 11 [Tetum].

83   Ibid.

The International Commission of Jurists considered that sub-s (2) should be qualified to take into account the ability of each adult and child, whilst also suggesting that the Catholic education system should be explicitly recognised alongside the public education system.[84]

In the context of discussions of children's rights, the Working Group on Child Rights for East Timor's Constitution supported recognition of the right to free primary education and access to secondary education and training for all children, regardless of citizenship. Support for their draft clause was also forthcoming from the Human Rights Unit of UNTAET.[85] Whilst not specifically addressing the right to education, the SRSG noted that under international human rights law, human rights were applicable to all persons, with distinctions made only in relation to political rights and certain economic rights.[86]

---

84 International Commission of Jurists (Australian Section), 'Commentary on the Draft Constitution Proposed for East Timor by the Constituent Assembly', undated, 11. The ICJ also suggested substituting language of 'intends to be' for 'tends to be'.

85 For details of the clause from the Working Group and support from the Human Rights Unit of UNTAET, see the discussion under 'Section 18' above.

86 Comments attached to the letter from the UN SRSG and Transitional Administrator, Sergio Vieira de Mello, to heads of the political parties, 22 February 2002.

Section 60
(Intellectual property)

The State shall guarantee and protect the creation, production and commercialisation of literary, scientific and artistic work, including the legal protection of copyrights.

(Official translation of the final text)

Drafting history

Thematic Committee I text

There was no equivalent in the text of Thematic Committee I.

Systematisation and Harmonisation Committee draft text used in the plenary debate

There was no equivalent provision in the draft text produced by the Systematisation and Harmonisation Committee. The subject of copyright was raised by Quitéria da Costa (UDT) during debates on s 59 of the Constitution, but was not at that point accepted. This section was proposed for inclusion by Armando da Silva (PL) during the debates on Part IV of the Constitution (Economic and Financial Organisation) on 18 January 2002. It was later moved to the Bill of Rights part of the Constitution.

Plenary debate (18 January 2002)

Most speakers referred favourably to this section – seeing that it would protect the rights of, for instance, artists, musicians, scientists and writers.[87] The question arose as to whether the section would safeguard both individual and communal rights. Adérito de Jesus Soares (FRETILIN) expressed some hesitation over the scope of the section, stressing that it was important to protect not only the rights of individuals, but also the rights of the community. In some countries, the rights of indigenous peoples, for instance, were not properly respected. He did not want the situation where the Constitution permitted the appropriation of communal rights by an individual. Certain dances and music originated from particular communities and their collective rights should also be protected. Adaljiza Magno (FRETILIN), speaking in favour of the provision,

---

87 Those speaking in favour included Jacob Xavier (PPT), António Ximenes (PDC), Mari Alkatiri (FRETILIN) and Manuel Tilman (KOTA).

considered that traditional culture was addressed in s 57 (what became s 59) of the Constitution – a provision which dealt with the State promoting, protecting and valuing cultural heritage. Jacob Xavier (PPT) distinguished between the rights of the community over a particular dance (for example, the *tebe-tebe*), and the rights of the individual who recorded the dance. Mari Alkatiri (FRETILIN) considered the section would protect not just individuals, but also traditions and communal property. However, if in the future there was a need, there could be further legislation on this point. Rui Meneses (PD) raised the need to cover foreigners who were inventors, as well as citizens. He also queried how the State would apply the protection to products going outside its borders. Adaljiza Magno (FRETILIN) and Manuel Tilman (KOTA) queried the appropriate placement of this section, with Magno suggesting it was more appropriate to place it with economic, social and cultural rights, rather than in Part IV of the Constitution. Mari Alkatiri (FRETILIN) proposed that the Systematisation and Harmonisation Committee decide on the placement of the section, if it was approved. Voting for the section proceeded on this basis.

Voting on the section during the plenary session

The new section was adopted in a vote of 76:0:1.

Version finalised prior to the public consultation process

Section 60
(Intellectual property)

The State shall guarantee and protect the creation, production and commercialisation of literary, scientific and artistic work, including the legal protection of copyrights.

(Identical to final)

Representations and submissions

District consultations: No comments on this section appear in the summary of District Consultations prepared by the Systematisation and Harmonisation Committee.

Submissions listed in the Systematisation and Harmonisation Committee's Consultations Report: None listed.

Other submissions made during the process: The Haburas Foundation proposed that the section protect 'communal intellectual rights' in addition to intellectual copyright. The examples given were of the production of *tua sabu* (traditional alcohol) or *banin ben* (honey) in the Beheda-Ilimanuk community. Protection of the communal rights was necessary, otherwise individuals or businesses could carry out research for their own patenting of such rights.[88]

Yayasan HAK suggested the addition of another subsection: 'The State shall recognise and guarantee collective community ownership of traditional East Timorese works and promote the development of production and creativity.'[89]

An earlier HAK submission had recommended a broader formulation to recognise the individual's right to freedom of artistic, literary, technical and scientific creation, and for the State to protect the right to intellectual property.[90]

The Asia Foundation suggested patents might be mentioned as well as copyright.[91]

---

88 Haburas Foundation, 'Comments and Recommendations on the Draft Constitution of the Democratic Republic of Timor-Leste', 4 March 2002 [Bahasa Indonesian].
89 Yayasan HAK, 'Draft Proposals for the Constitution of East Timor', received by the Assembly on 15 March 2002, 12 [Bahasa Indonesian].
90 Draft Bill of Rights included in Yayasan HAK, 'Civil and Political, Economic, Social and Cultural Rights', undated, received by the Assembly on 22 October 2001, art 25.
91 The Asia Foundation, 'Discussion Paper on Draft of East Timorese Constitution', March 2002, 7.

Section 61
(Environment)

1. Everyone has the right to a humane, healthy, and ecologically balanced environment and the duty to protect it and improve it for the benefit of the future generations.

2. The State shall recognise the need to preserve and rationalise natural resources.

3. The State should promote actions aimed at protecting the environment and safeguarding the sustainable development of the economy.

(Official translation of the final text)

Drafting history

Thematic Committee I text

Section 50
(Environment)

1. *Everyone has the right to a humane, healthy, and ecologically balanced environment and the duty to protect it and improve it for the benefit of the future generations.*

2. *The State shall recognise the need to preserve and rationalise natural resources.*

3. *The State should promote, in accordance with its capacities, actions aimed at protecting Nature, [and] safeguarding the sustainable development of the economy.*[92]

Commentary: This provision was based in part upon art 50 of the FRETILIN Project with additions from an NGO's suggestions.

Subsection (1) was based on Haburas Foundation's proposal and was approved unanimously in a vote of 20:0:0.[93]

---

92   The Portuguese text referred to '*acções de defesa da Natureza*', which could be translated as 'actions to protect nature'. However, given the final translation of the Constitution, the phrase 'actions aimed at protecting nature' has been adopted here.

93   This was the only NGO submission directly referenced in the report of the thematic committee.

There was a slight variation between the FRETILIN Project version and the adopted version of sub-s (2), with the addition of the adjective 'natural' before resources. The Bench also suggested removing 'in accordance with its capacities' in sub-s (2), but this was rejected: 4:12:4.

The section as whole was adopted in a vote of 18:0:2.

Systematisation and Harmonisation Committee draft text used in the plenary debate

Section 58

(Environment)

1. *Everyone has the right to a humane, healthy, and ecologically balanced environment and the duty to protect it and improve it for the benefit of the future generations.*[94]

2. *The State shall recognise the need to preserve and rationalise natural resources.*

3. *The State should promote, in accordance with its capacities, actions aimed at protecting Nature, [and] safeguarding the sustainable development of the economy.*[95]

Plenary debate (22 December 2001)

The Systematisation and Harmonisation Committee suggested that sub-s (2) be amended to add a reference to the State needing to take 'appropriate measures' for preserving and rationalising natural resources.[96] According to Manuel Tilman (KOTA), the intention was for the State to be obliged not merely to recognise the necessity for conservation, but to actually take steps to implement and protect natural resources. Agreement was expressed by Clementino Amaral (KOTA) and Jacob Xavier (PPT), whilst Cipriana da Costa Perreira (FRETILIN) and Lú Olo (FRETILIN) thought this matter could be satisfactorily addressed in later legislation. Lú Olo noted that there would be a special department to take such measures. Lú Olo underlined the importance of this section for the future of Timor, noting that the environment had become depleted with the concentration of people in areas and the limitations on people's ability to

---

94 The English Assembly translation omitted the reference to 'humane' environment contained in the Portuguese text.

95 The English Assembly translation of this text translated *'natureza'* as 'environment', but it would seem more appropriate to refer to 'nature'. The term for environment was only introduced in sub-s (3) after the plenary debate.

96 This had been a suggestion of Mario Carrascaláo (PSD) during deliberations of the Systematisation and Harmonisation Committee: author's observation, 27 November 2001.

move around during Indonesian times. People had destroyed the environment, chopping down trees and the forests. Thought needed to be given to the future of the environment for Timor's future life.

Eusébio Guterres (PD) suggested eliminating the limiting phrase 'in accordance with its capacities' in sub-s (3), so that the obligation to promote and to protect nature would be expressed without qualification.[97] Lú Olo (FRETILIN), however, thought there was no need to delete the phrase, since the State could only take measures according to its capacity. No specific amendment was put in relation to this point.

Several speakers, including Mariano Sabino Lopes (PD), referred to the protection of the environment being not simply a matter for the State but also for citizens. Rui Meneses da Costa (PD) gave a practical example, noting that whilst people could chop trees, they had to be encouraged to replant them.

Only one proposal was put forward, that advanced by the Systematisation and Harmonisation Committee – to add a reference to the State needing to take 'appropriate measures' for preserving and rationalising natural resources. This proposal failed in a vote of 21:42:12.

Voting on the section during the plenary session

Vote for the section as a whole: 73:0:2.

Version finalised prior to the public consultation process

Section 61

(Environment)

1. *Everyone has the right to a humane, healthy, and ecologically balanced environment and the duty to protect it and improve it for the benefit of the future generations.*

2. *The State shall recognise the need to preserve and rationalise natural resources.*

3. *The State should promote, in accordance with its capacities, actions aimed at protecting the environment and safeguarding the sustainable development of the economy.*

Commentary: This text substituted the term 'environment and', instead of 'nature' in sub-s (3), but otherwise the text remained identical.

---

97   Agreed by Quitéria da Costa (UDT) and Rui Meneses da Costa (PD).

Representations and submissions

District consultations: No comments on this section appear in the summary of District Consultations prepared by the Systematisation and Harmonisation Committee.

Submissions listed in the Systematisation and Harmonisation Committee's Consultations Report: None listed.

Other submissions made during the process: Prior to the Assembly's deliberations, the National Planning and Development Agency of the East Timor Transitional Administration circulated a discussion paper on 'The Environment and the Constitution in East Timor' (September 2001). While not putting forward specific text as a recommendation, the discussion paper highlighted clauses from other Constitutions, including on the topics of the right to a clean and healthy environment, and the right to compensation for violation of this right.

A very detailed draft text was suggested by the environmental rights NGO the Haburas Foundation. Its draft text read:

1. Everyone has the right to a healthy and ecologically balanced environment, and the duty to protect and improve the environment for future generations.

2. In order to guarantee the right to a healthy and ecologically balanced environment, it is the duty of the State, in consultation with the people and local communities:

    (a) to prevent, and mitigate the harmful effects of, environmental degradation;

    (b) to preserve and restore ecological systems and biological diversity for future generations;

    (c) to establish, maintain and protect a system of terrestrial and marine conservation areas that is compatible with traditional uses of natural resources;

    (d) to provide formal and informal environmental education and to increase environmental awareness;

    (e) to recognise, respect and develop traditional culture and laws that benefit the environment; and

(f)   to ensure that the environment is utilised and managed in an ecologically sustainable way and for the benefit of all citizens.[98]

In its final submission, Haburas recommended deleting 'in accordance with its capacities' from sub-s (3), fearing that this relegated protection of the environment to a secondary status, and that the provision was 'rubbery'.[99]

Post-consultation plenary debate

The Systematisation and Harmonisation Committee, in their report on the consultations, recommended eliminating the expression 'in accordance with its capacities' from sub-s (3).

The phrase 'in accordance with its capacities' was removed from sub-s (3) by consensus agreement.

---

98   Haburas Foundation, 'Environment and the Constitution', submitted to the Assembly on 22 October 2001, 2.

99   Haburas Foundation, 'Comments and Recommendations on the Draft Constitution of the Democratic Republic of Timor-Leste', 4 March 2002 [Bahasa Indonesian].

Additional sections suggested in submissions

There were a number of other clauses suggested by submissions of civil society and international organisations. Topics included:

An Applications clause. Yayasan HAK, for instance, put forward a clause stating:

Section 1
(Application)

1. The State must respect, protect, promote and fulfil the rights in the Bill of Rights.

2. The Bill of Rights applies to all law, and binds the legislature, the executive, the judiciary and all organs of State.

3. A provision of the Bill of Rights binds a natural or a juristic person if, and to the extent that, it is applicable, taking into account the nature of the right and the nature of any duty imposed by the right.

The Human Rights Unit suggested further consideration might be given to the coverage of the constitutional rights; that is, whether they extended to private and public actors, and ways in which existing obligations on government covered protection of persons in the private sphere.

Right to a nationality (Human Rights Unit, UNTAET)

Right to a name/identity (Yayasan HAK)

Right to access information

Yayasan HAK, for instance, suggested inclusion of a section which would give a broad ranging right of 'access to any information held by the State'. It also supported a right to receive written reasons and the right to appeal against any administrative action which adversely affected a person's interest. The Haburas Foundation also advocated for the right to information, suggesting a more detailed text:

1. Everyone has the right of prompt access to all information and documents that are held by the State, subject to matters of national security.

2. National legislation shall be enacted to give effect to the right to information, and may provide for reasonable measures to alleviate the administrative and financial burden on the State.

Similarly, the Human Rights Unit supported a right to information concerning government/administrative action which would cover everything from laws, to judgements to administrative decisions.

Administrative rights (Yayasan HAK)

Right to use language of choice in the private sphere and in the expression and conduct of cultural life (Yayasan HAK)

Regulation of traditional law

The Women's Charter of Rights for East Timor sought explicit recognition of women's equal rights to inheritance, the State's duty to regulate to reduce the dowry system in traditional law, and for women to be guaranteed the right to participate in traditional decision-making processes. REDE Feto Timor Lorosae sought a sentence in the Constitution stating that the rights in the Constitution were 'directly applicable' to traditional law.

Freedom from gendered exploitation

The Women's Charter of Rights also sought recognition of 'freedom from exploitation' under which they asked the State to prohibit prostitution and slavery.

Freedom from slavery (Human Rights Unit, UNTAET)

Right to a full and fair public hearing by an impartial tribunal of all rights and obligations (Human Rights Unit, UNTAET)

Right to an adequate standard of living (Human Rights Unit, UNTAET)

Right to rest and leisure (Human Rights Unit, UNTAET)

Right to seek asylum (Human Rights Unit, UNTAET and UNHCR)

Rights of ethnic and linguistic minorities (Human Rights Unit, UNTAET)

Right to freely participate in the cultural life of the country (Human Rights Unit, UNTAET)

Right to water and sanitation (Yayasan HAK)

Annexes

Annex I. Bill of Rights in the Constitution of the Democratic Republic of Timor-Leste (Portuguese)

PARTE II

DIREITOS, DEVERES, LIBERDADES E GARANTIAS FUNDAMENTAIS

TÍTULO I

PRINCÍPIOS GERAIS

Artigo 16
(Universalidade e igualdade)

1. Todos os cidadãos são iguais perante a lei, gozam dos mesmos direitos e estão sujeitos aos mesmos deveres.

2. Ninguém pode ser discriminado com base na cor, raça, estado civil, sexo, origem étnica, língua, posição social ou situação económica, convicções políticas ou ideológicas, religião, instrução ou condição física ou mental.

Artigo 17
(Igualdade entre mulheres e homens)

A mulher e o homem têm os mesmos direitos e obrigações em todos os domínios da vida familiar, cultural, social, económica e política.

Artigo 18
(Protecção da criança)

1. A criança tem direito a protecção especial por parte da família, da comunidade e do Estado, particularmente contra todas as formas de abandono, discriminação, violência, opressão, abuso sexual e exploração.

2. A criança goza de todos os direitos que lhe são universalmente reconhecidos, bem como de todos aqueles que estejam consagrados em convenções internacionais regularmente ratificadas ou aprovadas pelo Estado.

3. Todas as crianças, nascidas dentro ou fora do matrimónio, gozam dos mesmos direitos e da mesma protecção social.

Artigo 19
(Juventude)

1. O Estado promove e encoraja as iniciativas da juventude na consolidação da unidade nacional, na reconstrução, na defesa e no desenvolvimento do país.

2. O Estado promove, na medida das suas possibilidades, a educação, a saúde e a formação profissional dos jovens.

Artigo 20
(Terceira idade)

1. Todos os cidadãos de terceira idade têm direito a protecção especial por parte do Estado.

2. A política de terceira idade engloba medidas de carácter económico, social e cultural tendentes a proporcionar às pessoas idosas oportunidades de realização pessoal através de uma participação digna e activa na vida da comunidade.

Artigo 21
(Cidadão portador de deficiência)

1. O cidadão portador de deficiência goza dos mesmos direitos e está sujeito aos mesmos deveres dos demais cidadãos, com ressalva do exercício ou do cumprimento daqueles para os quais se encontre impossibilitado em razão da deficiência.

2. O Estado, dentro das suas possibilidades, promove a protecção aos cidadãos portadores de deficiência, nos termos da lei.

Artigo 22
(Timorenses no estrangeiro)

Os cidadãos timorenses que se encontrem ou residam no estrangeiro gozam da protecção do Estado para o exercício dos direitos e estão sujeitos aos deveres que não sejam incompatíveis com a ausência do país.

Artigo 23

(Interpretação dos direitos fundamentais)

Os direitos fundamentais consagrados na Constituição não excluem quaisquer outros constantes da lei e devem ser interpretados em consonância com a Declaração Universal dos Direitos Humanos.

Artigo 24

(Leis restritivas)

1. A restrição dos direitos, liberdades e garantias só pode fazer-se por lei, para salvaguardar outros direitos ou interesses constitucionalmente protegidos e nos casos expressamente previstos na Constituição.

2. As leis restritivas dos direitos, liberdades e garantias têm, necessariamente, carácter geral e abstracto, não podem diminuir a extensão e o alcance do conteúdo essencial dos dispositivos constitucionais e não podem ter efeito retroactivo.

Artigo 25

(Estado de excepção)

1. A suspensão do exercício dos direitos, liberdades e garantias fundamentais só pode ter lugar declarado o estado de sítio ou o estado de emergência nos termos previstos na Constituição.

2. O estado de sítio ou o estado de emergência só podem ser declarados em caso de agressão efectiva ou iminente por forças estrangeiras, de grave perturbação ou ameaça de perturbação séria da ordem constitucional democrática ou de calamidade pública.

3. A declaração do estado de sítio ou do estado de emergência é fundamentada, com especificação dos direitos, liberdades e garantias cujo exercício fica suspenso.

4. A suspensão não pode prolongar-se por mais de trinta dias, sem impedimento de eventual renovação fundamentada por iguais períodos de tempo, quando absolutamente necessário.

5. A declaração do estado de sítio em caso algum pode afectar os direitos à vida, integridade física, cidadania e não retroactividade da lei penal, o direito à defesa em processo criminal, a liberdade de consciência e de religião, o direito a não ser sujeito a tortura, escravatura ou servidão, o direito a não ser sujeito a tratamento ou punição cruel, desumano ou degradante e a garantia de não discriminação.

6. As autoridades estão obrigadas a restabelecer a normalidade constitucional no mais curto espaço de tempo.

Artigo 26
(Acesso aos tribunais)

1. A todos é assegurado o acesso aos tribunais para defesa dos seus direitos e interesses legalmente protegidos.

2. A justiça não pode ser denegada por insuficiência de meios económicos.

Artigo 27
(Provedor de Direitos Humanos e Justiça)

1. O Provedor de Direitos Humanos e Justiça é um órgão independente que tem por função apreciar e procurar satisfazer as queixas dos cidadãos contra os poderes públicos, podendo verificar a conformidade dos actos com a lei, bem como prevenir e iniciar todo o processo para a reparação das injustiças.

2. Os cidadãos podem apresentar queixas por acções ou omissões dos poderes públicos ao Provedor de Direitos Humanos e Justiça, que as apreciará, sem poder decisório, dirigindo aos órgãos competentes as recomendações necessárias.

3. O Provedor de Direitos Humanos e Justiça é eleito pelo Parlamento Nacional, por maioria absoluta dos Deputados, para um mandato de quatro anos.

4. A actividade do Provedor de Direitos Humanos e Justiça é independente dos meios graciosos e contenciosos previstos na Constituição e nas leis.

5. Os órgãos e os agentes da administração têm o dever de colaboração com o Provedor de Direitos Humanos e Justiça.

Artigo 28
(Direito de resistência e de legítima defesa)

1. Todos os cidadãos têm o direito de não acatar e de resistir às ordens ilegais ou que ofendam os seus direitos, liberdades e garantias fundamentais.

2. A todos é garantido o direito de legítima defesa, nos termos da lei.

TÍTULO II

DIREITOS, LIBERDADES E GARANTIAS PESSOAIS

Artigo 29
(Direito à vida)

1. A vida humana é inviolável.

2. O Estado reconhece e garante o direito à vida.

3. Na República Democrática de Timor-Leste não há pena de morte.

Artigo 30
(Direito à liberdade, segurança e integridade pessoal)

1. Todos têm direito à liberdade, segurança e integridade pessoal.

2. Ninguém pode ser detido ou preso senão nos termos expressamente previstos na lei vigente, devendo sempre a detenção ou a prisão ser submetida à apreciação do juiz competente no prazo legal.

3. Todo o indivíduo privado de liberdade deve ser imediatamente informado, de forma clara e precisa, das razões da sua detenção ou prisão, bem como dos seus direitos, e autorizado a contactar advogado, directamente ou por intermédio de pessoa de sua família ou de sua confiança.

4. Ninguém pode ser sujeito a tortura e a tratamentos cruéis, desumanos ou degradantes.

Artigo 31
(Aplicação da lei criminal)

1. Ninguém pode ser submetido a julgamento senão nos termos da lei.

2. Ninguém pode ser julgado e condenado por um acto que não esteja qualificado na lei como crime no momento da sua prática, nem sofrer medida de segurança cujos pressupostos não estejam expressamente fixados em lei anterior.

3. Não podem aplicar-se penas ou medidas de segurança que no momento da prática do crime não estejam expressamente previstas na lei.

4. Ninguém pode ser julgado e condenado mais do que uma vez pelo mesmo crime.

5. A lei penal não se aplica retroactivamente, a menos que a nova lei beneficie o arguido.

6. Qualquer pessoa injustamente condenada tem direito a justa indemnização, nos termos da lei.

Artigo 32

(Limites das penas e das medidas de segurança)

1. Na República Democrática de Timor-Leste não há prisão perpétua, nem penas ou medidas de segurança de duração ilimitada ou indefinida.

2. Em caso de perigosidade por anomalia psíquica, as medidas de segurança poderão ser sucessivamente prorrogadas por decisão judicial.

3. A responsabilidade penal é insusceptível de transmissão.

4. Os condenados aos quais sejam aplicadas pena ou medida de segurança privativas da liberdade mantêm a titularidade dos direitos fundamentais, salvas as limitações inerentes ao sentido da condenação e às exigências próprias da respectiva execução.

Artigo 33

(*Habeas corpus*)

1. Toda a pessoa ilegalmente privada da liberdade tem direito a recorrer à providência do *habeas corpus*.

2. O *habeas corpus* é interposto, nos termos da lei, pela própria ou por qualquer outra pessoa no gozo dos seus direitos civis.

3. O pedido de *habeas corpus* é decidido pelo juiz no prazo de oito dias em audiência contraditória.

Artigo 34

(Garantias de processo criminal)

1. Todo o arguido se presume inocente até à condenação judicial definitiva.

2. O arguido tem o direito de escolher defensor e a ser assistido por ele em todos os actos do processo, determinando a lei os casos em que a sua presença é obrigatória.

3. É assegurado a qualquer indivíduo o direito inviolável de audiência e defesa em processo criminal.

4. São nulas e de nenhum efeito todas as provas obtidas mediante tortura, coacção, ofensa à integridade física ou moral e intromissão abusiva na vida privada, no domicílio, na correspondência ou em outras formas de comunicação.

Artigo 35
(Extradição e expulsão)

1. A extradição só pode ter lugar por decisão judicial.

2. É vedada a extradição por motivos políticos.

3. Não é permitida a extradição por crimes a que corresponda na lei do Estado requisitante pena de morte ou de prisão perpétua, ou sempre que fundadamente se admita que o extraditando possa vir a ser sujeito a tortura ou tratamento desumano, degradante ou cruel.

4. O cidadão timorense não pode ser expulso ou expatriado do território nacional.

Artigo 36
(Direito à honra e à privacidade)

Todo o indivíduo tem direito à honra, ao bom nome e à reputação, à defesa da sua imagem e à reserva da sua vida privada e familiar.

Artigo 37
(Inviolabilidade do domicílio e da correspondência)

1. O domicílio, a correspondência e quaisquer meios de comunicação privados são invioláveis, salvos os casos previstos na lei em matéria de processo criminal.

2. A entrada no domicílio de qualquer pessoa contra sua vontade só pode ter lugar por ordem escrita da autoridade judicial competente, nos casos e segundo as formas prescritas na lei.

3. A entrada no domicílio de qualquer pessoa durante a noite, contra a sua vontade, é expressamente proibida, salvo em caso de ameaça grave para a vida ou para a integridade física de alguém que se encontre no interior desse domicílio.

Artigo 38
(Protecção de dados pessoais)

1. Todos os cidadãos têm o direito de acesso aos dados pessoais informatizados ou constantes de registos mecanográficos e manuais que lhes digam respeito, podendo exigir a sua rectificação e actualização, e o direito de conhecer a finalidade a que se destinam.

2. A lei define o conceito de dados pessoais e as condições aplicáveis ao seu tratamento.

3. É expressamente proibido, sem o consentimento do interessado, o tratamento informatizado de dados pessoais relativos à vida privada, às convicções

políticas e filosóficas, à fé religiosa, à filiação partidária ou sindical e à origem étnica.

Artigo 39
(Família, casamento e maternidade)

1. O Estado protege a família como célula base da sociedade e condição para o harmonioso desenvolvimento da pessoa.

2. Todos têm direito a constituir e a viver em família.

3. O casamento assenta no livre consentimento das partes e na plena igualdade de direitos entre os cônjuges, nos termos da lei.

4. A maternidade é dignificada e protegida, assegurando-se a todas as mulheres protecção especial durante a gravidez e após o parto e às mulheres trabalhadoras direito a dispensa de trabalho por período adequado, antes e depois do parto, sem perda de retribuição e de quaisquer outras regalias, nos termos da lei.

Artigo 40
(Liberdade de expressão e informação)

1. 1. Todas as pessoas têm direito à liberdade de expressão e ao direito de informar e ser informados com isenção.

2. O exercício da liberdade de expressão e de informação não pode ser limitado por qualquer tipo de censura.

3. O exercício dos direitos e liberdades referidos neste artigo é regulado por lei com base nos imperativos do respeito da Constituição e da dignidade da pessoa humana.

Artigo 41
(Liberdade de imprensa e dos meios de comunicação social)

1. É garantida a liberdade de imprensa e dos demais meios de comunicação social.

2. A liberdade de imprensa compreende, nomeadamente, a liberdade de expressão e criação dos jornalistas, o acesso às fontes de informação, a liberdade editorial, a protecção da independência e do sigilo profissional e o direito de criar jornais, publicações e outros meios de difusão.

3. Não é permitido o monopólio dos meios de comunicação social.

4. O Estado assegura a liberdade e a independência dos órgãos públicos de comunicação social perante o poder político e o poder económico.

5. O Estado assegura a existência de um serviço público de rádio e de televisão que deve ser isento, tendo em vista, entre outros objectivos, a protecção e divulgação da cultura e das tradições da República Democrática de Timor-Leste e a garantia da expressão do pluralismo de opinião.

6. As estações emissoras de radiodifusão e de radiotelevisão só podem funcionar mediante licença, nos termos da lei.

Artigo 42
(Liberdade de reunião e de manifestação)

1. A todos é garantida a liberdade de reunião pacífica e sem armas, sem necessidade de autorização prévia.

2. A todos é reconhecido o direito de manifestação, nos termos da lei.

Artigo 43
(Liberdade de associação)

1. 1. A todos é garantida a liberdade de associação, desde que não se destine a promover a violência e seja conforme com a lei.

2. Ninguém pode ser obrigado a fazer parte de uma associação ou a nela permanecer contra sua vontade.

3. São proibidas as associações armadas, militares ou paramilitares e as organizações que defendam ideias ou apelem a comportamentos de carácter racista ou xenófobo ou que promovam o terrorismo.

Artigo 44
(Liberdade de circulação)

1. Todo o indivíduo tem o direito de se movimentar e fixar residência em qualquer ponto do território nacional.

2. A todo o cidadão é garantido o direito de livremente emigrar, bem como o direito de regressar ao país.

Artigo 45
(Liberdade de consciência, de religião e de culto)

1. A toda a pessoa é assegurada a liberdade de consciência, de religião e de culto, encontrando-se as confissões religiosas separadas do Estado.

2. Ninguém pode ser perseguido nem discriminado por causa das suas convicções religiosas.

3. É garantida a objecção de consciência, nos termos da lei.

4. É garantida a liberdade do ensino de qualquer religião no âmbito da respectiva confissão religiosa.

Artigo 46
(Direito de participação política)

1. Todo o cidadão tem o direito de participar, por si ou através de representantes democraticamente eleitos, na vida política e nos assuntos públicos do país.

2. Todo o cidadão tem o direito de constituir e de participar em partidos políticos.

3. A constituição e a organização dos partidos políticos são reguladas por lei.

Artigo 47
(Direito de sufrágio)

1. Todo o cidadão maior de dezassete anos tem o direito de votar e de ser eleito.

2. O exercício do direito de sufrágio é pessoal e constitui um dever cívico.

Artigo 48
(Direito de petição)

Todo o cidadão tem o direito de apresentar petições, queixas e reclamações, individual ou colectivamente, perante os órgãos de soberania ou quaisquer autoridades, para defesa dos seus direitos, da Constituição, das leis ou do interesse geral.

Artigo 49
(Defesa da soberania)

1. Todo o cidadão tem o direito e o dever de contribuir para a defesa da independência, soberania e integridade territorial do país.

2. O serviço militar é prestado nos termos da lei.

TÍTULO III

DIREITOS E DEVERES ECONÓMICOS, SOCIAIS E CULTURAIS

Artigo 50
(Direito ao trabalho)

1. Todo o cidadão, independentemente do sexo, tem o direito e o dever de trabalhar e de escolher livremente a profissão.

2. O trabalhador tem direito à segurança e higiene no trabalho, à remuneração, ao descanso e às férias.

3. É proibido o despedimento sem justa causa ou por motivos políticos, religiosos e ideológicos.

4. É proibido o trabalho compulsivo, sem prejuízo do disposto na legislação sobre a execução de penas.

5. O Estado promove a criação de cooperativas de produção e apoia as empresas familiares como fontes de emprego.

Artigo 51
(Direito à greve e proibição do lock-out)

1. Os trabalhadores têm direito a recorrer à greve, sendo o seu exercício regulado por lei.

2. A lei define as condições de prestação, durante a greve, de serviços necessários à segurança e manutenção de equipamentos e instalações, bem como de serviços mínimos indispensáveis para acorrer à satisfação de necessidades sociais impreteríveis.

3. É proibido o *lock-out*.

Artigo 52
(Liberdade sindical)

1. O trabalhador tem direito a organizar-se em sindicatos e associações profissionais para defesa dos seus direitos e interesses.

2. A liberdade sindical desdobra-se, nomeadamente, na liberdade de constituição, liberdade de inscrição e liberdade de organização e regulamentação interna.

3. Os sindicatos e as associações sindicais são independentes do Estado e do patronato.

Artigo 53
(Direitos dos consumidores)

1. Os consumidores têm direito à qualidade dos bens e serviços consumidos, a uma informação verdadeira e à protecção da saúde, da segurança e dos seus interesses económicos, bem como à reparação de danos.

2. A publicidade é disciplinada por lei, sendo proibidas todas as formas de publicidade oculta, indirecta ou enganosa.

Artigo 54
(Direito à propriedade privada)

1. Todo o indivíduo tem direito à propriedade privada, podendo transmiti-la em vida e por morte, nos termos da lei.

2. A propriedade privada não deve ser usada em prejuízo da sua função social.

3. A requisição e a expropriação por utilidade pública só têm lugar mediante justa indemnização, nos termos da lei.

4. Só os cidadãos nacionais têm direito à propriedade privada da terra.

Artigo 55
(Obrigações do contribuinte)

Todo o cidadão com comprovado rendimento tem o dever de contribuir para as receitas públicas, nos termos da lei.

Artigo 56
(Segurança e assistência social)

1. Todos os cidadãos têm direito à segurança e à assistência social, nos termos da lei.

2. O Estado promove, na medida das disponibilidades nacionais, a organização de um sistema de segurança social.

3. O Estado apoia e fiscaliza, nos termos da lei, a actividade e o funcionamento das instituições de solidariedade social e de outras de reconhecido interesse público sem carácter lucrativo.

Artigo 57
(Saúde)

1. Todos têm direito à saúde e à assistência médica e sanitária e o dever de as defender e promover.

2. O Estado promove a criação de um serviço nacional de saúde universal, geral e, na medida das suas possibilidades, gratuito, nos termos da lei.

3. O serviço nacional de saúde deve ser, tanto quanto possível, de gestão descentralizada e participativa.

Artigo 58
(Habitação)

Todos têm direito, para si e para a sua família, a uma habitação de dimensão adequada, em condições de higiene e conforto e que preserve a intimidade pessoal e a privacidade familiar.

Artigo 59
(Educação e cultura)

1. O Estado reconhece e garante ao cidadão o direito à educação e à cultura, competindo-lhe criar um sistema público de ensino básico universal, obrigatório e, na medida das suas possibilidades, gratuito, nos termos da lei.

2. Todos têm direito a igualdade de oportunidades de ensino e formação profissional.

3. O Estado reconhece e fiscaliza o ensino privado e cooperativo.

4. O Estado deve garantir a todos os cidadãos, segundo as suas capacidades, o acesso aos graus mais elevados do ensino, da investigação científica e da criação artística.

5. Todos têm direito à fruição e à criação culturais, bem como o dever de preservar, defender e valorizar o património cultural.

Artigo 60
(Propriedade intelectual)

O Estado garante e protege a criação, produção e comercialização da obra literária, cientifica e artística, incluindo a protecção legal dos direitos de autor.

Artigo 61
(Meio ambiente)

1. Todos têm direito a um ambiente de vida humano, sadio e ecologicamente equilibrado e o dever de o proteger e melhorar em prol das gerações vindouras.

2. O Estado reconhece a necessidade de preservar e valorizar os recursos naturais.

3. O Estado deve promover acções de defesa do meio ambiente e salvaguardar o desenvolvimento sustentável da economia.

Annex II. Members of Thematic Committee I and the Systematisation and Harmonisation Committee

Thematic Committee I

Office holders

Paulo Assis Belo (PD): President

Adalgisa Soares Ximenes (FRETILIN): Secretary

Vicente Soares Faria (FRETILIN): Rapporteur

Members

Flávio Guterres da Silva (FRETILIN)

Rosária Corte Real (FRETILIN)

Josefa P Soares (FRETILIN)

Maria José da Costa (FRETILIN)

Manuel Sarmento (FRETILIN)

Luisa da Costa (FRETILIN)

Joaquim B Soares (FRETILIN)

Maria Avalziza Lourdes (FRETILIN)

Gervásio Cardoso (FRETILIN)

Lú Olo (FRETILIN)

Joaquim dos Santos (FRETILIN)

Paulo Alves (PD)

Lucia Lobato (PSD)

Vidal Riak (PSD)

Maria Valadares (ASDT)

Clementino dos Reis Amaral (KOTA)

Arlindo Marçal (PDC)

Aires Francisco Cabral (PNT)

Systematisation and Harmonisation Committee

Office holders

Adérito Soares (FRETILIN): President

Vicente Guterres (UDC/PDC): Secretary

Manuel Tilman (KOTA): Rapporteur

Members

Adalgisa Ximenes (FRETILIN)
Adaljiza Magno (FRETILIN)
Ana Pessoa (FRETILIN)
António Cardoso (FRETILIN)
Cipriana Pereira (FRETILIN)
Flávio da Silva (FRETILIN)
Francisco Branco (FRETILIN)
Francisco Soares (FRETILIN)
Jacinto Maia (FRETILIN)
Januário Soares (FRETILIN)
Jacob Fernandes (FRETILIN)
Joaquim Amaral (FRETILIN)
Joaquim dos Santos (FRETILIN)
José Lobato (FRETILIN)
José Reis (FRETILIN)
Lourdes Alves (FRETILIN)
Mari Alkatiri (FRETILIN)
Maria Solana (FRETILIN)
Maria Viegas (FRETILIN)
Orsório Florindo (FRETILIN)

Rosária Corte-Real (FRETILIN)
Rui António (FRETILIN)
Vicente Faria (FRETILIN)
Aquilino Fraga Guterres (PD)
Eusébio Guterres (PD)
Mariano Sabino Lopes (PD)
Paulo Assis Belo (PD)
Lucia Lobato (PSD)
Mario Viegas Carrascalão (PSD)
Milena Pires (PSD)
Feliciano Fatima (ASDT)
Francisco Xavier do Amaral (ASDT)
Pedro Gomes (ASDT)
António Ximenes (PDC)
Aires Francisco Cabral (PNT)
Armando Jose da Silva (PL)
Jacob Xavier (PPT)
Pedro da Costa (PST)
Isabel Fereira (UDT) (replaced by Quitéria da Costa)

Source: Constituent Assembly records.

Annex III. Members of the Constituent Assembly

Office holders

Francisco Guterres ('Lú-Olo') (FRETILIN): President

Francisco Xavier do Amaral (ASDT): Vice-President

Arlindo Marçal (PDC): Vice-President

Members

ASDT

Afonso Noronha

Feliciano Alves Fatima

Jacinto de Andrade

Maria da Costa Valadares

Pedro Gomes

FRETILIN

Adalgisa Maria Soares Ximenes

Adaljiza Albertina Xavier Reis Magno

Adérito de Jesus Soares

Alfredo da Silva

Ana Maria Pessoa Pereira da Silva Pinto

António Cardoso Machado

António Cepeda

Arão Noé de Jesus da Costa Amaral

Armindo da Conceição Silva Freitas

Augusto da Conceição Amaral

Cipriana da Costa Pereira

Constância de Jesus

Elias Freitas

Elizario Ferreira

Flávio Maria da Silva

Francisco Carlos Soares

Francisco Kalbaudi Lay

Francisco Lelan

Francisco M.C.P. Jcrónimo

Francisco Miranda Branco

Gervásio Cardoso de Jesus da Silva

Gregório Saldanha

Jacinto Maia

Jacob Martins dos Reis Fernandes

Januário Soares

Jerónimo da Silva

Joaquim Amaral

Joaquim Barros Soares

Joaquim dos Santos

José Andrade da Cruz

Josefa A. Pereira Soares

José Maria Barreto Lobato Gonçalves

José Maria dos Reis Costa

José Soares

José Manuel da Silva Fernandes

Judit Ximenes

Lourdes Maria Mascarenhas Alves

Luisa da Costa

Madalena da Silva

Manuel Sarmento

Marí Alkatiri

Maria Avalziza Lourdes

Maria Genoveva da Costa Martins

Maria José da Costa

Maria Solana da Conceição Soares Fernandes

Maria Teresa Lay Correia

Maria Teresinha da Silva Viegas e Costa

Mario Ferreira

Miguel Soares

Norberto José do Espirito Santo

Osório Florindo

Rosária Maria Corte Real de Oliveira

Rui António da Cruz

Vicente Soares Faria

Independent

António da Costa Lelan

KOTA

Clementino dos Reis Amaral

Manuel Tilman

PD

Aquilino Ribeiro Fraga Guterres ('Ete Uco')

Eusébio Guterres

Samuel Mendonça

Mariano Sabino Lopes ('Assa Nami')

Paulo Alves Sarmento ('Tuloda')

Paulo Assis Belo ('Funu Mata')

Rui Meneses da Costa ('Lebra')

PDC

António Ximenes

PL

Armando da Silva

PNT

Aires Francisco Cabral

Aliança da Conceição Araújo

PPT

Ananias do Carmo Fuka

Jacob Xavier

PSD

Fernando Dias Gusmão

Leandro Isac

Lucia Maria Lobato

Mario Viegas Carrascalão

Milena Pires

Vidal de Jesus ('Riak Leman')

PST

Pedro Martires da Costa

UDC/PDC

Vicente da Silva Guterres

UDT

João Viegas Carrascalão

Quitéria da Costa

Source: Listing of names and signatures appended to the text of the Constitution reproduced in *Jornal da República*, 2003, Série 1, No 1, 1st Suplemento.

Annex IV. List of reviewed submissions to the Constituent Assembly

Submissions concerning the process

Assembly Watch Team (on Renetil letterhead), Letter to the President of the Constituent Assembly, 29 October 2001 [Tetum]*

Assembly Watch Team, Letter to the President of the Constituent Assembly, 31 January 2002 [Bahasa Indonesian]*

NGO Working Group on the Constitution, 'Recommendations to the Constituent Assembly', undated, circa October 2001 [English], from the files of the Human Rights Unit, UNTAET.

NGO Working Group on the Constitution, 'Clarification', 5 October 2001 [Tetum]*

US Congress (eight members: Dennis J Kuinich, Barbara Lee, Chris Smith, Anthony D Weiner, Tammy Baldwin, Bernard Sanders, Lane Evans, Sam Farr), Letter to the President of the Constituent Assembly, 10 January 2002*

Submissions concerning the substance of human rights clauses

Transitional Government

Dr Rui Maria de Araújo (Minister for Health), Letter to the President of the Constituent Assembly concerning a proposal for inclusion of material relating to health in the Constitution of East Timor, 29 October 2001 [Portuguese]*

Dr Rui Maria de Araújo (Minister for Health), Letter to the President of the Constituent Assembly, 26 February 2002, received by the Assembly 5 March 2002. [Portuguese]*

Isabel Ferreira (Adviser to the Chief Minister on Human Rights), and Maria Domingas Alves (Adviser on the Promotion of Equality), Letter to the President of the Constituent Assembly, 21 November 2001 [Portuguese]*

José Ramos Horta, Minister of State and for Foreign Affairs and Cooperation, Letter to the President of the Constituent Assembly, 25 February 2002 [Portuguese and English]*

Domingos Maria Sarmento, Vice-Minister for Justice, Letter to the President of the Constituent Assembly, 2 March 2002 [Portuguese]*

National Planning and Development Agency, The Environment and the Constitution in East Timor: Discussion Paper, September 2001 [English]*

NGOs

Article XIX, 'Note on the Draft Constitution of the Democratic Republic of East Timor of 9 February 2002: Focus on Provisions Affecting Freedom of Expression', London, February 2002 [English]*

The Asia Foundation (Patrick McAuslan), 'Suggested Draft of a Property Clause for the Constitution of East Timor', 29 October 2001 [English], from the personal files of the Chair of the Systematisation and Harmonisation Committee.

The Asia Foundation (Anthony Regan), 'Provedor for Justice: Some Comments on Proposals', 7 December 2001 [Portuguese]*

The Asia Foundation, 'Comments and Suggested Amendments to East Timor's Draft Constitution of 9/02/2002', undated but with a cover letter to the President of the Constituent Assembly dated 8 March 2002 [English]*

The Asia Foundation (Yash Ghai and Jill Cottrell), 'Discussion Paper on Draft of East Timorese Constitution', March 2002, [English]*

Committee for Child Rights in East Timor's Constitution, 'Draft Articles on Child Rights for East Timor's Constitution', 18 October 2001 [English and Portuguese]*

Church-Constitution Working Group submission on letterhead of the Centre for Peace and Development, Letter to the President of the Constituent Assembly, January 2002, received by the Assembly on 23 January 2002 [Portuguese and English]*

Consumers International, Regional Office for Asia and the Pacific, 'Proposed Constitutional Provision on Consumer Protection for East Timor', undated [English], from the files of The Asia Foundation

East Timor Study Group, 'Debate on the Draft Constitution: Positive and Negative Implications for the Future of East Timor', 20 February 2002 [Tetum]*

Haburas Foundation, 'Environment and the Constitution Draft Position Paper', undated, circa October 2001 [English]*

Haburas Foundation, 'Environment and the Constitution', presented to the Assembly on 22 October 2001 [English]*

Haburas Foundation, 'Comments and Recommendations on the Draft Constitution of the Democratic Republic of Timor-Leste', 4 March 2002 [Bahasa Indonesian]*

International Commission of Jurists (Australian Section), 'Commentary on the Draft Constitution Proposed for East Timor by the Constituent Assembly', undated [English], from the files of the Human Rights Unit, UNTAET

National Committee of Rights of Children of Timor Leste (CNDCTL), undated, received by the Assembly on 24 October 2001 [Tetum]*

REDE Feto Timor Lorosae, Letter to members of the Constitutional Commission 1 'Fundamental Rights, Duties and Freedoms', 22 October 2001 [Portuguese]*

REDE Feto Timor Lorosae, Letter to the President of the Constituent Assembly (with the subject heading 'General considerations from the East Timor Women's Network (REDE) regarding the draft Fretilin Constitution'), 31 October 2001 [English]*

Timor Lorose'a Journalists Association (TLJA)/Internews, 'Submission to the Constituent Assembly on Articles in the FRETILIN Draft Constitution of May 2001 concerning freedom of expression', undated, but with an attached handwritten note indicating that it was sent to members of the Assembly on 26 November 2001 [English]*

TLJA, 'New Proposals of the Timor Lorosa'e Journalists Association', undated [Portuguese], from the personal files of the Chair of the Systematisation and Harmonisation Committee

TLJA, 'Submission on Freedom of Expression', 7 March 2002 [English]*

TLJA, Letter to members of the Assembly on International Women's Day (8 March 2002) [Portuguese], from the personal files of the Chair of the Systematisation and Harmonisation Committee

Yayasan HAK, 'Civil and Political, Economic, Social and Cultural Rights', undated, received by the Assembly on 22 October 2001 [English]*

Yayasan HAK, 'Draft Proposals for the Constitution of East Timor', received by the Assembly on 15 March 2002 [Bahasa Indonesian]*

Women's Charter of Rights in East Timor [Bahasa Indonesian and English]*

Working Group for Child Rights in East Timor's Constitution, 14 November 2001 [English], from the files of the Human Rights Unit, UNTAET

UN

Human Rights Unit, UNTAET, 'Submission of the Working Group on Future Human Rights Institutions to the Constituent Assembly', 30 October 2001 [English and Bahasa Indonesian]*

Human Rights Unit, UNTAET, 'Thematic Committee One's Proposals For the Protection of Human Rights in the Constitution: An analysis by the HRU', 14 November 2001 [English and Bahasa Indonesian]*

Human Rights Unit, UNTAET, 'Summary of select technical comments concerning the East Timorese draft Constitution and its treatment of human rights', December 2001 [English], from the files of the Human Rights Unit, UNTAET

UN High Commissioner for Human Rights (Mary Robinson), Letter to the President of the Constituent Assembly, 19 December 2001, with a cover letter from the SRSG, 3 January 2001 [English and Portuguese]*

UNHCR, Letter to members of the Constituent Assembly, 6 December 2001 [English and Portuguese]*

Special Representative of the Secretary-General (SRSG)/Transitional Administrator, Letter addressed to heads of the political parties with attached comments, 22 February 2002 [English and Portuguese]*

Steering Committee of CAVR, 5 December 2001 [Portuguese]*

(Copies of submissions marked with an asterisk (*) can be found in the files relating to the Constituent Assembly in the National Parliament of Timor-Leste.)

Other submissions collected

Additional options papers prepared by consultants for The Asia Foundation and provided to the Assembly Secretariat/committees were collected. However, they were not necessarily in general circulation and so are not included in the list above. The titles of these papers include:

- Categories of Laws that may be Required to Implement the Draft Constitution
- Additional Anti-Corruption and Accountability Mechanisms for East Timor's Constitution
- Constitutional Provisions for the Judiciary: Some Fundamental Principles
- Is it consistent with international human rights standards to preclude those who acquire citizenship from the diplomatic and military services?
- Detention, arrest and habeas corpus.

Select references

Primary material

Documents relating to the constitutional process collected from the files of the:

- National Parliament of Timor Leste, in particular:
  - Written records of the thematic committees, the Systematisation and Harmonisation Committee, and other records of the Constituent Assembly (relating to the plenary sessions and the District consultations).
  - Copies of constitutional texts; and submissions received by the committees or the Assembly. Records were held variously in the cabinets of the Secretariat of the National Parliament, and/or the Archival Unit.
  - Recordings of the plenary sessions of the Constituent Assembly for 12–22 December 2001; 18 January 2002.
  - Constituent Assembly Daily Press Releases.
- Personal collection of the Chair of the Systematisation and Harmonisation Committee, Adérito de Jesus Soares.
- Human Rights Unit, UNTAET.
- UNICEF (Timor-Leste) and communication with (then named) UNIFEM (Timor-Leste).
- UNTAET, Daily Press Briefings.
- The Asia Foundation (Timor-Leste office, and the personal collection of TAF consultant, Anthony Regan of The Australian National University).
- OXFAM.
- Yayasan HAK.
- Personal Collection of Fr Frank Brennan SJ (former Director of the Jesuit Refugee Service, Timor-Leste, and adviser to the Church-Constitution Working Group).
- Contemporaneous reports of UNTAET to the Security Council, and of the High Commissioner for Human Rights (2001–02).

Secondary material

Aucoin, L and Brandt, M, 'East Timor's Constitutional Passage to Independence', in United States Institute for Peace, (LE Miller (ed)), *Framing the State in Times of Transition: Case Studies in Constitution Making* (USIP, 2010) 245.

Baltazar, A, 'An Overview of the Constitution Drafting Process in East Timor' (2004) *East Timor Law Journal* 9.

Binchy, A, 'The Constitution of Timor-Leste in Comparative Experience' in W Binchy (ed), *Timor-Leste:Challenges for Justice and Human Rights in the Shadow of the Past* (Clarus Press, 2009) 261.

Brandt, M, *Constitutional Assistance in Post-Conflict Countries: The UN Experience: Cambodia, East Timor and Afghanistan* (UNDP, 2005).

Braithwaite, J, Charlesworth, H, Soares, A, *Networked Governance of Freedom and Tyranny*, (ANU E Press, 2012).

Comissão de Acolhimento, Verdade e Reconcilição de Timor Leste (CAVR), *Report of the Commission on Reception, Truth and Reconciliation* (2005).

Carter Center, *The East Timor Political and Election Observation Project: Final Project Report* (April 2004).

Charlesworth, H, 'The Constitution of East Timor' (2003) 1 *International Journal of Constitutional Law* 325.

Devereux, A, 'Searching for Clarity: A case-study of UNTAET's application of international human rights norms' in N White and D Klaasen (eds), UN, *Human Rights and Post Conflict Situations* (Manchester University Press, 2005).

Direitos Humanos – Centro de Investigação Interdisciplinar, (coordinator: Pedro Carlos Bacelar de Vasconcelos), *Constituição Anotado: Republica Democrática de Timor Leste* (Empresa Diario do Minho, 2011).

De Sousa, L, 'Some Facts and Comments on the East Timor 2001 Constituent Assembly Election' (2001) *Lusotopie* 299.

Garrison, R, *The Role of Constitution-Building Processes in Democratisation: Case Study: East Timor* (IDEA, 2005).

Goldstone, A, 'Building a State and 'State-building': East Timor and the UN, 1999–2012', in M Berdal and D Zaum, *Political Economy of State Building: Power after Peace* (Routledge, 2013) 209.

Goldstone, A, 'UNTAET with Hindsight: The Peculiarities of Politics in an Incomplete State' (2004) 10(1) *Global Governance* 83.

Ingram, S, 'Building the wrong peace: Reviewing the United Nations Transitional Administration in East Timor (UNTAET) through a political settlement lens', (2012) 64(1) *Political Science* 3.

Lutz, N, 'Constitutionalism as Public Culture in East Timor', Paper presented at the Law and Society Association meeting, Pittsburgh, 2003.

Morrow, J and White, R, 'The United Nations in Transitional East Timor: International Standards and the Reality of Governance' (2002) *Australian Yearbook of International Law* 1.

Pires, M, 'East Timor and the Debate on Quotas', Regional Workshop on the Implementation of Quotas: Asian Experiences, Jakarta, September 2002.

Soares, D B, Maley, M, Fox, J and Regan, A, *Elections and Constitution Making in East Timor* (ANU, 2003).

Timor-Leste Legal Education Project, *An Introduction to Constitutional Law in Timor-Leste*, supported by USAID, The Asia Foundation and Stanford Law School (undated).

UNDP, *Ukan rasik a'an: East Timor – the way ahead* (UNDP, 2002).

Wallis, J, *Constitution Making during State Building* (Cambridge University Press, 2014).

Walsh, P, 'East Timor's political parties and groupings: Briefing Notes', ACFOA Development Issues 9 (ACFOA, 2001).

www.ingramcontent.com/pod-product-compliance
Lightning Source LLC
Chambersburg PA
CBHW061242270326
41928CB00041B/3371